Social and Biological Roles of Language

The Psychology of Justification

Social and Biological Roles of Language

The Psychology of Justification

Richard Totman

The University of Sussex
Laboratory of Experimental Psychology &
Centre for Research on Perception & Cognition
Brighton, England

1985

ACADEMIC PRESS, INC.

(Harcourt Brace Jovanovich, Publishers)

London Orlando San Diego New York
Toronto Montreal Sydney Tokyo

ACADEMIC PRESS INC. (LONDON) LTD.
24–28 Oval Road
LONDON NW1 7DX

United States Edition published by
ACADEMIC PRESS, INC.
Orlando, Florida 32887

British Library Cataloguing in Publication Data

Totman, Richard
Social and biological roles of language
1. Social psychology
I. Title
302'.01 HM251

Library of Congress Cataloging in Publication Data

Totman, Richard.
Social and biological roles of language.

Includes bibliographical references and index.
1. Social psychology. 2. Stress (Psychology)
3. Mental health. 4. Adjustment (Psychology) I. Title.
HM251.T67 1985 302 84-14509
ISBN 0-12-696080-1 (alk. paper)

PRINTED IN THE UNITED STATES OF AMERICA

85 86 87 88 9 8 7 6 5 4 3 2 1

For
Felicity-Ann

Contents

Preface

There is a Wittgensteinian air about much of what is happening in and around social psychology at the present time. Attribution theory, ethogenics, semiology, and sociolinguistics each reflect a growing awareness of the role which language plays in governing social life. This focus on language naturally raises the question of the suitability of the technical scientific language which social psychologists use as a medium for the expression of social phenomena when these phenomena themselves appear closely tied to the speaking practices of communities of individuals.

One of the exciting things about contemporary social psychology is that its discussions seem to be entering more cosmopolitan ground. Traditional research programmes have been justly criticised for their insularity; because of the incommensurability of their categories and distinctions, researchers do not talk to each other. This book is written in the hope that the days of insularity may be coming to an end and that the way is open to a sharing of debates about matters of social importance among those schooled in different academic subjects. It is divided into three parts. In the first part, the social psychologist's title to a specialist vocabulary and methodology is questioned, and the assumption that research based on an ideal of specialism can, in principle, reflect general social laws and truths is challenged.

The more theoretically constructive project of the book begins with Part II. The argument is developed that theories in social psychology have evolved not as a result of specialist research programmes but on different grounds. Their course has more to do with a changing metaphysics than with data—specifically, a changing perspective on men and women as rational, freely choosing, moral agents. Relatedly, our conception of what is meant by "social" has changed too.

One particular development in the recent history of social psychology is a convergence of its aims and interests with those of medicine. This is discussed in Part III, which comprises about half of the book. I have felt for some time that medicine and social psychology are close relations. Both have as their starting points the distinction between adaptive and maladaptive states of the individual—as a biological entity on the one hand, and as a social one on the other. The discussions in this part revolve around the idea, for which there is now considerable support, that the social adaptation of the individual is linked to his or her biological survival. The chapters in the third part of the book draw on a growing, multi-disciplinary literature concerned with stress and coping in relation to health.

The increasing use of epidemiological data in social research and the appearance of the relatively new discipline of psychoneuroimmunology are indications of a new era in the development of social psychology. The significance of these changes is not to be underestimated; they open up the enquiry on the nature of human socialness enormously, extending it to the concerns of medicine, sociobiology, and physiology and to those of sociolinguistics and philosophy. In this book I want to emphasize the role of social psychology as the centrepiece in these developments in that it embraces the notion of the person as both organism and institution.

The book is deliberately wide-ranging in its design. While I would have liked to deal more thoroughly with specific areas of research and specific sub-disciplines, to have done so would have been to interfere with the continuity of the argument. The resulting (very long) volume would not have been the book I wanted. In places in the text where coverage is brief I have included what I consider to be key references so that the reader can explore work in a particular area in greater depth.

I am grateful to the following for their helpful comments on a draft of this book: George Brown, David Caudrey, Andrew Chidley, Rona Davies, Raymond ffoulkes, Rom Harré, Joe Kiff, Barbara Kugler, Keith Oatley, Stuart Sutherland, and Felicity-Ann Totman. I also owe a debt of gratitude to Rona Davies for drawing the diagrams and to Helen Holland for the typing.

Introduction and Plan of the Book

When I first started doing social psychology, in the late 1960s, I was intrigued by the theories but could not see the point of the research. The theories, it seemed to me, had a life of their own, a vitality and interest that was dissipated by the laborious stream of technical data collected on their behalf. It was not just that these data were often inconclusive. Certain theories had an immediate intuitive appeal in that they seemed to fit with what I knew of the social world from my own participation in it. On the few occasions when I summoned sufficient courage to venture this opinion to my superiors they produced what seemed at the time a knockdown argument: psychologists must at all costs avoid making personal assumptive (and probably prejudiced) judgments. Until it is tested, a theory or hypothesis remains speculation. Theory can only become fact through consensus and the only path to consensus is the systematic and replicable collection of objective data. The alternative is a chaotic muddle of fact and myth.

I believed that as I became more familiar with the subject this attitude would change. and I would come to understand the importance of the link between theories and data. But the longer I searched the literature for clear examples of theories formed, modified, or abandoned on the basis of data, the more my initial impression was reaffirmed. I became convinced that theories stood or fell not as a result of the findings of the specialist empirical research that was done but on different, less obvious grounds. I could not see how the "facts" produced by psychologists in the laboratory or in the field were any more "objective" than my own intuitions. The role of data, rather than to confirm or refute theories, seemed to be to transform the interesting social issues explored in theories into debates over technical matters which fast became so disconnected from the original issue as to be irrelevant to the social world that everyone knows.

In psychology, despite some strong criticisms in the 1970s of the laboratory experiment as an appropriate means of searching out social phenomena, support for this sceptical attitude to research remains thin. Discussions on the subject still mainly converge around empirical data. In the history and philosophy of science, however, as well as in social anthropology and sociolinguistics, there is growing disquiet about the reverencing of objective facts in the social sciences. To some extent the critical arguments have been anticipated by French and German writers in the structuralist tradition. Among philosophers of science this concern extends to the physical sciences as well. The insights of Wittgenstein in *Philosophical Investigations* and the theories of Heidegger and Dewey foreshadow some strong caveats issued by contemporary philosophers. All three came to reject the ideal for the philosophy of science as the establishment of a foundational "theory of knowledge" against which the legitimacy of claims to knowledge in other subjects can be measured. Feyerabend (1981) sees in the teaching and application of science today a pale copy of the imaginative and innovatory enterprise that used to be science. He finds much wrong with the modern tendency to apply automatically a scientific methodology without looking on this activity itself as a cultural practice, rooted in unexamined assumptions. Rorty too, in his book *Philosophy and the Mirror of Nature,* views the preoccupation of science and psychology with "accuracy of representation" as deeply reactionary and as overdue for change: "the notion of 'accurate representation' is simply an automatic and empty compliment which we pay to those beliefs which are successful in helping us do what we want to do" (1980, p. 10).

I have divided the text of this book into three parts. In Part I I examine the role of research in social psychology, and in particular the grounding assumption that the evolution of theories depends on the research that is done in connection with them. There is surprisingly little support for this assumption. Theories *do* progress and evolve in a logical manner, but this does not appear to happen as a result of the technical data of research. It is quite a different tide that carries them.

The more constructive project of the book begins with Part II, which includes Chapters 3 and 4. Chapter 3 is an attempt to identify the basis on which theories in social psychology do evolve, if it is not through the data of specialist research. A continuity is found in the principle theories since the mid-1950s, which is independent of these data. Theoretical changes over this period reflect, and indeed may well have influenced, how we think about people as freely choosing moral agents. They chart a gradual but highly significant change in metaphysical commitment on the nature of action and free choice. The point is that this change and this continuity can be illuminated without recourse to the findings of research that spin off along the way.

The line of theory in question runs from consistency theories, cognitive dissonance theory and forced compliance, through self-perception theory to attribution theory and ethogenics. My claim is that the categories and relations in these theories were and indeed are empirically tested but not in the sense of being stood up against the technical data and statistics of research. They are tested and their preeminence determined rather like works of literature are "tested;" by being measured against people's own experience in the social world.

But this is only part of the story. People are constantly found talking to each other, and ideas and beliefs are continually being aired in conversation. The real terrain of assessment involves the social structures and relations that lurk in the ordinary language we speak. In ascribing a primary social role to language my approach converges with and draws on Wittgenstein's demonstration that there is an indissoluble link between the speaking practices and the rules and institutions of a community. The same idea is behind the concept of a "speech community" as this appears in studies in sociolinguistics. The upshot of my argument about social psychology theories is that the good theories are those which receive most discussion and whose categories and distinctions overspill their professional boundary and are taken up into more general usage. New concepts and expressions, in becoming part of the corpus of ordinary speech, affect meanings in a language in a subtle way and in doing so affect the lives of the speakers of that language. The technical, "scientistic" language into which hypotheses and findings are typically put in social psychology is largely self-defeating because its supposedly specialist definitions and distinctions are rarely free of ordinary-language associations, and ordinary language is the vehicle of lay expressions of the social order. To use Wittgenstein's famous term, specialist (psychological) "language games" which pretend to be superior commentaries on the institutions of social life are effective only inasmuch as they are taken up widely and thus themselves in due course become institutions of ordinary life.

Attribution theory differs from previous approaches in social psychology in that its subject matter is the explanations people themselves produce for their actions. The analysis has, as it were, gone one "meta-stage" beyond older analyses. It has shifted from explanations of actions to explanations of people's explanations of actions. The changing metaphysics which is visible in more than 30 years of social psychology theory is a movement toward greater relativism in our conception of action, choice, and meaning. It yields a view of the social world as pluralistic: as made up of different incommensurable or only partly commensurable subcommunities each with its own inviolable criteria of objectivity and truth—each with its own inviolable language games. Identifying this change sets the stage for a reassessment of the nature of "social behavior." Saying that a person attributes his or her action to a goal or a motive, and that goals and motives and the systems of talk of which they form a part themselves emanate from the community, implies that an individual, in acting and choosing, aligns himself or herself with a particular sector of the community: that sector which is constituted on the basis of that particular class of attribution. In playing a particular language game, the individual actively participates in the moral order which lays claim to language games of this kind. At the centre of the discussion of human socialness in Chapter 4, therefore, is the idea that accountable action is socially binding. It represents the lifeline between the individual and the social community. Loyal to a tradition in social psychology which began with Festinger's cognitive dissonance theory, I have referred to this process of moral accountability as *justification* throughout the book.

In the social psychology of the 1980s there is growing interest in the possibility that social forces may have a bearing on physical health and may influence a person's susceptibility to life-threatening illness and death. In Chapters 5, 6, 7, and 8, which make up Part III of the present book, this idea is discussed from the perspective of the theory of social behaviour developed in Part II. The idea of an indissoluble connection between the deployment of words and the institutions of human social life remains the lynchpin of this discussion. The concerns of social psychology are, or ought to be, close to those of medicine. Both disciplines are based on the distinction between adaptive and maladaptive functioning of the individual as a biological unit on the one hand, and as a social one, on the other. I believe that the direction in which modern social psychology is travelling is toward concerns similar to those of medicine and that the way is now open to a sharing of many of the problems and discussions within the two fields. The issue of the individual's ability to cope with the stresses which result from the deprivations and demands of the present age and that of the consequences for health of a breakdown in coping have been until quite recently the province of physiologists, behaviourists, and psychoanalysts. Now they are being taken up in social psychology. One of my aims is to discuss this development and to show that the problems of stress and coping and the concerns of medicine are connected in an intimate way with the global project of social psychology. One cannot study a breakdown in adaptive social functioning without considering what adaptive social functioning means. One cannot have a theory of social stress without a theory of normal, nonstressful social living.

In Chapter 5, recent work on the relation between psychosocial factors and physical health and survival is reviewed. This leaves little doubt that such a relation exists. Social forces are consistently implicated as risk factors for premature illness, suicide, drug abuse, accident proneness, and victimisation. What is particularly interesting from the point of view of a social enquirer is that descriptions of the social determinants of each of these organismically destructive states often show at least an intuitive similarity. Excessive rates of all these conditions are found, for example, in recently bereaved people. Other studies concur that the supportive community has a health-protecting function. The possibility is therefore opened up that there is an *essential* link between the social adaptation and the biological survival of the individual.

Such a contingency has a Darwinian ring to it, and in Chapter 6 physiological interactions which may have evolved as mediators of the social stress effect are discussed. This chapter begins with a brief discussion (more an illustration) of some of the physiological hypotheses that are currently receiving attention. The comparatively new discipline of *psychoneuroimmunology* reflects the now acknowledged view that the immune system, active in the causation and prevention of a vast number of chronic degenerative conditions, including cancer, is not as autonomous as has traditionally been assumed. The competence of the immune response and the efficacy of immune surveillance mechanisms are critically dependent on neurohormonal, neurotransmitter, and neuropeptide activity, and therefore on activity in the cortex associated with the production of these chemicals. Underlying the present keen interest in these matters is the theme that endogenous factors such as neuroimmune interaction play a much bigger role in the control of health, illness, and death than has been credited in the past.

Sociobiology makes a prima facie case that man's inherited socialness is the key to his health and survival, both as a species and ipso facto as individual men and women. My aim in Chapters 5 and 6 is to develop the argument that the evolution of language has produced a unique form of socialness in which the bond between individual and collective is primarily a symbolic rather than a physical one. Cases of excess risk of illness and death very often involve circumstances that can be represented as a detachment of the individual from the community. But because of the symbolic nature of human communities—because these are based on structures of meanings that only arise as a consequence of a linguistic ability—this detachment needs to be viewed not so much as a physical isolation of the individual but as a symbolic or semiotic isolation. The at-risk case—the individual outsider—is the person who is cut off from any of the systems of moral accountability that make up a complex society.

Throughout the discussion in these chapters reference is repeatedly made to the pluralistic nature of human societies. Societies are seen as composites of different, not fully reconcilable, sub-cultures, groups, and cliques. In the process of accounting through which we endow actions with meaning and justify them, we are justifying them *against* alternative morally less expedient courses of action. Social psychology's focus on the process of attributing actions is itself a kind of illustration that the social world must be pluralistic in order for choice and action to be possible. Another route to the same conclusion is to imagine an ideal world in which everyone is agreed on the rules of conduct, morality, style, etc. Such a world would not contain the scope for choice and action because there would be no alternatives to choose and act against. There would be no potential courses to exclude. The idea of division and opposition as inherent features of macrocommunities is central to the theory of human social life developed in this book. The moral implications of this idea and its counterpart—the negotiation between people of opposing views—are taken up and analysed from both a social and a psychological angle in Chapter 7.

It will be apparent that the general perspective adopted in this book has much in common with the ethogenic position taken by Harré. Ethogenics starts from the principle that accounting for an action—explaining and justifying it—is as much a part of acting as the physical performance itself. The accounts people give of their own actions, in their own words, are treated as unassailable. Like the accounts collected by traditional social anthropologists, people's explanations are not fully interpretable and are not subject to prior, outside standards of validity. Harré's emphasis, however, is on the negotiation of accounts: the creative resolutions that can arise out of confrontations between different rhetorics, vocabularies, and speaking styles. In elaborating the theory of choice and action that runs through the discussion of health and survival in Part III of this book, I shall be concerned with the other side of this coin; the important implications for the understanding of social life that result from the irreconcilable aspects of social worlds predicated on different Wittgensteinian language games. Whereas Harré is concerned with the commensurability that can be forged between the different discourses of different kinds of people, my primary interest is in the aspect of human social behaviour that works against the commersuration and conciliation of mutual perspectives. But my objective is not symmetrical with that of ethogenics. It is certainly not my wish or evil aim to work out how to set up and preserve barriers between groups of people. Rather, my interest as a psychologist is in the necessary nature of the divisions inherent in communities that are built on words and the implications this has for individual biological survival.

That all macrocommunities are shot through with division and opposition I do not consider needs much proving. Most work in the social sciences is concerned, directly or indirectly, with how to knock down these hazardous boundaries between people and how to engineer compromises and reconciliations. In no way would I want to criticize or impede this important aim. However, the point of departure of this discussion is the view that while through our sustained efforts we may be able to prevent social differences and conflicts from getting out of hand, and even to achieve breakthroughs, we can never abolish social boundaries altogether. To do so would negate the possibility of personal choice and attributed action. It is in the nature of people living together in large groups to organise themselves into smaller groups because the contradistinctive quality of these smaller groups is what furnishes the individual with a prescriptive basis for acting and with his or her personal armory of justifications. Social opposition is the source of personal choice and the condition on which it is possible for the individual to act and to establish and maintain a sense of personal identity.

In a fever of trying to find ways of removing barriers between people and communities of people it is necessary to give some thought to what would be lost if these barriers were altogether to disappear; if some social magician was suddenly to organise things so that all social forms were suddenly to become commensurate. It is true that if this happened there would be no more misunderstanding and probably no more wars, but my contention is that this state of affairs is as imponderable and unreal as the state of affairs that would prevail in the world of material objects if friction was suddenly to disappear. In mechanics friction is a fact of life. In the social world I believe the situation to be somewhat similar with respect to social barriers. Just as physicists study the sources and effects of friction because it is there, so it is important for social enquirers to study the sources and effects of the divisions and incommensurabilities in our societies. This project is not as pessimistic as it may sound. One of the conclusions toward which it draws us, for example, is that the real weapons of the world are words and language. Few would want to deny that it is best kept that way.

The final chapter, Chapter 8, returns to the psychology of the individual and considers what the theory developed in the book has to say about the individual's resources for coping with and defending against social stress. Again, the role of language as inextricably bound to the workings of the social world, and the life-protecting quality of active participation of the individual in a system of moral accountability form the springboards for this discussion. Coping is equated with social support and defined simply as justified action.

It is often remarked that there is not much exchange of ideas between the different disciplines of the social sciences. Sociologists and psychologists, for example, do not talk to one another very much. One reason for this is that the concepts and distinctions in one subject often do not translate easily into another subject. We academics, in our own departments, like to play our own rather insular language games. My interest in the relation of social adaptation to biological survival stems from a hope that the questions that surround this issue can provide a meeting point for ideas within and even beyond the social sciences. The scale of the kind of theory building that is needed to account for this relation is impressively large. It stretches to medicine and the life sciences on one side and sociolinguistics and philosophy on the other.

Part I

1

The Data of Social Psychology

The Scientist's Privileged Access

Although much is spoken and written about science and scientists, agreement is far from universal about what science is and what exactly it is that scientists do. The most widely held idea of a scientist, one broadly endorsed by historians and philosophers of science, is of someone who is prepared to give closer and more systematic attention to some aspect of the world than the layman. A scientist notices details and irregularities in the environment that others miss and finds fault with explanations that get by in ordinary everyday life. For these purposes, the scientist is continually making physical aids which extend the limits of normal perception and make accessible states and events which would otherwise remain hidden. Microscopes and staining techniques allow biologists to observe organic structure that is invisible to the naked eye; physicists use bubble chambers and accelerators to study the behaviour of otherwise unstudyable particles, and so on. Hypothesis testing in the physical sciences is heavily bound up with the development of investigative instrumentation.

Piaget believed that the way in which a scientist operates is similar in many respects to the way in which children come to know the world in the course of normal mental development. He showed that children continually test and progressively refine and revise their ideas through the balanced interplay of two functions: the assimilation of marginally new information to established hypotheses and the accommodation of established hypotheses in the wake of radically new and challenging experiences. Just as improvements in the scientist's knowledge of the world are made possible by the constant development of new instrumentation and reagents, the child's progressively more sophisticated understanding of the world goes hand in hand with the maturation of the neural structures that underlie perception, cognition, and language.

Social scientists, by contrast, have neither the specialist sensory hardware of the physical scientist nor the transforming neurological apparatus of the growing child. They have access to data-processing facilities and statistics for sorting collected information, but there is nothing equivalent to the investigative instrumentation on which growth of knowledge in the physical and natural sciences depends. They must use the same sensory and interpretative apparatus that is constantly available to everyone else.

Perhaps the absence of instrumentation is one of the reasons for the scepticism expressed by many who work in the physical sciences as to whether social enquiry can ever really be called a scientific enterprise. The value of descriptive studies—surveys, epidemiological correlations, and anthropological reports—can be appreciated easily enough. By and large, their findings can be expressed in terms that are accessible to ordinary folk (e.g., "early heart disease is more prevalent among low-income earners") But the value of representing naturally arising social phenomena as the data of causes and effects, using a specialist, technical vocabulary, is less obvious. How can the social investigator be at an advantage over the layperson when he or she has neither specialist extensions to the senses nor private access to information? I believe there is indeed a case to answer that the "technical" knowledge that has been accumulated in traditional social psychology research tells us little we did not, in some intuitive sense, already know. Sometimes it even tells us things that we know to be false—artifacts of the "experimental" method.

The main argument of the first part of this book is that the value of social psychology does not lie in the technical data of empirical research: research aimed at relating social phenomena to other social phenomena in a specialist language of causes and effects. The psychological measurements that are made in an effort to do this, whether in the laboratory or the field, are not like the measurements of physics or chemistry. There can be no counterintuitive findings from this kind of study, no findings that are an improvement on knowledge that is already in the culture being researched.

It is very easy to play wise after the event and with hindsight to dismiss much of what has been done as unnecessary. But how many of the findings from social psychology research are truly noteworthy? How many can be called milestones in the subject comparable to the many textbook experiments in physics and chemistry? How many experiments are even remembered other than fleetingly by undergraduates working for exams and those who teach them? Unless of course they are highly controversial, like Milgram's studies in which people were encouraged by an experimenter to administer electric shocks to others.

A reciprocal query must also be raised about why it is that the best-remembered achievements in the social sciences are those that are not based on quantitative data. The most renowned social scientists—Freud, Marx, Hegel, Durkheim, Lévi-Strauss, Keynes, and Piaget, to take just a few examples—are the very individuals whose work would not merit serious attention under the canons of experimental research adhered to in the social science departments of today.

Criticisms of Experimentation

The 1970s have seen some strong attacks on traditional experiments in social psychology (see, e.g., Gilmour and Duck, 1980), and I do not want to recapitulate these at length here. Among the most prominent are the criticisms of Harré from the position that he calls ethogenics (Harré, 1979, 1983; Harré and Secord, 1972). Harré reflects a widening opinion in his view that the classic experimental method which relies on holding all but one condition constant, varying this condition, and looking among the consequences for a lawful covariate, is inapplicable to social enquiry: "If the conditions of social action are a structure of internally related elements, then this condition for the application of the experimental method can never be met. The extraction of an element from the structure and its separation from the relations in which it stood to other elements would, if it were internally related to them, change the nature of the element. It would be no longer what it was in the natural condition" (1979, pp. 102–103).

Harré's criticisms of traditional methods are made from the outside. They are the criticisms of a philosopher of science who, in the philosophical tradition of Peters, Melden, Strawson, and Hampshire, sees the reasons people give for the things they do as the stuff of social life and who is committed to a reflexive, nonmechanistic conception of human beings and a structuralist account of human social behaviour. Social psychology is seen not as a branch of natural science, having to do with natural laws, but more as a branch of philosophical ethics—Aristotle's ethical science—having to do with illuminating social rules and the moral orders that lie beneath them.

In the first two chapters of this book I am concerned with assessing traditional methods from the inside, looking at the problems set themselves by researchers, and focusing on the language—the psychologese—that has grown up out of the requirement of representing social phenomena in terms of empirical data. It is this language, posing as a precise and technical science, that masks the emptiness of much of what is said in social psychology. My aim is to investigate this specialist language. I shall try to show that research and theory in social psychology are essentially unconnected: that technical empirical findings have little bearing on the often quite interesting issues raised in theories and do not govern which theories are kept and which discarded.

Reasons and Causes

Psychologists and philosophers remain divided over the issue of the real business of social enquiry; in particular, whether its proper province is the human being as a reasoning, moral agent, or as a set of mechanisms subject to the laws of causal necessity. In social psychology something of a reaction has built up against the traditional causal–deterministic model and many share the feeling that people should be regarded as deliberating and reflexive agents and not as machines (see, e.g., Brenner, 1980; Gilmour and Duck, 1980). But the two types of models are probably not as incompatible as they are often made out to be. In our dealings with computers we are happy talking about a machine performing operations and the same machine being controlled by its software. Both are legitimate ways of speaking. Each has its own vocabulary and grammar which is not transferable to the other. We tend to talk about a machine doing things when we are trying to make sense of the work that is being produced and about causing it to do things when we want to design or change some aspect of its functioning. As with people, explaining a machine's performance by giving reasons ("It did it this way so as not to have to go through the search again") relies on a normative knowledge of the kinds of things certain kinds of machines do.

Harré is an enthusiastic champion of the agentive view of humans. For him the best kind of data are to be got from autobiographies. The social worlds of individuals are revealed principally by listening to them talk and "negotiating" with them the accounts that they give. The reflexive model on which this approach rests has shown itself to be a sensitive and sympathetic approach to understanding other people and its popularity is growing. However, if we want to try, for instance, to build a general theory of the way in which social forces affect the health and survival of the individual, then it is necessary to accept some kind of causal, or functional, relation as already there, implied, in this aim. Actions and personality traits are sometimes talked about as produced, for example, by genes and environmental conditions. Insightful as it may be, there seems no reason to be bound by the reflexive model of humans to the exclusion of all other styles of analysis. Ethogenics is firm about treating acts and actions as autonomous, but sometimes for some purposes it may be appropriate to view people as mechanisms.

Jargon of Research

Whether working in the laboratory or in the field, social psychologists like to use a lot of jargon. People are subjects. Attitudes, likings, and preferences are points on a normal distribution. Quite complex social interactions are treatments. Not performing tasks to the experimenter's specification is failure. Deviations from expected patterns is response bias. Trying to please an experimenter is responding to demand characteristics. Pleasure and pain are positive and negative affect. Challenging experiences are life events and all kinds of reactions, including illnesses, are responses. Even death itself has been described fantastically by one group of authors as "mortality experience" (Medalie et al., 1973).

The social researcher has no specialist instrumentation to extend the senses, so what is it that entitles him or her to this specialist vocabulary? How, we might ask, is the social science of today different from the theologies of the past? Let us look at the claim that the difference lies in the incorporation of a scientific methodology and that research produces objective data as a result of objective hypotheses.

The first thing to notice about jargon words, especially those that have ordinary language connections, is that far from being precise, they are often very ambiguous. A good example is the concept of stress. Over the past two decades there has been a great deal of interest in relating stressful experiences in a person's life to physiological activity, especially reactions that could conceivably be linked to the onset or exacerbation of organic pathology. Here are a few of the many situations that for the purpose of research have been defined as stressful: crowding, isolation, being overworked, being underworked, overload, underload, overstimulation, understimulation, receiving electric shocks, group pressure, working for exams, having a child who is dying of leukaemia, changing jobs, parachuting, bereavement, moving house, watching films of people being circumcised without anaesthetics, working on unsolvable anagrams, and listening to bursts of white noise.

These examples speak for themselves. It is not difficult to appreciate how all these could be stressful. But fixing on a situation that we know from our experience is going to cause a person anxiety and discovering that corticosteroid levels are elevated, or that some other physiological balance is upset adds nothing much to our *psychological* understanding of stress, or of anything else. Abelson (1977) makes a similar point:

> To sum up the matter roughly and provisionally, to the degree to which a psychologist tries to be scientific in a way analogous to physicists and biologists, to that degree his procedure is self-defeating, for it will not produce positive *psychological* knowledge. Experimental psychologists are very scientific in this sense, and that is probably why they have added little to our knowledge of *human* motivation, although they have found out a great deal about physiology and animal behavior. (p. 1)

In the case of work on stress, it would be much better from the point of view of psychology if we were to concentrate on the intuitions that led these investigators confidently to infer that such diverse experiences are all stressful. In other words, as well as searching for physiological correlates of stressful states it is interesting to think about the social and cultural signs that caused independent authors to select radically different circumstances in the lives of individuals and link these in the common term *stressful life events*. Just why and in what sense can all these different encounters be said to be stressful? The idea of experimenters confidently deploying the term *stress* in their specialist research programmes has an air of objectivity about it. But this merely helps to mask the difficulty inherent in using the term as a lynchpin of research design. Some empty statements have been produced, clothed in scientistic rhetoric, about what stress is. Mandler, for example, defines stress in the following way: "a situation is defined as stressful if and when the interpretative cognitive activities of the organism transform input in such a way that a percepible internal change results" (1979, p. 184). Antonovsky (1979), himself critical of the stress concept as a basis for investigation, captures the problem in his remark, "All social environments are inherently stressful" (p. 87).

Every piece of research must be selective and in this sense theory based. A researcher has to have certain definitions and preconceptions in order to start out. It is not possible to study the behaviour of neutrons, for example, without having some idea of what neutrons are and how theoretically they differ from other particles. My criticism of the technical empirical research that is done in social psychology is not that it is linked to theory but that the resolutions of theoretical issues and the answers to questions raised in hypotheses are not achieved through the data of this kind of research. In the following sections I try to show that research conclusions are typically of one or two forms. They are either trivially circular in that they represent entailed properties of the problem as this was laid out, or they are trivially obvious; disguised reiterations of uncontroversial pieces of common sense.

These two charges turn out to be related insofar as the jargon of research relies for its sense on ordinary meanings.

Research and Common Sense

How far is the allegation of "no advance on common sense" supported by what has been achieved so far in social psychology (see Joynson, 1974)? How well does a gloss of the main conclusions from research programmes, such as might be found in any standard introductory text, stand up to the challenge of obviousness? How, for example, would a layman react to a simplified summary of the principle findings of the research done over the past three decades?

An introductory text leaves us with impressions of the following kind. We find that research has shown societies and groups to be highly structured, with different individuals occupying different social roles; that there are leaders, followers, Machievellians, introverts, extraverts, conformers, deviants; that people are characteristically full of prejudice and hold stereotypes of others; and that in groups pressure to conform can be very strong and can affect what the individual says and does in a powerful way. This theme is recapitulated in research on "risky-shift;" people will do more daring things with others than when by themselves. Studies of non-verbal communication show that a great deal of social interaction and cuing goes on without words. Programmes of training in social skills have been developed which apparently help people overcome their feelings of inadequacy in social situations.

Discussions of attitudes and attitude change figure prominently in most standard texts. Research in this area indicates that people like most, and associate with, others of similar attitudes and opinions to themselves and that the introduction of choice, effort, public commitment, and involvement are conducive to attitude change, and that people are subject to cognitive dissonance and so are preoccupied with trying to justify their decisions and inject consistency into their actions. Bem's studies, and subsequent research on the "overjustification effect" show that giving someone a tangible reward can undermine his or her motivation. Milgram's experiments are usually featured because their conclusion—that people are prepared to do very cruel things to one another when they can defer responsibility—has a sensational appeal.

No introductory text is complete without an elaborate discussion of the social psychology of the social psychology experiment itself. Orne's discovery of the power of demand characteristics makes it plain that special forces are at work in the psychologist's laboratory so that a subject will try to guess the experimenter's wishes and produce reactions in accordance with what he or she believes the experimenter wants. The study of "social situations" has been taken up and developed recently as more attention is being paid to social influences on individual behaviour in face-to-face encounters. Social "episodes" are likened to staged scenes and it is fashionable to talk about rules and scripts governing performance. Argyle, Furnham, and Graham, (1981) define a *situation* as "the sum of the features of a social occasion that impinge on an individual person" (p. 3).

Most contemporary texts are written in the language of attribution theory. Schachter and Singer's experiments are usually to be found in this section. These showed that people, when artificially physiologically aroused by being injected with adrenalin and when misinformed about the effects of the drug, look round for cues to label their feelings. If they see someone whom they believe has been similarly treated exhibiting anger, they too will become angry. But if it is euphoria they see the other experiencing, they too will report feelings of euphoria. The conclusion from these classic studies is that emotions contain a cognitive element: people look round for social cues for an appropriate label for their emotional state (Schachter and Singer, 1962).

Studies in attribution theory offer further conclusions. For example, there are at least a dozen studies that support the prediction that people are inclined to make face-saving attributions; they find ways of avoiding blaming themselves for bad consequences and will try to point to mitigating circumstances in order to excuse themselves. In the jargon of attribution theory, people prefer *internal* (or *dispositional*) attributions for positive outcomes and *external* (or *situational*) attributions for negative outcomes. Other research has shown that these face-saving attributions are more likely when action is committed publicly, when perceived choice and perceived responsibility are high, under high ego-involvement conditions, and so on.

With hindsight it is easy to embark on a sarcastic commentary on the achievements in any subject. Many theories and generalisations seem obvious once they become part of established knowledge. Does it not seem trivially obvious to us in the twentieth century, for example, that the extension of a spring is proportional to the load applied to it? This relation seems almost built in to the meanings of the terms *load* and *extension.* Yet, Hooke's law was undoubtedly a major step forward in the physics of the 1670s. Nonetheless, it is a sobering exercise to strip away the jargon from some of the more cherished findings of social psychology and look at them in plain terms. Most can be adequately expressed in this manner and a surprising proportion of them appear unremarkable, to say the least.

Our layman might be excused for having thoughts of the following kind: (1) anyone who knows about the Nazi treatment of Jews in the Second World

War, the British treatment of their prisoners in the Boer War, or, for that matter, any persecution of any minority group at any point in history, would not be surprised by Milgram's findings, (2) people are, of course, forever trying to justify the choices they have made and make their actions appear sensible and consistent, (3) it is common knowledge that every trick in the book is used to avoid blame and gain credit, (4) attitudes by definition generate behaviour and the fact that people of like attitude tend to associate with one another is implicit in the concept of attitude itself—birds of a feather flock together, (5) on the other hand, we know it is not just a one-way process and that actions can design attitudes too—the mask becomes the man.

Even the less immediately obvious findings, such as those of Schachter and Singer in relation to emotion, have their everyday counterparts. As we jokingly surprise a friend with a dig in the ribs from behind, his or her emotion can be watched as it changes from fear to anger or humour, depending on the circumstances, either of these reactions being more appropriate to the situation than the original one of fear.

Notwithstanding the caution about hindsight, it is difficult to avoid the feeling that much of the research in social psychology concerns itself with problems that are no more than self-evident social truths dressed up in numbers, formulae, and fancy words. There is a natural tendency for any accredited academic subject to want to preserve its professional autonomy, and resorting to scientistic rhetoric is one way of foiling outside critics. I believe that most social science subjects have been guilty of this manoevre over recent years. Why, for example, do social psychologists take so little account of the distinctions of law when there are good reasons for regarding these as bearing intimately on social life? What counts as legally and morally reprehensible action changes with time and place, but the concepts of responsibility and recrimination are themselves sufficiently inured to merit serious attention from psychologists. Are there really any grounds for preferring the comparatively new attribution-theory distinction between internal and external attributions (a distinction which, incidentally, is interpreted in widely different ways by different authors; Antaki, 1982) to the older and more tried distinction between actions for which an individual can be held responsible and actions for which he or she cannot (see Locke and Pennington, 1982)?

"Technical" Data

It could be argued that any selective and superficial tour through the research literature like the one I have just provided is bound to leave a misleading impression and that the value of research can only be appreciated at a finer level, looking at things such as the exact conditions under which conformity effects occur, the specific factors affecting magnitude of attitude change, and the precise circumstances in which defensive attributions are resorted to. To many involved in research the conclusions that I have listed in the previous section will seem like generalisations of the grossest kind and will not be considered in any way representative of the real findings.

The first thing to be said about the finer-grain findings of research is that these tend to be the most jargon-ridden. This is inevitably so, defenders of traditional methods will say, because these are the findings that touch on fresh social truths, the relationships that require new precision psychological terms and definitions. The latter are put forward as objective descriptions of social phenomena. Hypotheses are impressive-sounding and technical but tautological. It is usually possible to excavate the answer to the question raised in the hypothesis from the sense of the hypothesis itself. Consider the following passage: "The findings of several social psychological and clinical studies indicate that explicit external or environmental response-reinforcement contingencies, particularly when perceived as influence attempts, tend to undermine the individual's sense of self-initiation and responsibility for behaviour" (Sonne and Janoff, 1982, pp. 88–89). The authors go on to recommend that "the clinician hold to the principle of least powerful reward or punishment."

The message here is the tautology that attempts at persuasion become more apparent as they are made more obvious and the message to the clinician is little more than "people don't like to be pushed if they see what you're doing is pushing them."

The second thing to notice about this precision research is that its jargon, its technical language, is rarely properly independent of ordinary speech in that it relies for its sense on structures that support everyday conversation; exactly those structures in fact which constitute lay expressions of the social order.

The application of attribution theory to clinical problems is a field in which there are plenty of technical expressions. In a review of "attributional style therapy," Layden comments: "Overall, the processes examined here indicate that low self-esteem individuals have a negative self-image and a number of strategies that maintain this self-image" (Layden, 1982, p. 69). This statement involves two tautologies: (1) low self-esteem people think little of themselves, and (2) all structures (self-images included) resist change.

Consider also the recommendations for treatment that are arrived at in the conclusion section of the same paper:

> Because high self-esteem persons externalise failure, in the present research I have chosen to train individuals with low self-esteem to increase the salience of external causes

> for failure. External attributions lessen the feeling of responsibility for failure and the self-blame that failure engenders.
>
> Clearly, there is, however, another possible approach that might be beneficial; that is to decrease the stability of the perceived causes for failure. Making an internal cause unstable promotes a sense of control. (Layden, 1982, p. 69)

What is being said in this passage is that it does people good to feel they are not personally responsible for failures (increasing the salience of external causes for failure), and that it may be a good idea to tell people they can do better if they try (decreasing the stability of the perceived causes for failure). But doesn't every good friend know the comfort in "Don't be daft, it's not your fault" (encouraging the externalisation of failure)? And don't all parents from time to time say to their child, "Well done; all your own work too!" (promoting the internalization of success)? And what about that old school-report chestnut, "could do better if s/he tried." So entrenched in our culture are these moral enjoinders that they find mythological expression in legends and literature, and in cant slogans like "if at first you don't succeed, try, try again!."

Not infrequently psychological hypotheses contain words that have both an ordinary and, so we are led to believe, a technical meaning. The following passage illustrates the type of problem that arises when this is the case:

> What effect does stress have upon self-esteem? Disapproval treatment, rejection or negative feedback, which many individuals interpret as being stressful, when used in laboratory research has produced lowered self-esteem. Ludwig and Maher (1967) found that seventh and eighth-grade boys, when given disapproval treatment for performing various physical tasks, showed lowered self-esteem. Gibby and Gibby (1967) explored the effects of academic failure upon seventh-grade students. Under the failure situation, students regarded themselves less highly and believed they were not as highly regarded by others. Wilcox and Mitchell (1977), using a role-playing exercise, found that rejected college students showed a decrease in self-esteem. (Williams, 1980, p. 20)

On a superficial reading the author of this passage may appear to be reviewing findings of some value. A closer look though, with an eye to the reliance on ordinary-language meanings of the key words and phrases shows the blandness of what is being said. We do not need research to tell us that "disapproval treatment," "rejection," and "negative feedback" engender "lowered self-esteem." Or that in a "failure situation" people regard themselves "less highly." The relationships are entailed and trivial because the meanings of the terms are mostly accessible at an ordinary level. "Stress," "disapproval treatment," and "lowered self-esteem" are made to appear like professional terms with exact technical meanings but in fact they are not. With this illusion blown away, the "findings" here are exposed as a straight duplication of everyday consensus.

Midgley (1981) levies exactly the same charge against many of the discussions in sociobiology:

> It is simply not possible to use words of strong everyday import in a private and peculiar sense. . . The whole nature of language prevents such a detachment of meaning from habitual background. Anyone using words like this must mislead his audience. What is more serious, unless he is exceptionally sharp and sophisticated, he will certainly mislead himself. (p. 525)

These examples are illustrations of the point that the answers to questions raised in social psychology research often lie buried in the questions themselves. Insofar as this is so, the "findings" of this research achieve no more than to direct attention to a fragment of the structure on which our ordinary language and conversation is based and hence a fragment of the order by which social life is lived. My two criticisms, of tautology and obviousness in the interpretation of data, turn out not to be properly independent of one another because most hypotheses contain neither pure technical jargon nor straight imported ordinary language but a mix of both.

The Experiment as Illustrative Anecdote

McGuire (1973) and Shotter (1981) have both expressed the opinion that psychological studies are often advertisements for hypotheses disguised as empirical testings. McGuire writes:

> . . . we social psychologists have tended to use the manipulative laboratory experiment not to test our hypotheses but to demonstrate their obvious truth. . . . We tend to start off with a hypothesis that is so clearly true (given the implicit and explicit assumptions) and which we have no intention of rejecting however the experiment comes out. Such a stance is quite appropriate, since the hypothesis by its meaningfulness and plausibility to reasonable people is tautologically true in the assumed context. (1973, pp. 446 and 448)

Bruner agrees: "We researchers . . . suppress our presuppositions in communicating our findings and then feign surprise when we state our final conclusions" (1982, p. 313).

Shotter (1981) is critical of the studies reported by Nisbett and Wilson (1977) and Nisbett and Bellows (1977), which showed that after their participation in an experiment as subjects, people were unable to pinpoint accurately the factors that had influenced their behaviour. This finding is held up by Nisbett and Wilson as surprising and significant. But Shotter disagrees:

> But how should we react to these 'findings'? Firstly, when the confusing and misleading language in which they are reported is clarified the results are, in one sense, I think, trivial. They merely report once again the already well-known fact that while we do many things in social life, intelligently and intelligibly, in quite skillful ways, it is quite normal not to be able to report upon how we do them. (p. 175–176)

The data of social psychology, while a clear target for this kind of criticism, may not be the only such target. There is concern among some philosophers of science as to the value of much of the empirical work that is done in physical and natural science departments. Laudan makes a similar point to McGuire's: "Changes in, and debates about, scientific theories often turn on conceptual issues rather than on questions of empirical support" (1981, p. 144).

Feyerabend, who acknowledges the value of post-Galilean scientific endeavour as a source both of stability and progress in Europe, draws a comparison between the teaching of science now and the teaching of religion in the nineteenth century. He follows a discussion of the problems of deciding between theories whose concepts are incommensurable with these remarks:

> It is good to be constantly reminded of the fact that science as we know it today is not inescapable and that we may construct a world in which it plays no role whatever (such a world, I would venture to suggest, would be more pleasant than the world we live in today). What better reminder is there than the realization that the choice between theories which are sufficiently general to provide us with a comprehensive world view and which are empirically disconnected may become a matter of taste? (1981, p. 160)

And Rorty, in a thoroughgoing critique of epistemology, aligns himself with Kuhn (1978), saying: "We do indeed need to give up the notion of 'data and interpretation' with its suggestion that if we get to the *real* data, unpolluted by our choice of language, we should be 'grounding' rational choice" (1980, p. 325). Setting the argument in sharp focus, he states: "The application of such honorifics as 'objective' and 'cognitive' is never more than an expression of the presence of, or the hope for, agreement among enquirers" (1980, p. 335).

The "Non-obvious" Finding

Tajfel and Fraser (1981) are among many psychologists who argue that while it is not difficult to find examples of restatements of the obvious in social psychology, this is only to be expected in any comprehensive programme of research aimed at separating fact from superstition in folk explanations. Non-obvious relations, they claim, are the exception to the rule, but are nevertheless sometimes brought to light. This goes against my argument which is that non-obvious findings are *in principle* impossible in social research which resorts to a technical language to express a causal connection between two or more variables of the social world. To be non-obvious and go against the prevailing consensus would mean going against the relations in ordinary talk and ordinary talk is simultaneously the custodian of this consensus and the source from which hypotheses are drawn. The would-be researcher does not operate like the legendary Martian, starting out to study our societies with no presuppositions. Such a researcher's hypothesis is culled from his or her own experience in the social world as actor, observer, listener, and commentator. He or she does not randomly select a dimension as potentially of interest. It cannot possibly be done because how, other than on the basis of personal experience can he or she even decide what counts as a "dimension" in social life quite apart from any hunch about which dimensions might be relevant to the particular problem chosen for study. To get to the stage of hypothesis formation, a researcher must have called on personal accumulated knowledge and experience, first, to segment the social world into meaningful analytic slices and second, to pick one of these as the centrepiece of his or her investigation.

The testing of social hypotheses is indeed an empirical matter but not in the sense of taking objective measurements. What is up for measurement is the quality of the articulated hypothesis as an insightful commentary on some aspect of the social world. But the testing that ensues, and which determines whether a hypothesis survives, has no more to do with data than the "testing" of a novel, play, piece of music, or work of art. The way things happen in social psychology indeed bears out Rorty's view that a theory or hypothesis succeeds not on account of its proven status as an objective truth but simply because there is agreement between people about it. Agreement is reached in dialogue, so we might say that the success of a theory or hypothesis can be judged by how much discussion it gets. Put another way, the value of a theory or hypothesis lies in its power to code, in an edifying way, some aspect of social life. Because social life and the conversational language spoken by the people living it are so intimately bound together, social theories and hypotheses can be thought of as commentaries on ordinary forms of talk. The more incisive the commentary, the more appealing the hypothesis.

The same spirit of relativism is to be found in McGuire's constructivism (1980), Gergen's generative theory (1978), and Brenner's (1982) plea for multiplicity in theories of action. McGuire explains his position in the following way:

> The (alternative) Constructivist paradigm can be introduced by the outrageous assertion that it supposes that all hypotheses are true: in Blake's words, "Everything possible to be believ'd is an image of truth". That is to say, if a reasonable person guided by some plausible theory formulates the hypothesis that people like best those most similar to themselves then it should be taken for granted that *ipso facto* the hypothesis is true. But so would the opposite hypothesis be true if it also could be derived by a reasonable researcher from a plausible theory. (1980, p. 78)

The argument is perhaps helped by the philosophical distinction between correspondence and coherence theories of truth. Correspondence theory, based on a realist metaphysics, maintains, roughly, that hypotheses are accepted or rejected according to the accuracy with which they depict phenomena in the real world. Coherence theory, based on a rationalist metaphysics, holds that a hypothesis is measured against other hypotheses and stands or falls according to the range, elegance, and internal consistency of its explanatory premises. The way in which research is approached in social psychology suggests an assumptive commitment to the correspondence view. But this assumption does not seem to hold up when we look at theories and hypotheses and what actually happens to them. Taking a long view of what is regarded as progress in the social sciences, it is tempting to say that the growth of knowledge more closely approximates the course described in coherence theory. Yet this distinction has only a limited use to us because on the one hand I am supporting a correspondence version in holding that hypotheses are matched against our distilled experience of the social world, and on the other, a coherence version in the view of hypotheses as edifying precis of aspects of ordinary talk. Both positions can be supported on the assumption on which the main arguments of this book rest; that there is an equivalence between systems of talk and the institutions of social life.

What support is there for such an equivalence? There is some support within social psychology in the radical positions taken by writers such as McGuire, Gergen, and Shotter. There is implicit support in the traditions of ethnomethodology and ethogenics. Harré's work is built on this assumption. But the strongest support comes from outside psychology. Douglas (1980) considers it a well-established principle of social anthropology that thought and accounting practices are embedded in institutions. She traces this notion particularly in the writings of Evans-Pritchard. The speech act theory of Austin and Searle (Searle, 1969) emphasises the agentive character of utterances, construing language as a rule-governed, institution-bound form of intentional behaviour. The idea of social order as inherent in discourse is more or less taken for granted among French philosophers in the structuralist tradition. Among the very first voices in this chorus was, of course, that of Marx who insisted that definitions of problems are themselves not free of the influence of history.

Wittgenstein's "Language Games"

One of the most original and thorough versions of this argument was set out by Wittgenstein in his later works, particularly *Philosophical Investiga-*

tions (1953). Wittgenstein's theory of language is developed from the basic intuition that the meaning of utterances is established by their practice in a community: "If we had to name anything which is the life of the sign we should have to say that it was its *use*" (1958, p. 4). Behind this statement is a refusal to divorce the study of a language from the study of those who speak it.

Wittgenstein developed the concept of language games to refer to systems of communication that are rehearsed between individuals. In the idea of language games lies his thesis that talk is based on rules and rules are the property of institutions. To establish this, he attacked the notion of private languages—the possibility that an esoteric, introspective commentary could arise which is intelligible only to the speaker. From the impossibility of private languages he argued that there is a binding link between the individual's social world, and his or her speech and mental life. Wittgenstein locates objectivity in the practice of language, and thus—in the tradition of Durkheim—in the institutions that make up society. Other sign systems such as mathematics are different kinds of language games played by a different kind of player. Russell wanted to reduce mathematics to logic. Wittgenstein asks, "Why logic?" and attempts to reduce both mathematics and logic and all other forms of signal-based communication between people to language games. In linguistically sophisticated societies many different kinds of language games are played, the multiplicity of language games reflecting the network of communities that makes up these complex societies. Mathematics, logic, and forms of talk are all, in Wittgenstein's eyes, to be seen as anthropological phenomena. Words, sentences, and symbols come to have value and meaning only on account of their shared nature and only in context of the institutions that govern their usage. Institutions are there lurking in the background even in the least-pretentious exchanges between people—even in such things as small-talk about the weather. Bloor (1983) gives a good account of Wittgenstein's theory of language games and the empirical possibilities that are raised by the concept.

Bringing Wittgenstein's analysis to bear on what social scientists do in the name of research, one could say that in their involvement with measuring instruments and a methodology imported from classical physics, social investigators are caught up in a peculiar, insulated set of language games; ones in which usage, and hence meaning, is mostly restricted to a small community of people who have taken it upon themselves to speak psychologese. But social investigation is special in that its subject matter—people and the things they do—*includes* the social investigator and his or her measuring devices. Why should the language games that are set up in connection with these activities add up to a better commentary on social life than anyone else's? The pursuit of objectivity in the data that are collected smacks of essences in a way that Wittgenstein would not have cared for. It suggests that the construction and rigorous testing and refining of measuring instruments (psychological scales, etc.) will eventually yield an apocalyptic language game—one to which all others are answerable and to which only social scientists, by virtue of their specialism, possess the title.

Successful Social Knowledge

If we accept the fully blown relativist position that talk is constitutive of human social life, then the effectiveness of a theory or hypothesis—the extent to which it influences social matters and the way people think—comes to the same thing as its success in introducing new expressions and meanings into our language and everyday talk. We might say a good social science hypothesis is one that intrudes on ordinary discourse and, to use Rorty's phrase, "extends the conversation." The better the hypothesis, the greater the amount of discussion it provokes and the deeper its effect on conversational talk. Wittgenstein's argument goes against the assumption that the most significant theories and hypotheses are those that best predict the "data". It establishes a case that the best theories and hypotheses are those that engineer the biggest changes in the words we use and the way we speak, and ipso facto in the world in which we live. Change is possible, and indeed vital, in Wittgenstein's theory and comes about by people using new words, and using old words in new ways.

The idea of progress as change is one that finds favour with Gergen. He defines his generative theory of social behaviour thus: "The generative theory is one that challenges the guiding assumptions of the culture, raises fundamental questions regarding social life, fosters reconsideration of that which is "taken for granted" and thereby furnishes fresh alternatives for social action" (1980, p. 261).

Conclusion

To sum up, I have suggested that the empirical data of social psychology generated as a result of the specialist measurement of social "variables" and interactions between them are inherently trivial. If the data clearly support a hypothesis, people will say, "That's obvious"; if the data clearly refute it, they will say the same. One can make a hypothesis look technical so that it is less easily reduced to ordinary terminology and therefore less readily available to the layman but the more technical it is made, the more tautological seem to be the findings and conclusions that spring from it. One of the reasons for this is that the supposedly technical psychological terms still often rely for their sense on ordinary meanings. When findings are ambiguous the cry "methodological problems" invariably goes up, but there is seldom much wrong with the method of studies as far as it goes. What is wrong is that there should be an enjoinder to this kind of method at all because it is not within the capacity of such method to produce genuinely controversial, counterintuitive findings. Such findings would have to run against the collectively negotiated intuitions—the prevailing language games—of the community, and these are both constitutive of the life of the community and at the same time contributary to the conceptual base from which hypotheses are drawn. The claim that a piece of research has produced counterintuitive findings therefore contains a contradiction. It implies both that such findings do and that they do not relate to the social world which is the object of study.

Anything that leads to new distinctions and further discussion is of course good in that by expanding the enquiry it builds upon existing knowledge. I believe that the exchange of ideas between social investigators can and does do this but that being bound to a system in which ideas cannot get a hearing other than in published research reports actually works against the constructive process.

Importing the method of classical physics makes social psychology look respectably scientific and licenses the social investigator to use scientistic rhetoric in commenting on a culture of which he or she is part. Where both the "variables" are social phenomena there can be no new findings. The social measurements of cause-and-effect research are expendable without any loss to the subject, even without loss of the empirical ideal that motivates the rational, systematic investigator. For discussions between social scientists *are* answerable to an empirical standard associated with testing of a more satisfactory kind than can be done under the dry patronage of independent and dependent variables. Hypotheses are tested by being fitted anecdotally to real life and by being negotiated by people in ordinary conversation. The winners are those that excite the most talk and those whose categories filter through into ordinary discourse. There can be no objection to specialist psychological terms per se as a speculative shorthand, as long as they are not linked to the collection of data and as long as the pretence that concepts have real objective counterparts which it is the task of research to find is dropped. History confirms that the mark of a good social hypothesis is its power to make an academic conversation overflow its sectoral, professional precinct and spill over into other walks of social life so as, in the long run, to affect the relations between words and thus subtly to alter the way in which people talk. For Wittgenstein, speaking practices and the institutions of society come down to the same thing, and to alter the talk is to alter the people themselves. In the past, in what we call the social sciences, it is precisely those ideas that have done this that have survived longest and that command the greatest respect.

2

Theories as Independent of Research

My aim in this discussion of research is not so much to expound on how social psychology should conduct itself as to offer an alternative account to the one generally held of how it does proceed, and to discuss how it continues to get by as an interesting subject. The way the textbooks would have us believe knowledge advances—step by step, systematically from one research initiative to the next, the result of a focused collective effort—is a misrepresentation of what really happens. I am not prescribing a future course so much as commenting on the past and present one. In this chapter and the next I shall look at the history of social psychology theories and try to prove that their pre-eminence does not depend on the findings of the research that is done in connection with them.

Language, Knowledge, and Change

There are plenty of examples from history to show that informal, intuitive conceptions of phenomena are an adequate basis for acting on these phenomena. People were able to construct good sentences before the rules of grammar were outlined by Chomsky, and they could reason before Aristotle extracted the rules of logic. Cathedrals were built in the absence of the applied mathematics which is a prerequisite for a career in civil engineering today.

The same is true of discussion in the social sciences. For example, the word "unconscious" was in the vernacular before Freud, but it is probably fair to say that this term was not used as widely and in quite the same sense as it is today, along with other Freudian words that have become commonplace, like "neurotic," "repression," and "identification." The altered sense and widened circulation of these words affect our attitudes and how we react to other people. Coveney (1967) draws attention to the effect that Freud's essay on infantile sexuality has had on our image of the child. The romantic picture of childhood innocence idealised by Rousseau is undermined by Freud's account of the psychosexual stages and the Oedipus complex (another phrase that has found its way into modern dictionaries).

Class conflict was undeniably in evidence long before Marx. However, the outcome of Marx's theories was a new frame of reference for the representation of this and other matters connected with the distribution of social power and the psychology of work. The meanings of the words "class" and "capital," among others, have not been the same since. Psychology too has been quite successful in introducing new words into our ordinary talk and putting a new slant on existing words—anxiety, role, intelligence, personality, paranoid, phobia, loss, deprivation, depression, and behaviour are a few examples. Moscovici (1976) has described the process by which academic concepts and explanations percolate into the ordinary speech of a culture so that they become part of this speech.

But this is only the tip of the iceberg, for more is at stake than the meanings of individual words. Linguists generally concur with Saussure's important insight that language must be treated as an integral structure, the elements of which (the unitary concepts) get their meaning by virtue of the complex and arbitrary relation in which they stand to other elements (Culler, 1976; Saussure, 1916). The idea of words as immutable one-to-one labels for stable properties of the outside world will not do. This point is often illustrated by words standing for colours. One cannot know what is meant by the word "yellow" without being able to appreciate the limits, or boundaries, of the concept; without being able to distinguish yellow from cream, orange, or brown, and so on. The concept of yellowness does not arise independently of other colour concepts. The old teaser; "How do I know that when you say you see red I am not seeing green, or blue, or some other colour?" is easily dealt with if we think of learning a language as learning a set of distinctions rather than a set of labels.

The interconnectedness of concepts is arbitrary in the sense that the spectrum of conceptual possibilities can be divided up by the words of a language in a theoretically limitless number of ways. Like Wittgenstein, Saussure regards the way in which meanings are allocated—although this seems natural to us because as members of a culture we are so well practiced in using words in particular ways—as rooted in shared assumptions and conventions. For example, the distinction in English between "food" and "kitchen" is not at all the same as the distinction in French between the nearest dictionary equivalents, "nourriture" and "cuisine." Saussure calls the abstract structure of forms underlying speech *la langue* and distinguishes this from the physical performance of utterances which he calls *parole. La langue* is the "social product": a set of linguistic forms "deposited by the practice of speech in speakers who belong to the same community; a grammatical system which, to all intents and purposes exists in the mind of each speaker" (Saussure, 1973, p.30). The distinction between *la langue* and *parole* has much in common with Chomsky's distinction between the competence and performance aspects of language. *La langue* can be identified with the unspoken rules of Wittgenstein's "language games."

The Saussurian conception of a language as a system of culturally taught distinctions and relations, rather than a set of labels for particular entities each of which is characterised by some kind of distinctive essence, bears the implication that it is not possible to alter the meaning of one concept without affecting the meanings of others related to it by virtue of their mutual positions in the structure of *la langue.* To change the meanings of individual words in a language or to introduce new words or new meanings, is to affect the whole fabric of meanings on which the language rests, or at the very least to affect a big part of it. The sounds and meanings of languages change over time and occasionally go through periods of drastic transformation. The best social science hypotheses, I believe, are not those that stimulate the most research but those that generate the most discussion. In doing so they subtly introduce new meanings which, if taken up at all widely by the speakers of a language can be said to involve a slight shift in the axis of *la langue.* If, as I am suggesting, a hypothesis in social psychology is two things at the same time—a description of social life and a commentary on ordinary speech—then if this commentary is a good one it will itself come to be incorporated into ordinary speech and, in becoming part of that corpus, will force an accommodation in the conservative structures that are the basis of that corpus' stability.

I have argued that the technical talk that goes with the traditional empirical research of social psychology comes down either to common sense or to a species of jargon that by its nature contains tautologies and can be characterised as little more than the playing of novel language games by an exclusive club of "specialist" members. If this is so; that is; if social psychology research is just scientistic ritual with no bearing on anyone except those who practice it, one would expect all the major programmes of research eventually to come to be regarded as historical curiosities: specious addenda to the new ideas of the time. Is it possible to find examples that would contradict this? Are there any striking findings, findings whose definitive nature has brought the state of knowledge to a turning point? Is there any research in the subject comparable to the great text book experiments of physics and chemistry? My reading has not yet led me to any. More significant perhaps is that the reading of reviewers of the major research programmes does not seem to have done so either. Let us briefly explore the fate of the research done in connection with the classic theories of social psychology.

The History of Research and Theory in Social Psychology

Cognitive Dissonance Theory

When cognitive dissonance theory was first put forward by Festinger in 1957, it was hailed as an exciting new development because many of its predicitions seemed to run counter to common sense and to the laws of Skinnerian behaviourism. The focus of the theory was the psychological consequences of making a decision. Its main proposal was that after taking an important decision, like buying a new car, people are subject to cognitive dissonance—a kind of motivating regret which they strive to allay using a variety of strategies. They overstate the virtues of the selected alternative and underplay its disadvantages; they understate the virtues of the rejected alternative and play up its disadvantages; they avoid information that conflicts or is *dissonant* with the decision they have made, and so on. At the heart of the theory and its subsequent reworkings is the very simple commonsense notion that people are preoccupied with accounting for their actions and justifying their decisions. This notion, and the others that lead from it and make up the detailed theory, fit extremely well with our intuitions about justifications and the face-saving purposes they serve. Consideration of the detailed theory and in what sense it *was* innovative must be left until the next chapter. At this stage I simply want to draw attention to the theory's career and the way in which the received attitude toward it changed during the years of its popularity. Not for long was cognitive dissonance theory reckoned to be offering counterintuitive predictions. As Aronson (1968) later pointed out, its uncommonsensical nature was no more than an illusion and its non-obvious predictions dissolve on a closer look at the theory's conceptual structure.

Nevertheless a lively controversy followed the publication of the theory over what seemed to be crucial differences between the predictions that it offered about the optimum conditions for attitude change and the predictions offered by Skinnarian reward–incentive theory. Cognitive dissonance theory seemed to be saying that dissonance and attitude change are inversely proportional to an individual's perception of coercive influences. whereas reward–incentive theory held that attitude statements, in common with other behaviours, are shaped through schedules of reward and punishment. The two sides in the debate polarised and the leading protagonist's names were, for a time, on the tip of every undergraduate tongue along with details of the experiments that were done in an attempt to confirm or refute the predictions of one or other theory (e.g., Elms and Janis, 1965; Rosenberg, 1965). But it gradually became apparent and was eventually generally acknowledged that the two theories were not really offering different predictions at all (Zajonc, 1968). And this conclusion emerged more in spite of than because of all the research that had been so painstakingly worked through.

Although somewhat neglected now, it should not be forgotten that cognitive dissonance theory and the research on attitude change that it spawned were the main concerns of social psychologists for over a decade. In his review of cognitive dissonance theory in the 1968 *Handbook of Social Psychology,* Zajonc writes:

> No theory in social psychology has stimulated more research than the theory of cognitive dissonance. Articles in this area constitute the modal category in journals publishing results of social-psychological research. . . If there is any one theoretical formulation that has captured the imagination of social psychologists during this decade, it is beyond any doubt Festinger's theory of cognitive dissonance. (p. 359)

A tremendous rush to do experiments followed the publication of the theory in 1957. In 1964 Chapanis and Chapanis published a comprehensive review of the studies completed by this time. Their conclusion was that overall the data that had been collected did not support the theory. More revealing though was the doubt expressed in this paper about the relevance of much of the research to the theory's predictions. Ambiguities in the theoretical postulates themselves as well as the ubiquitous "methodological problems" were blamed for the difficulties experienced in putting the theory to the test in experiments.

Other authors echoed the Chapanis's criticisms (plenty of examples can be found in the enormous *Sourcebook,* edited by Abelson et al. in 1968), but interest in the theory remained at a high level nevertheless. The published research was criticised as ambiguous and inconclusive but it was always assumed that the ambiguities that had come to light would be resolved by doing more research. More was done, but few findings were at all widely received as having fulfilled their goal of confirming or refuting that part of the theory with which they ostensibly dealt. Whenever confidence was expressed it was later undermined by an alternative interpretation of the data. Yet, despite all the non-supportive and ambiguous findings, cognitive dissonance theory survived virtually unscathed, its popularity undiminished, well into the 1970s and it still provides the inspiration for some research initiatives today.

The main forum for discussion of the issues raised in cognitive dissonance theory was, undeniably, published research reports. It is also true that conceptual reworkings of the theory, such as that of Brehm and Cohen in 1962, were tied in with debates about research design. But these debates were concerned less with interpretations of figures and statistics as objective measures than with the meaning of experimental procedures to subjects. For example, in the experiment by Aronson and Mills (1959), college girls underwent one of two kinds of initiation in order to become participants in a group discussion on the psychology of sex: "mild" and "severe". In the severe condition the girls had to read aloud a list of obscene words. It was predicted, and duly confirmed, that those in the severe initiation condition would rate the discussion as more interesting than would the others. They would suffer cognitive dissonance at having elected to read out obscene words which they would be motivated to reduce by saying to themselves, "It was worth it because the discussion was really interesting."

Chapanis and Chapanis, however, argued that reciting the obscene words may have itself aroused the girls, or alternatively, that the girls may have been relieved when they found the subsequent discussion inocuous. To test out these possibilities, Gerard and Mathewson (1966) followed the same general procedure but used electric shocks rather than obscene words and discussions about cheating at exams instead of discussions about sex. It was found that those in the severe initiation condition still rated the discussion more favourably than the others.

What subjects really thought about these bizarre procedures will probably never be known. But it is clear that the scope for interpretation of their experiences is enormous and the number of possible explanations of the data is legion.

Discussions about experiments were not discussions about hard facts but about anecdotal social situations. There is nothing to indicate that its reworkings and the popularity that cognitive dissonance theory continued to enjoy were in any way linked to the findings of the experiments that were carried out—the supposedly objective quantitative comparisons. The research that was published in connection with the theory carries no more than a historical curiosity value for us now. If we remember particular studies it is as descriptive embellishments of the theory. But most of them have been forgotten.

Numerous references can be found throughout this period in the life of social psychology to the inconclusive nature of specific research initiatives, but no-one saw the wider implication of this. No-one alluded directly to the lack of correspondence between research and theory that was characteristic of these years. Zajonc, however, looking back on a decade of research on cognitive dissonance theory comes quite close in the following passage: "Dissonance research has not strengthened the basic statements and postulates that generated it, it has not clarified them, it has not brought them closer to the data level, and it certainly has not been integrated into a neat unified system" 1968, p. 390). In his concluding remarks Zajonc acknowledges the intellectual value and "conceptual bravado" of dissonance theory and the discussions it provoked and notes that the theory has had profound consequences for social psychology and for the way we think about the relations between attitudes, cognition and behaviour. But he capitulates to the research model and the progress-through-data ethic in saying: "Soon, however, someone must settle down to the routine work of consolidating the information produced by this imaginative albeit swashbuckling approach, of resolving the methodological ambiguities still outstanding, and perhaps eventually pulling some of the main results together" (1968, p. 391). No-one of course has yet settled down to this mythical task.

Self-perception Theory

The next major upheaval in social psychology came in 1967 when Bem published what became known as *self-perception theory.* Ostensibly a radical departure from the notion of cognitive dissonance as an internal drive state, self-perception theory proposed that a person observes and evaluates his or her own actions in the same way that one might observe and evaluate the actions of others. Inferences are drawn about personal motivation in a detached, rational kind of way. If a source of coercion is apparent, then the action is retrospectively labelled *caused,* and personal motivation remains unaffected ("such-and-such made me do it"). If no source of coercion is apparent, a motive is inferred ("I must have done it because I wanted to").

Upon the publication of self-perception theory history repeated itself. A fierce controversy immediately blew up over what seemed to be a direct conflict between the predictions of self-perception theory and those of cognitive dissonance theory. Again, for a time, it appeared that research provided the best means of resolving the quarrel, and again there was a rush to do experiments aimed at deciding which of the two theories was correct. But again, it gradually became apparent that this issue was unlikely to be resolved through research and again, the tone of discussions switched from talk of hypothesis testing to talk of the two opposing positions "remaining untested" (Kiesler, Collins, and Miller, 1969), of a "logical impasse" between the two theories (Nisbett and Valins, 1971), and of a "truce between the two models" (Zanna and Cooper, 1976). Looking to the data of empirical research to settle theoretical differences once more proved to be based on vain hope.

Attitudes and Behaviour

At about the same time, a related controversy blew up over the two competing hypotheses; (1) attitudes cause behaviours and (2) attitudes are the result of behaviours. In the end, this problem too seemed to hang more than anything else on definitions and a compromise was proposed. It was agreed that both hypotheses were true (McGuire, 1976). Once again, the contribution made by the research that was done is questionable. A case can be made (as it eventually was) that this issue, like the others, reduces to a debate whose course and resolution has nothing whatsoever to do with the collection of data. A consideration of the logic of ordinary accounting practices gives us the same answer by a much less tortuous route. Consider the statement, "I sent the flowers because I'm fond of her". In our culture this represents a perfectly legitimate and readily understandable explanation. The simple fact that explanations of this form *are* universally intelligible itself is a sufficient basis for inferring the obvious correctness of hypothesis 1. It is incontrovertibly true that being fond (an attitude) can make you send flowers (a behaviour). It is true inasmuch as this account and others like it exemplify a familiar currency of speech: they make sense. That they do make sense ipso facto implies a shared acceptance of the relationship that attitudes can cause behaviours—a universal playing of this particular language game. If people did not have this knowledge, this explanation would be nonsensical, which it clearly is not. Likewise, the sense of remarks such as, "I cycled all that way so I suppose I must be fond of her", relies on a consensual intuition of the obverse relation; it is reasonable to say that behaviour can sometimes determine attitudes. The logic of ordinary accounting practices allows us to anticipate the eventual conclusion in respect of hypotheses 1 and 2 without even contemplating doing an experiment.

Research fares no better in separating the conditions under which attitudes follow behaviour from those under which behaviour follows attitudes. For instance, a reasonable a priori case can be made for the "finding" that behaviour is more likely to be the source of attitudes when it is done in public. Publicly witnessed acts are not as easy as private ones to forget, deny, or mentally distort. Because they are the subject of a consensus their meaning is more firmly "fixed".

Attribution Theory

In the late 1970s discussions of cognitive dissonance theory and self-perception theory gave way to a new set of ideas which became known as *attribution theory.* In fact, these ideas were not all that new, being based on the writings of Heider in the 1940s and 1950s (Heider, 1958). It is interesting to ask whether at this stage attitudes towards traditional research changed at all in the light of the ineffectiveness of the findings accumulated in connection with cognitive dissonance theory and self-perception theory. Was there any departure from the reflexlike tendency to fall back on "data" as the main way of resolving theoretical differences?

Criticism of the classic experimental design—the creation of artificial social situations in psychological "laboratories" and the controlled manipulation and observation of "variables"—had certainly grown more vociferous by this stage. Many social psychologists had come to feel that merely acknowledging the existence of special situational influences at work in the psychology experiment ("demand characteristics" as these were originally described by Orne, 1962) was not enough. Harré and Secord's book *The Explanation of Social Behaviour* (1972) is a landmark in this tide of reaction against the failure of social psychology experiments as faithful analogues of the kinds of social meetings and confrontations that make up ordinary life.

In general, present-day researchers proceed more cautiously than their counterparts in the 1960s and 1970s. But a strong push to do research—to come up with data of some kind—remains very much at the centre of social psychology. Potter (1981) has actually recorded an increase in the number of laboratory studies relative to other published papers in the *British Journal of Social and Clinical Psychology* during the decade prior to 1981. I remember the message of a poster at Nuffield College, Oxford, directed at postgraduate researchers in the social sciences: "What are you going to do with your data when you have collected it?" One is still not allowed to feel one is doing any real work unless engaged in the business of producing data. Perhaps this is not surprising in that courses and careers are run on the ideal of a scientific method and the bodies that fund them are necessarily conservative and self-perpetuating. As Feyerabend (1981) has pointed out in relation to scientific research in general, this is bound to express itself in the persistent censorship of alternative methodologies.

Has the gap between theory and research closed at all? I believe the situation has not changed very much despite the reaction against the laboratory as an appropriate place to search out social life. Echoes of the past are still to be heard.

The Learned Helplessness Model

Seligman's theory of learned helplessness (Garber and Seligman, 1980) has enjoyed considerable popularity in psychology over recent years and is one of the most widely discussed contemporary approaches to the problem of clinical depression. In 1978 a volume of *Journal of Abnormal Psychology* was specially dedicated to the theory and its reformulation in the language of attribution theory. The substance of the theory need not concern us here. What is of interest is the scepticism expressed independently by three sets of authors in this volume (Buchwald, Coyne, and Cole, 1978; Heusmann, 1978; Wortman and Dintzer, 1978) as to whether the experimental findings presented in other parts of the same volume in fact count as tests of the model—whether they are really relevant to it or not. Their comments are all too reminiscent of previous research reviews. The source of unease is not so much the direction that findings take but uncertainty as to whether there is any contingent link between them and the model on which they are presumably based.

Other Attribution Theory Predictions

There are plenty of other recent examples of the pattern repeating itself. The *divergent perspectives hypothesis* is widely regarded as one of the more solid of the original predictions made from attribution theory. This states that people typically explain their own actions by referring to situational pressures, or demands, ("I did it because circumstance dictated"), whereas dispositional explanations are preferred in explaining the actions of others ("she did it because she's that kind of person"). Van der Plight, in a painstaking review of the divergent perspectives hypothesis, concludes: "Because of a number of interpretational ambiguities, the prevailing procedures do not provide clear evidence regarding the dispositional versus situational locus of attributions to one's self and others" (1981, p. 117).

Regan (1978), writing about studies of interpersonal attraction, again working within the guidelines of attribution theory, concludes: "From the preceding review of the relationship between attribution and attraction, no simple, overall perspective emerges" (p. 229). Cotton (1981) concludes a review of Schachter's theory of emotion with these words: "Schachter's theory is not supported by the research, but the available evidence does not necessarily disprove the theory either" (p. 389).

Experiments using "misattribution" techniques to treat pathological symptoms have been especially popular and yet findings are notoriously difficult to replicate. Valins and Ray's (1967) treatment of snake phobia has been "repeatedly not replicated" (Brehm, 1976, p. 161). And Storms and Nisbett's (1970) well-known treatment of insomniacs has turned out unrepeatable too, as have attempts to use the same technique to modify speech anxiety and smoking (Antaki and Brewin, 1982). And what about this indictment of Kelley's ANOVA version of attribution theory? "A whole decade of research stimulated by Kelley's attribution theory has hardly scratched the surface of the problem of how people understand and explain the complex behaviour and interactions of their fellow men and women" (Newcombe and Rutter, 1982, p. 163).

It is important to stress that these examples are not just the few isolated fruits of a hard search through the psychological literature. They are fairly typical of the concluding remarks of research reviews. Tacked onto the end of them is usually the assurance that future research will succeed where past has failed. But it does not seem to. Instead, "future research" moves on to the next set of issues which it has become fashionable to "investigate". My intention here is not, however, to prove beyond question that no piece of empirical data in the subject has ever contributed usefully to the growth of knowledge. The exhaustive cover of the research literature this entails would be a superhuman task and would make very tedious reading. The quotations and examples in this chapter are given as illustrations of the point that the concept of specialist empirical research in social psychology whose aim is to discover causal ties between two or more social "variables" is *in principle* a misguided one. History confirms that progress in the subject, and probably in other social science subjects too, is not linked to this kind of research. If the problems posed by competing theories and hypotheses were genuinely resolvable by doing controlled tests then it would be possible to discern some overall coherence and continuity in the process of data collection, or at least a few milestones in research, like those of physics. But there is no such coherence and continuity and there are no such milestones.

The criticism of traditional research that I am putting forward is itself an empirical matter. It can be tried out by any critical reader of the research literature with the target of re-expressing relationships demonstrated in empirical studies in ordinary notation. The test is whether such re-expression is reliably possible, and whether in applying the rule of "reducing" meanings in this fashion, tautologies are laid bare and the relationships in data are found to be trivial.

"Conclusive" Research

There are, or course, occasions in social psychology when it is claimed that data clearly support a particular theory or hypothesis or clearly refute it. But as I argued in the previous chapter, it is hard to find examples of such definitive research in which findings are neither derivable from the sense of the hypothesis nor a disguised reiteration of common sense.

Miller (1980), for example, has presented a review of research concerned with the stress arising from the absence of personal control. Two hypotheses to explain why having control over a stressful experience decreases its unpleasantness are compared. One is called the *minimax hypothesis,* the other, the *internality hypothesis*: "only minimax specifies conditions under which individuals will choose to relinquish rather than retain control, and these predictions are supported by the experimental evidence" (Miller, 1980, p. 94). Here is a straight claim that research, in accord with the idealised model of research given by the physical sciences, has come up with a clear directive between two rival hypotheses. But let us look at these hypotheses. Both are concerned with the way an individual reacts in an unpleasant situation. The minimax hypothesis holds that people like to have control so as to "minimise the maximum danger to themselves." The internality hypothesis says that people like to have control so they can regulate when an unpleasant event occurs and fit it in with the moment-to-moment fluctuations in their mood. In this way they can reduce its subjective unpleasantness. Miller, after describing a series of quite complicated experiments, most of which involve people being given electric shocks under different experimental conditions, concludes that the minimax hypothesis is supported over the internality hypothesis. The details of these experiments and the reasoning behind them need not concern us. The point is that the minimax hypothesis is favoured because it makes a successful prediction that the internality hypothesis does not. The prediction in question says that there are some circumstances in which an individual prefers not to have control over an unpleasant situation; specifically, circumstances in which there is an opportunity to yield control to a person of superior expertise, one who the individual thinks is better placed than himself or herself to minimise the unpleasant outcome. The internality hypothesis, on the other hand, predicts that given the choice people will never relinquish control whatever the circumstances. Here is how Miller sums up the results of these studies:

> To summarize, although individuals generally choose to retain control over aversive stimulation, they only do so as long as they believe their own response is the most stable factor for limiting the maximum danger to themselves. When they believe that another individual has a more stable response for minimizing the maximum danger, then they relinquish control to that other person. (1980, p. 95).

This conclusion is trivial on two levels. It is trivial in that most of it can be derived from the sense of the pivotal word "danger." Although sometimes people deliberately court it, "danger" connotes a power to hurt and defines something that people generally strive to avoid. To say that people will do all kinds of things in order to avoid danger, including, if necessary, relinquishing control, is merely to restate the meaning of the term. On the other hand, as Miller points out, there may be a mental condition under which the threat to an individual's feelings of personal identity involved in the relinquishing of control constitutes a greater psychological danger than the danger contained in the external challenge. But this amounts to little more than saying that some people, in some circumstances, find it hard to hand over control.

Miller's conclusion is also trivial because it is no advance on common knowledge. We know that people sometimes go to the doctor, that they usually refer their legal problems to a solicitor and that they would probably not, if the opportunity arose, choose to take over the controls of an aircraft from an airline pilot. There are numerous circumstances in everyday life in which control of a difficult situation is delegated to others, sometimes even at the expense of some loss of face. Who needs data and statistics to tell them this happens?

There are two additional points to note about this example. The first is that it contains a considerable amount of jargon; the jargon of attribution theory and also the lingering old behaviourist jargon of "aversive stimulation" and "responses." In this supposedly social context these words are not only unnecessary but potentially misleading. They give the impression that something special and precise is being said. Behaviourist terms have undisputed explanatory power when applied to the field of data for which Skinner designed them; that of automatic behaviours in the sense of chains of limb movements, but they are out of court in a social psychology whose concern is meanings and the moral orders in which meanings are to be found. Wrongly applied, out of context, they make it appear that something has been explained when in fact it has not.

The second point to note is that when the jargon is done away with and plain terms are substituted the problem becomes more obviously resolvable without recourse to research. As we have seen, the minimax hypothesis can be supported against the internality hypothesis by empirical testing of a different kind; by seeing how well each measures up to our own experience of the world and by trying them out on other people in conversation: by asking people what they think. The problem posed by the two conflicting hypotheses has a compelling solution, albeit an uncontroversial one, based on the consensus of observation that is accessible in ordinary discourse. The specialist "psychological" language in which problem and solution are represented here is no more than a smoke screen for the absence of novelty and the perpetuation of the data-collection ethic.

Conclusion

These examples from the attribution theory literature are enough to show that the same basic problems are present in contemporary research programmes as dogged the older ones. The history of the subject right up to the moment supports the argument that the technical data accumulated in the name of specialist empirical research do not affect the careers of theories and that these data are quite unlike the data of the sciences that rely on instruments of exploration. Doing experiments is at its most imaginative thinking up anecdotal illustrations of theories, and at its least, cementing one's membership of a discoursively closed club. A better guide to the success of a theory seems to be how much discussion it gets and how much agreement there is between people as to the sharpness of the commentary it represents on a social world of which we and our activities must be considered part.

If theories in social psychology do progress and evolve in a constructive manner, as I believe they do, we must ask, What is the current that carries them if it is not the data of empirical research? It would certainly seem that theories follow from one another with some kind of logical continuity. If this is so, it should be possible to point to the source of this continuity if it is not data and statistics. It is with this purpose in mind that I now turn to a consideration of the philosophical import of the main line of social psychology theory since the 1950s.

Part II

3

Action and Free Choice: Social Psychology Theories as Metaphysics

If the specialist empirical research of social psychology is irrelevant to social life, can we say the same about social psychological theories? I believe we cannot. In this chapter we return to the main theories of the past 30 years with two aims. The first is to support the argument of the first part of this book by showing that there is indeed a continuity and progression in the evolution of this theory but that this answers to a changing metaphysics rather than to accumulated data. In charting the course of the main theories without recourse to the data and statistics of research (although the logic of forced compliance studies is considered in some detail), I am strengthening the case that this kind of data is unnecessary.

My second, perhaps more constructive, aim is to identify this changing metaphysics as a movement toward greater relativism in our conception of free choice and truth. The way in which psychological theories of action have evolved reflects a gradual but highly significant transformation in our understanding of the individual as a choosing, moral agent. The line of theory that I take to be the mainstay of the social psychology of this time ranges from Festinger's cognitive dissonance theory and the application of this theory in a procedure that became known as "forced compliance," through Bem's self-perception theory, to attribution theory and Harré's ethogenics.

Forced Compliance

The basic proposals of Festinger's cognitive dissonance theory were outlined in the previous chapter. The theory is about making choices, and it rests on the principle that people are constantly motivated to justify the decisions they have taken and achieve consistency between the things they do and the things they say. A lively interest in attitudes and how to change them has always surrounded the theory. The commerical advantages of knowing how to manipulate people's attitudes are only too obvious. Dissonance theory, as it became known, was clearly very relevant to the investigation of techniques of attitude change. One particular research design, known as the forced compliance paradigm, came to epitomise studies of the effect of cognitive dissonance on attitudes and attitude change. Forced compliance defined a procedure which, it was claimed, could be used to manipulate not only attitudes but also feelings of hunger and thirst and even the experience of pain (Zimbardo, 1969).

The pattern of all forced compliance experiments is the same. An experimenter asks the subjects if, as part of a psychological experiment, they are prepared to commit themselves to a procedure deliberately concocted to involve discomfort, embarrassment, or some other privation. A subject might be asked, for example, if, in the interests of the research he or she is prepared to go without food or drink for a day or so, suffer electric shocks, or give a talk to other students one a topic known to be unpopular, such as the desirability of conscription. Subjects are always given a false cover story of the experiment's purpose, the real purpose being simply to confront them with a difficult choice. The choice in question is between obliging the experimenter and undergoing the discomfort of acting counter-preferentially on the one hand, and suffering the embarrassment of having to refuse the experimenter's request on the other. One might ask why subjects ever agree to what are really rather unreasonable requests. The reason they do is because the social situation is specially structured to make it awkward for them to refuse. For one thing the experimenters in forced-compliance studies are usually psychology professors and the subjects their students.

The reasoning behind forced-compliance designs is that the subjects who comply with the experimenter's request will suffer dissonance ("Why did I agree to do these awful things?") and will try to justify this decision by, as it were, unconsciously aligning their own private attitudes with the course of action that has been "chosen." So the student who gives a talk extolling the virtues of conscription, providing he or she is convinced that there was a choice involved in doing this, ends up a little more in favour of conscription than before. The student is thereby in a position to justify the option taken and reduce dissonance with platitudes like, "One must look at both sides of the coin and I suppose there are some arguments for conscription after all," or "Maybe in some circumstances it's not necessarily a bad thing." Likewise, the student who agrees to go without food for an extended period actually ends up less hungry as a consequence of feeling he or she has chosen to do this. The same unconscious justifying mechanisms cause hunger to be mentally "controlled" ("I really didn't mind going without food because actually I didn't feel hungry anyway"). It seems this unconscious control does not stop at face-saving statements like these but extends to measurable physiological changes. There is not much difference between feeling not hungry and being not hungry and not only do such subjects appear not hungry from what they say, their blood chemistry suggests that they really are less hungry than similarly starved subjects who have not had so much choice in the matter and for whom dissonance and the need to justify their decision does not arise (Zimbardo, 1969).

What are we to say is happening in these experiments? The success of the dissonance manipulation rests on two conditions: (1) the choice given to subjects must be made explicit and (2) no subject, or virtually no-one to whom a choice is put, must refuse to comply with the experimenter's request. If condition 1 is not met, then the precondition necessary for the arousal of dissonance—the subject's awareness of having made a choice—is not fulfilled and attitude change (or unconscious mental control over physiological processes) does not become a hypothetically necessary contingency. If condition 2 is not met, any variation from the norm in the attitudes of those subjects who were given a choice can logically be attributed to self-selection: those starting out most favourably disposed to the experimenter's request are those that agree to go along with it. On the face of it these two conditions appear contradictory; how can a person's action be determined and at the same time free? Nevertheless, we read from the successful forced-compliance studies that both conditions are met. Subtle, camouflaged pressures are put on subjects so that virtually no-one refuses to comply. But notwithstanding, everyone is left with the conviction that they have acted out of free choice.

The above is a description of what happens to a subject in the low-justification or high-dissonance conditions of these experiments. Typically, and as an integral part of the study, differential incentives for complying with the experimenter's request are introduced at a stage before the subject "decides" to comply. Subjects in the opposite high-justification (low-dissonance) condition are offered strong reasons why they should comply; sometimes they are paid, sometimes they are told that the experiment is part of an especially important scientific programme. In this way an olive branch for dissonance reduction is built into the situation which these individuals confront. They are supplied with a ready-made justification (e.g., "I did it because it paid good money" or "I did it for science"). It is anticipated that attitude change in a direction consistent with the act that has been performed will be greatest in those individuals not supplied with extrinsic rewards or encouragement—those in the low-justification (high dissonance) condition. The trick in these studies is to get a person to do something against his or her better judgement but leave him or her with the definite impression that the act was done out of free choice. By and large, as might be expected from the logic of the procedures themselves, forced-compliance studies have confirmed that attitude change is dependent on and proportional to the degree of personal commitment and free choice that a subject feels is attached to his or her decision (Brehm and Cohen, 1962; Linder, Cooper, and Jones, 1967).

It is worth considering a little more closely the seemingly paradoxical conditions on which the success of the forced-compliance trick depends. The experimenter must be able to count on virtually every subject complying with his or her request even though this is presented to subjects as an open choice. The efficacy of the experiment depends on near-total compliance. So, from the experimenter's point of view, a subject's compliance *must* be regarded as predictable and under the control of the camouflaged demands and oblique pressures that are deliberately built into the request. The experimenter's conception of a subject's behaviour is therefore necessarily deterministic. The way subjects will decide has to be seen as predictable and the result of the carefully planned and rehearsed manipulation. The fact that compliance with the request is the near-universal outcome is the vindication of the experimenter's causal–determinist position.

But the efficacy of the experiment also depends on subjects, at least those in low-justification conditions, being convinced, knowing in fact, that their compliance with the experimenter's request was freely chosen. The subject's conception differs from the experimenter's in an important way. The subject necessarily views his or her compliance as freely chosen and not as the result of someone else's calculated duplicity. The correctness of the subject's view is vindicated by an awareness that an explicit choice was put and the certain knowledge that he or she *could* at the time, at will, have responded by choosing not to comply.

An observer of forced-compliance experiments is therefore faced with two apparently conflicting accounts of the low-justification subject's behaviour. On the one hand, the experimenter is confident in the knowledge of having caused the subject's compliance because he or she can point to the conditions controlling the outcome. On the other, the subject is confident in the knowledge of having acted freely, because when the choice was put he or she could have chosen differently. Who is right and which of these two positions is the correct one?

Self-perception

Another way of looking at the forced-compliance scenario is to suggest, as Bem (1967) did in self-perception theory, that people look back on the choices they have made in a detached kind of way; in rather the same way that one individual might look back on and assess the choices of another. Without being especially motivated, a person considers the context in which he or she acted and retrospectively labels the action either as freely chosen or as constrained by circumstances and makes inferences about himself or herself correspondingly. Where no extrinsic constraints or pressures are visible, the conclusion of the subject is that volition was exercised and it was indeed he or she choosing and acting. A crude way of putting this is to say that in default of any alternative one has to conclude, "I did it because I suppose I'm that sort of person."

Self-perception theory is clearly saying something very similar to dissonance theory. Indeed, as was seen in the previous chapter, after a lot of hot air and research to try to disprove one theory or another, it turned out there was little to choose between them in terms of their predictions and interpretations of people's behaviour (Harré and Secord, 1972; Zanna and Cooper, 1976). Empirical studies were made of the "over-justification effect" (see Morgan, 1982). Their message—that tangible rewards undermine intrinsic motivation—is logically no different from the message of forced-compliance experiments. It is just expressed in a different jargon. From our point of view, whether a person can be reckoned to be going through the same rationalisations when reflecting on his or her own actions as when reflecting on the actions of others is of no great significance. Both theories concur that people do reflect on their actions and that these actions are endowed with significance through the accounts that are fitted to them. As participants in a socially pluralistic culture there are bound to be differences and disagreements between people about how an action is best explained. The negotiation of these differences makes up a large part of gossip and conversation. That the distinction between freely chosen and determined action is one of the main bones of conversational contention needs no proving because on it hangs that most absorbing of human preoccupations: the appropriation of blame and responsibility. It is to be expected that people are concerned with sorting actions into the fundamental categories "free" or "forced" and labelling them accordingly. Until this has been done there exists not even a preliminary basis for deciding on their meaning and their moral warrantability.

Applying the terminology of self-perception theory to the forced-compliance procedure, we can say that the viability of forced-compliance experiments depends on the subject and the experimenter labelling the subject's action in different ways. The subject reflexively labels his or her action as free, the experimenter labels it the product of social pressure. We must now return to the question of who is right.

Attribution

The growth of interest in attribution theory during the 1970s can partly be explained on the grounds that it offers a solution to dilemmas such as this. In fact, what it offers is less a solution than a way out of the problem. Attribution theory is not a theory in the strict sense; it is more an enjoinder to study the explanations and interpretations of phenomena which people themselves offer. The attribution analysis is built on the assumption that such naturally occurring explanations can be ordered into various theoretically meaningful categories. The most important of these (although paradoxically the most ambiguous) is the distinction between internal and external attributions—roughly the distinction between things done *by* and things done *to* a person (at least this is how Rotter, 1966 and Abramson, Seligman, and Teasdale, 1978 interpret Heider, 1958). The point of such categories is that they provide a framework in terms of which the psychologist can talk about *changing* a person's attributions. A student who is depressed because he or she has failed an exam might be encouraged to make an external attribution about the reason for the failure (e.g., bad luck the right questions didn't come up) rather than the more depressing internal attribution (e.g., stupidity). What is new and significant about the attribution analysis is that it endows the explanation that the person himself or herself offers with something of an authority of its own, independent of alternative, outside criteria.

Underlying the attribution analysis is a movement away from absolute standards of corrigibility and veracity toward a more relativist perspective. The primary data have become people's own perceptions and interpretations rather than the social world carved up and pre-emptively labelled according to the whim of the investigator. The radical proposal of attribution theory is that we abandon the study of social psychological phenomena as a priori essences and truths and concentrate instead on people's own accounts—their attributions. The field of study is to be augmented by a level, from the psychologist's explanations of actions to the psychologist's explanations of individual's explanations of actions. And in this very significant, albeit essentially philosophical, move the confrontation between alternative accounts, such as those of experimenter and subject in forced-compliance experiments, is sidestepped and the paradox over whether the subject's action is free or caused is resolved.

Several authors writing about attribution theory have drawn attention to the anti-objectivist, or relativist, logic on which the theory is founded. Weiner and Litman-Adizes note: "what matters is the contemporary evaluation of the physical and the social world, regardless of the veridicality of the source of one's beliefs" (1980, p. 51.). And Wilkinson writes:

> If we are attempting to study a person who actively interprets reality in her/his own terms, then her/his own account of those terms is the only acceptable primary source of data. It does not matter whether this account is "accurate" or "reliable" (whether or not we accept that there is a "correct" view); she/he acts on each situation as she/he sees it, and it is this—or whatever she/he chooses to tell us of this—that is significant. (1981, p. 216).

A similar point is made by Brenner, this time about the attributions of social psychologists themselves:

> Given that there may be an indeterminate number of fruitful ways of making sense of action, it is most likely, I think, that employing just one mode of description, based on just one particular theoretical perspective, will lead to an incomplete, if not partly invalid, understanding of the action. . . contrary to the current fashion, we must try to underplay in social psychology the relevance of *particular* theories of action. (1982, p. 221)

Douglas (1980) makes what is essentially the same point from the perspective of a social anthropologist:

> An expectation that ideas can somehow be mapped out apart from the institutions in which they work is (similarly) misleading. Again, to present the general relation between ideas and institutions as a feasible field of enquiry, leaving out the persons and intentions that generate both, is another form of the general fallacy. (Reprinted by permission of John Farguharson Ltd. p. 60)

More general invitations to less a priori perspectives such as this touch on the arguments of philosophers of science such as Rorty and Feyerabend, which were outlined in Chapter 1.

Because it does not stipulate loyalty to one particular perspective, attribution theory allows us to talk without contradiction about one person causing another to perform a self-initiated or freely chosen act. In the forced-compliance paradigm and self-perception theory lay the seeds of a new psychological conception of action, a less absolutist version than that traditionally adhered to. In attribution theory this achieves much more direct expression: previously non-negotiable mental processes like free choice become individual perceptions, or labellings, which vary systematically over different conditions and which themselves can be studied and manipulated. The attributional description of forced compliance runs something like this: for dissonance to be aroused and attitude change effectively contrived the subject must make an internal attribution in respect of his or her compliance with the experimenter's request. The decision must be attributed to volition. Contrastingly, it is equally necessary for the occurrence of dissonance and attitude change that the experimenter makes an external attribution. The subject's decision must be attributed to carefully worked out pressures and undercover manipulations. The principle which all but crystallised in attribution theory is that these two accounts can be treated as quite compatible. According to the idealised attribution model, the fact that the experimenter sees himself or herself as coercing the subject does not invalidate the subject's own impression. The free choice the subject experiences is in no sense an illusion. It is the cornerstone of the "theory" of the action that he or she constructs, and in the relativist language of the attributionist, this "theory" is to be treated with the same respect as the experimenter's. The two positions are not mutually exclusive but are both tenable in the new "meta" level of analysis.

To the proponents of attribution theory the preceding points may seem pedantically obvious. But a great deal hangs on this apparently innocent shift in perspective. To start with, accepting this analysis means accepting that the achievement of attribution theory is much more an achievement of an intellectual kind than an achievement of research in the sense of collecting objective data. A major claim made for the theory is that it stands out from other social psychology theories as a source of applied techniques. Here at last we are repeatedly told is a theory that can actually be used to help people. So, we must turn next to the question of what the analysis of attribution theory that I am offering here has to say about the theory's practical potential. I believe that attribution theory may be potentially valuable as a source of applied techniques but that its value consists entirely in an ethical shift that is forced by the logic of the new approach.

One of the consequences of acknowledging the veridical equivalence of people's own accounts is to make available, or at least to render permissible, manipulations in the interest of psychological change that were previously considered ethically taboo. By far the most significant of these manipulations, shiftily executed and poorly explained in old forced-compliance experiments, is to coerce an individual into underwriting a commitment and leave him or her with the impression that he or she has acted out of free choice. In the new attributional system, of course, the word "impression" is out of court. As long as the subject's explanation, or attribution, is held in the same esteem as the experimenter's—so long as the two accounts are treated as equally "primary"—then criticism that the subject has been deceived or conned is simply irrelevant. It is irrelevant ipso facto because attribution theory is built on the premise that both accounts are unassailable. Each, in its own right, is equally authoritative and therefore equally true. To take a moral stand and censor such manipulations as "deception" requires identifying one position, the experimenter's say, as uniquely authentic and judging the subject's against it. But such a move is specifically disqualified by the banishing of extrinsic, absolute criteria against which different accounts can be measured. In attribution theory people's explanations are to be taken at face value. The issue of mendacity does not, indeed cannot, arise. By augmenting the analysis from the level of raw explanations (the psycholgist's ad hoc ones, that is) to the level of explanations of explanations, its axiomatic status is changed in such a way that the conditions of warrantability and truth applicable to the old system cannot be carried over to the new because they are logically divorced from it. It is not that the truth value and hence the morality of explanations is callously brushed aside; it is simply irrelevant in the new scheme.

An example from a different area may help to clarify this important point. Consider the two arithmetical statements: (a) $2 + 2 = 4$ and (b) $2 + 2 = 5$. We are easily able to recognise, from our knowledge of arithmetic, that (a) is true and (b) is false. But consider the two statements: (i) I heard him say, "$2 + 2 = 4$" and (ii) I heard him say, "$2 + 2 = 5$." These are no longer statements in mathematics and it can no longer be said that one is true and the other false. The original mathematical criteria of truth and falsity do not apply to the new statements as they did to (a) and (b). The criteria for judging the correctness of (i) and (ii) are different and require a different language than the language of mathematics. The system that gives (a) and (b) is incommensurable with that which gives (i) and (ii).

The same kind of transformation is involved in taking on the attributional approach, and the same irrelevancy of previously relevant evaluative criteria. I believe that attribution theory's radicalness, as well as its practical and therapeutic potential, derive *solely* from this property—its break from an absolutist conception of "true reasons" and its consequent freedom from previously inhibiting ethical considerations. The logic of attribution theory frees us to embark on techniques of manipulation in the interest of social change and help that bring into the open questions of moral and political expediency that were previously assumed by a psychology which reckoned its explanations, scales of meaning, and truths to be the essential ones.

Ethogenics

If attribution theory was a less self-conscious expression of the relativism that had been fermenting in forced-compliance experiments and self-perception theory, Harré's ethogenics brings it even more fully into the open through its basic premise that actions are given meaning through the verbal accounts of them which people offer by way of explanation and justification. Social structure is most richly revealed, according to ethogenics, in people's ordinary everyday talk. Unlike attribution theory, there is no pressure to sort people's accounts into a priori categories (internal–external, global–specific, etc.). The aims of ethogenics are therefore more biographical and novelistic than prescriptive. In ethogenics a person's own explanation of why he or she did something is completely sacred, as is the reading by others of the action even if their accounts differ. Conversational language provides a spectrum of possible reasons for an action and one reason has ascendency over another simply insofar as it is articulated and agreed in the community. To the ethogenic investigator an actor's explanation of his or her action must not be categorised or "translated" (although it may be "negotiated"). To keep intact the private social world of an individual, the accounts he or she gives of behaviour have to be preserved in his or her idiosyncratic vocabulary and style of talk:

> Only the actor himself can give an authoritative report of the monitoring of his own behaviour. We need *not* worry about the unreliability of the actor's reports. The fact that he is the ultimate *authority* does not entail that only he has access to his thoughts and feelings. Other people frequently have some access to the feelings of another, and, if they speak the same language, to his thoughts as well. (Harré and Secord, 1972, p. 8)

Shotter, making a similar point (1980), elaborates on what he terms the incorrigible and morally coercive nature of private social worlds:

> The nature of socially constructed realities is such as to render all Popper's (1963) strictures about falsifiability quite beside the point. . . Let me illustrate with an example: when the Azande of Africa are faced with important decisions, Evans-Pritchard (1937) tells us, decisions about whom to marry, or where to build their house, and so on, they consult a spirit oracle. They do it by first gathering a substance from the bark of a certain type of tree and then, after having prepared it in a seance-like ceremony, they feed it to a small chicken. The Azande have decided beforehand whether the death of the chicken will donote a 'yes' or a 'no' answer, and the oracle, working through the medium of the chicken's living or dying, gives them an unequivocal answer to their question.
>
> We, with our western "scientific knowledge", "know" that the tree bark used by the Azande contains a poison that kills some chickens but not all. Knowing the oracle's bark is "really" poison, *we* wonder what would happen when, for instance, someone else consulted the oracle about the same question and got a contradictory answer? What if the oracle is contradicted by later events?. . . What *we* would call contradictions are not contradictions for the Azande; they are only contradictions *for us,* as we view the events from within the reality of western science. While we look at oracular practices to determine whether oracles exist or not, the Azande *know* that oracles exist; that is the beginning premise of their particular mode of rationality. Everything that happens they experience as supporting that initial assumption in some way. (pp. 56–58)

The ethogenic investigator studies members of his or her own culture rather like an anthropoligist studies members of foreign cultures (see, e.g.,

Marsh, Rosser, and Harré's 1978 account of the customs and rituals of football fans). It could be said that the investigator studies people who speak the same language as himself or herself whereas the anthropologist studies people who do not. But this is only half the story. It is only true to the extent that the community of English speakers in England, for example, makes up a socially homogenous group all sharing the same vocabulary and styles of speaking, which of course they do not. The quasi-anthropological project of ethogenics is possible because macro-societies are pluralistic; they are collections of diverse, often opposed, social orders which touch only at points of universally shared convention and utterly standard figures of speech. To the ethogenist the social world is a matrix of diversified social orders superimposed on which are a lesser number of more general orders, and only superimposed on these is the category, "native speaker." It is ethogenics' concern with the diversity *within* a community of native speakers, and its treatment of this community as a small-scale replica of the world of different language speakers that gives rise to its complete break from absolutism and its reluctance to categorise people's private accounts.

Wittgenstein captures the flavour of culturally local communities in his idea of players of different kinds of language games. To try to design interpretative categories, in psychology or wherever, to which all the different kinds of language game are assimilable is merely to impose the rules of one's own language game on other people. But the point about different language games is that they are answerable to different incommensurable rules and hence define different incommensurable institutions.

In summary, a general movement toward greater relativism in social psychology has expressed itself in the main theories of action of the past 30 years. It was present in embryonic form in cognitive dissonance theory and forced-compliance experiments. It came to the forefront in the controversy surrounding self-perception theory. It was incorporated as the foundational principle of attribution theory and is most directly confronted and worked out in ethogenics.

Therapy

Social psychology is nothing if it cannot be applied in the world and one of the most promising areas of its application, if we are to believe contemporary writers, is therapy. Considerable hope is pinned on attribution theory as a source of therapeutic techniques. For this reason, and also because it allows me to focus my argument more sharply, I shall discuss attribution theory and the client–therapist relation in some detail.

There are, of course, many different styles of therapy founded on different ideologies and having different avowed objectives. But common to them all is the idea that the therapist must change some aspect of the client or the client's world so as to make him or her better fitted to live in it: healthier, happier, more adaptive, and perhaps more effective. The goal of prospective change—the creation of patterns incompatible with psychopathological behaviour—is in the nature of the therapist–client relationship. If there was no need for individuals to change in any way, they would not place themselves in the role of patient or client. What then are the options open to a modern therapist who wishes to apply the accumulated wisdom of social psychology? These can be summarised thus: (1) change the client's environment to make it more compatible with the client or (2) change some aspect of the client's psyche to make him or her more compatible with the world in which he or she must live.

Opportunities for a therapist to take the first of these alternatives are rare. By the time a person presents or is sent to therapy this possibility will almost certainly already have been explored and exhausted by the client himself or herself and by family and friends. In general, a therapist has to try to alter the person. Attitudes and attributions can of course be changed through straight argument and persuasion. The therapist could, for example, try to make a client less depressed by arguing that an undesirable behaviour or an unpleasant experience is under the control of external (circumstantial) rather than internal (personal) forces. But again, by the time client meets therapist the chances are this will already have been tried and the therapist may well have no more success than family and friends in making this viewpoint stick.

In the end, the therapist must draw on specialist knowledge and he or she can look to attribution theory as one source of suggestions as to what about the client needs changing. Attribution-based therapy is a catalogue of recommendations as to what kind of cognitive restructuring needs to be done. It does not tell us about the mechanism by which cognitive restructuring is achieved although it does, I have argued, philosophically legitimate the psychological theories that do. To find out how the person may be changed we must return again to the idea that was seeded in dissonance theory, exploited in forced-compliance experiments, and developed in self-perception theory and the notion that attitudes can follow actions. To anticipate my conclusion, what I am proposing happens in therapy, at least in directive therapy, when the therapist sets out deliberately to change the client in some way, is the same as what happens in forced-compliance experiments: the therapist contrives in the client actions, declarations, and commitments which the client executes and reflects on as self-initiated.

I have suggested in relation to forced-compliance experiments that this circumstance depends on the coexistence of two alternative "theories" of the subject's actions; the experimenter's necessary conviction that the subject's behaviour is the result of the hidden manipulations that are built into the experiment, and the subject's belief, or rather knowledge, that he or she is acting out of free choice. The same can be said of directive therapy. The therapist, to be effective, must endeavour to produce in the client adaptive thoughts and actions, and to do this must see himself or herself as instrumental in determining aspects of the client's behaviour. The client, on the other hand, if he or she is genuinely to change, must cling to the knowledge that all along he or she is choosing and acting freely. The metatheoretical point about attribution theory is that it obviates any conflict between these alternative points of view in its proposal that the therapist is making external and the client internal attributions about the locus of causality of the client's redirected commitments.

To give this argument any real force, the claim that enduring psychological changes do in fact follow from this special circumstance must be backed up. What support is there for the idea that the combination of a controlling therapist or experimenter and a freely choosing client or subject is the starting point of the kind of cognitive restructuring that is undertaken in therapy? For those putting their faith in it there is some experimental support in the results of forced-compliance experiments. The extent of change in these studies is, broadly speaking, proportional to the amount of personal responsibility or perceived choice on the part of the subject (e.g., Linder et al., 1967; Zimbardo, 1969). Further experimental support comes from studies stimulated by the controversy over whether attitudes cause actions or vice versa (e.g., Kahle and Berman, 1979; Kelman, 1974; McGuire, 1976). The general conclusion from this batch of studies is that there is no fixed direction of causality between attitudes and actions but that each has a bearing on the other. For our purpose it is sufficient to note that there is support for the contention that attitudes *can* take their cue from actions.

More significantly, there is good support from the line of theories of action to which I refer throughout this chapter. As I have tried to show, the logic of these is very similar and is based on the principle of a dialectic link between mental processes—attitudes, beliefs, values, styles etc.—and actions. The attribution theory assumption that people *do* make attributions and the ethogenic axiom that people reflect on and account for their actions are expressions of the same principle.

However, neither psychological research nor psychological theory are really needed to prove this point. Like so many psychological truths, this one too resides in the issue itself; in the sense of the concepts. The concept of action as distinct from behaviour implies intention and, potentially, justification. Intention and justification are not randomly based but are the expressions of rules of morality and convention (Peters, 1958). Any system of rules, to exist as such, must bear a permanence beyond that of a single instance of rule-following—a single action. This is simply to say that rules must have some tenure. The relative permanence of moral rules implies a relative permanence in the mental apparatus that is the prescriptive basis for acting. Hence, actions and cognitive structure cannot be conceptually dissociated. Winch (1958) puts it more succinctly: "Action with a sense . . . goes together with certain other actions in the sense that it commits the agent to behaving in one way rather than another in the future" (p. 50).

The reciprocal relation between action and cognition is acknowledged in people's everyday accounting practices. Imagine a person about to give an explanation of an action he or she has just committed. We can rank the difficulty of this prospective task from "very easy" (an explanation is quickly and effortlessly found) to "very difficult" (no explanation is readily at hand). Explanations are easy when the action can be construed as the clear consequence of obvious constraint, moral or extrinsic ("I did it because it is a requirement of my course" or "I did it to prevent further suffering"). If no such binding motives present themselves and the element of unconstrained free choice is strong, when we press for a reason we will probably get something like "I did it because I believed it was the right thing to do in the circumstances" or even "I did it because I'm that kind of person." These can be called the *default* or *end-of-the-line* explanations. In them, reference is specifically made by the individual to his or her psychology; to the self. If we pause to ask just how it is that explanation is achieved in such circumstances we are bound to say that it is achieved through an appeal to a culturally shared implicit knowledge of the necessary relation between cognition and action.

There are also thousands of examples in everyday life of sales routines, propaganda, initiation ceremonies, and techniques of interrogation that rely on getting the individual to perform preliminary actions which the cunning agent provocateur is quick to cast as self-initiated. To begin with such actions are often of a seemingly trivial and inconsequential kind. The theory, however, is always the same: small-scale self-attributed actions lay the foundation for more enduring commitments through the close interplay of actions and psychological structure. Consider the ritual that surrounds therapy itself. The initial investment the client is called on to make is by no means insignificant. Traditionally, in Britain a client cannot go directly to a psychotherapist but must first be interviewed by a doctor or social worker to determine eligibility. The client must travel to the clinic, perhaps making special arrangements. On arrival there are tedious administrative procedures to go through and probably periods of waiting. When eventually the client does get to meet the therapist the importance of the client's active involvement throughout the series is often explicitly referred to in timeworn cliches such as "The real initiative must come from you," "It's you who are going to have to do most of the work," and "You've already taken the most important step in coming to see me."

We have already observed that it is a fundamental principle of ethogenics that the same cognitive resources govern accounting for an action as govern acting itself. The notion of stable patterns in a particular individual's acting and accounting seems inescapable if we are to admit the possibility of character or persona. The premise on which ethogenics is built is therefore fully consistent with the assumption of the present argument; that there is an analytic link between freely chosen action and the less ephemeral resources of the individual which form the basis of his or her social presence.

Thus, psychological research and theory give empirical backing, everyday observation provides natural or anecdotal backing, and there is logical support, for the assumption of a necessary connection between freely chosen action and mental structure. In addition, attribution theory and ethogenics invoke a new relativistic way of conceiving free choice. With these constituents it is possible to put together a general theory of social influence in the following two propositions: (1) mental structure (the "person") changes through attributed, freely chosen action and (2) one person can engineer attributed, freely chosen action in another.

I have accounted for the progress of some of the theory in social psychology on the basis of a movement away from finite, objective construals of social behaviour. If this is correct, the potential application of attribution theory in therapy can be extended far beyond the treatment of abnormal or undesirable patterns of behaviour. There is now a substantial psychological literature linking enhanced risk of illness and self-destructive tendencies of all kinds with so-called stressful life events. How stressful events are defined has depended more on the intellectual persuasion of individual authors than anything else but there is no doubt that their significance lies in their socially disruptive effect in people's lives. Bereavement, job loss, role loss, separation from friends, moving home, poor adjustment to a new situation, culture shock, and the absence of social support are all descriptions of circumstances that research has linked with the onset or exacerbation of life-threatening symptoms of various kinds (this research and its implications are discussed in Chapters 5 and 6, this volume).

The failure to adapt to change which is implied in these examples can be pictured as an incompatability between the prescriptive psychological resources of an individual and his or her changed social world so that meaningful action is effectively blocked (Totman, 1982; see also Chapter 5, this volume). The task facing a therapist is to "reprogramme" the client so that there is compatibility between him or her and the new set of social conditions that prevail and so that the client becomes an effective member of a moral order. My proposal is that this is achieved principally through justified action; through the therapist (or counsellor or friend) engineering in the client appropriate (adaptive) acts and actions and encouraging their attribution to his or her own volition. This lays the groundwork for the establishment of new commitments and life projects; for the playing of new language games.

The intellectual advance that attributional and post-attributional approaches represent is in the premise that as commentators on the psychological mechanics of this process we are not answerable to the question of who is right; which version—client's or therapist's—is the correct one. They are alternative and compatible orders of explanation, each having its own different, incorrigible criteria of authenticity. In forgoing our title as intellectuals to the "correct" version, and in keeping the ideals of "adaptive behaviour" and "changing the client for the better" we enter the arena of moral and political debate in a fully fledged way.

Exactly this view of the incommensurable positions of client and therapist is taken by Draeger (1983) in an analysis of the therapeutic encounter from a phenomenological point of view: "There is no 'problem' of truth in psychotherapy, from a phenomenological point of view. . . . All productions of the patient are truthful in that they derive from personal experience" (pp. 373 and 375).

"Misattributions"

How is the view I have just reiterated tenable in the light of so much mention in the attribution literature of people's misattributions? A person is said to have made a *misattribution* when his or her rendered explanation is patently unconvincing against an alternative explanation. But to allow misattributions is to violate the assumption of coexistent equally authentic accounts on which I am saying attribution theory is based.

Recall the well-known study in which Storms and Nisbett (1970) successfully treated sleep disturbance using placebos. The subjects in this study were all insomniacs and were all given a placebo pill believing it to be a drug. Half were told that the side effects of the pill were similar to the kinds of things insomniacs typically suffer (racing heart, obsessive thoughts etc.) and the other half were led to expect different side effects, unrelated to insomnia. The prediction (confirmed in this study although not in subsequent replications) was that those in the first group who were able to attribute, or rather misattribute, their insomniac symptoms to the side effects of the "drug" would worry less about these symptoms, enjoy decreased emotionality, and so be able to get to sleep faster than the others as a result of the placebo. The point of interest to us is not the finding of the study but whether examples like this force us to admit the concept of misattribution. If they do, then my interpretation of attribution theory as a major step in the direction of the abandonment of absolute criteria of authenticity is seriously called into question.

From the point of view of the experimenter in Storms and Nisbett's study it seems fairly unambiguous; subjects are being fed a false explanation of their insomniac symptoms. The experimenter can say categorically that this explanation is false because he or she knows that the insomniac symptoms existed before the pill was administered and that they will probably persist again after it has been stopped; there is no necessary link between the pill and the symptoms. But this style of reasoning follows quite formal, scientific guidelines that are not applied so vigorously and consistently by non-scientists. Indeed, one can safely assume that in Storms and Nisbett's experiment subjects did not work things out along strictly rational lines. If they had, the prediction would not have been confirmed because they would not have accepted the experimenter's story so uncritically. Perhaps this is why the finding proved difficult to replicate with other subject groups. Within the frame of reference of the unscientific mode of thinking which it is darkly assumed the subjects in this study will employ, the belief that the pill caused insomniac symptoms—the misattribution that was contrived—is perfectly authentic. It is authentic simply on the grounds that the experimenter has passed information to the subject and the subject trusts the experimenter to tell the truth. The standards the subject uses to judge the validity of his or her attribution are, relative to his or her own scheme, his or her *Umwelt,* correct and unassailable.

But consider an imaginary development in this study. Suppose, after the study is over, one of the experimenters approaches a subject and owns up to the "true" nature of what has been happening; that the drug which was given and which improved sleep is no more than a sugar pill. Is not then the attribution that the subject has been led to make finally compromised and shown to be fallacious? Cannot the subject be made to see that the pill's effect was due to a misattribution? Here is a situation in which the two systems of explanation appear in direct conflict. How can we fail to resolve the issue in favour of the experimenter?

If we feel compelled to side with the experimenter it is because we ourselves are psychologists, or scientific empiricists, inasmuch as we take upon ourselves this particular kind of logico-empirical discourse; inasmuch as we choose to restrict ourselves to this particular kind of language game and ignore other kinds. Adopting the truly relativistic stand that I am arguing is demanded by a fully fledged attribution theory we must regard the efforts of the experimenter in imposing his or her account on the subject as no different from those of a salesman trying to push one particular product, or those of a committed evangelist advocating one particular fundamentalist position. The only proof any of these can offer of the authenticity of their statements is proof within their own rhetorical systems. The salesman's proof is his or her advertising aids and the selective information in the sales patter, the fundamentalist's, his or her biblical quotations, and the psychologist's, his or her logico-empiricist QEDs. How convincing any one of these is depends, in each case, on the professional props and rhetorical skills of the protagonist. We feel safe under the shelter of scientific rhetoric because over the centuries it has become deeply institutionalised:

> The excellence of science is *assumed,* it is not argued for. The same is true of the standards proposed by the methodology of research programmes. These standards are obtained by an analysis of modern science. Their excellence is therefore again assumed, it is not argued for. There is not a single argument to show that they are better than the standards that underlie the practice of magic. (Feyerabend, 1981, p. 205)

By and large people do not accept uncritically what is said by salespeople, evangelists, and sometimes even scientists. This being so we might expect the nonscientist subjects in Storms and Nisbett's experiment to resist the psychologist's explanation in various ways. Indeed, it is an interesting speculation that some subjects would simply not believe the experimenter's account of the "true" nature of the experiment. Should the experimenter insist on forcing home his or her version, he or she can be considered no different from the most doctrinaire propagandist, open to the accusation of upsetting pefectly adequate and adaptive, albeit maybe "intuitive" rather than strictly rational, moral mentalities. The ethics of deception and debriefing in such experiments gets a curious twist from the relativist metaphysics behind the attributinal approach.

Responsible for the effects obtained in this study is a contrast between two different kinds of people. Roughly, the empiricism and pragmatism of the experimenter is set against the trust and dependency of the subject. A necessary social distance exists between the two, this being at least in part a function of their reciprocal situational roles. I believe that the same device is at work more generally in directive psychotherapy. If so, we can suppose that the efficacy of this kind of therapy also depends crucially on the preservation of a social distance between the participants. While, up to a point, client and therapist enter into the same stream of discourse in order to be able to talk with one another, it is in the residual incommensurability of their respective *Umwelts* that the potential for change and treatment lies. Directive therapy works insofar as the client invokes moral, intellectual, and rhetorical criteria that are different from those of the therapist.

I believe Peterson has something of the same idea when he says:

> Cognitive therapy works because it weaves new strands into the web of belief in which depressed attributions are 'located', thereby changing the entire fabric. The therapist, as a trusted, admired, and expert figure, provides a different ground (thoughts cause emotions) against which the figures (attributions) appear differently than they have in the past. The determinants of attributions are changed, and so are the attributions themselves. (1982, p. 110)

To what extent such personal incommensurabilities are situational and ephemeral or more general and enduring in people's lives obviously depends on the setting of the particular encounter. In therapy, the element of ritual helps accentuate the situational difference and the specialist equipment, vocabularies and styles that are the professional endowment of practitioners work to sustain it in the longer run.

The clearest example of a therapeutic encounter whose success is dependent on the preservation of an attributional discrepancy between therapist and client is one in which therapy is specifically aimed at encouraging an individual to initiate actions. A reliable symptom of clinical depression is the apathetic inability to act in any respect. There are a large number of currently popular therapies designated "assertion training," "effectiveness training," and "personal control training," all of which place emphasis on the remedial consequences of self-initiated action per se (see Smith, 1980). In Seligman's (revised) learned helplessness model, a species of depression is identified which is said to be the result of a "helplessness cognitive set." Therapeutic programmes are attempts to break this set, including manipulations to encourage attributions of agency on the part of the client. Beneath these recommendations lies the same *fons et origo* that I have repeatedly described in this chapter. By getting the client to perform self-attributed actions, even if at first these are no more than of a menial kind, the stage is set for the establishment of larger-scale interests and moral projects. Here again, the psychological reprogramming implied in these moves relies on the perpetuation of different and incommensurable bases from which therapist and client draw their respective theories of the client's behaviour.

Conclusion

In this chapter I have traced the development of the most influential line of theory in social psychology since the 1950s. This is not the tale of a step-by-step progression, based on the steady accumulation of data, but rather that of a changing metaphysical commitment: a gradual shift in our way of thinking and talking about social beings. This chapter bridges the first and second parts of the book. Its link with the criticisms of research in Part I is my effort to exhibit a continuity in theory that is independent of research findings. I have several times discussed the form and design of experiments but have not needed to get involved in their findings. Its link with subsequent chapters is the identification of a tide of pragmatic relativism in social psychology which is the real carrier of thinking and theories over this period. Whether this trend is something unique to social psychology or whether it is one limb of a more broadly based intellectual movement is a question that will occupy the minds of historians of the future. But it is tempting to draw parallels between the change I describe in social psychology and current similarly relativistic trends in other academic subjects, particularly in the philosophy of science (Bloor, 1983; Feyerabend, 1981; Hollis and Lukes, 1982; Rorty, 1980).

4

Justification as the Source of Social Behaviour

"Social" Behaviour

I argued in the last chapter that the current intellectual drift in social psychology reflects a change in our conception of free choice. In modern theories, starting with attribution theory, free choice and personal commitment are conceived not as psychological absolutes but as individual perceptions which are subject to situational influence and can be, up to a point, manipulated and controlled. It must be stressed again that this move does not debase free choice by robbing it of moral significance. Many attributionists seem to think that to be true to attribution theory they must talk about "misattributions" and the "illusion of free choice." But it does not follow that because free choice is an individual perception it is an illusion. It can only be an illusion against another more authoritative perspective, and while the logic of attribution theory requires the idea of other perspectives, it does not seek to pit the perspicacity of one against that of another. Indeed, to do so would be an infringement of the theory's principle axiom. In the new scheme, free choice is neither an illusion nor is it divorced from considerations of conscience and moral responsibility.

The analysis of free choice offered in the last chapter leaves a number of questions unanswered. The most pregnant of these is: What are the conditions of an action's being free, or rather of its being attributed as free? This question will be explored in this chapter and with it the related question of what counts as "social behaviour" and "social meaning" in academic debate.

When the word "social" crops up in ordinary conversation it makes most people think in terms of activities carried on in the company of other people. To talk about someone's social life is to talk about the company they keep, and to say that someone is a very social or sociable person is to say that a fair proportion of their time is spent with other people.

Social scientists do not use "social" in quite this sense. In fact, it is rather difficult to work out precisely the meaning they do put on the term. Shaw and Costanzo (1982), in the introduction to their book reviewing social psychological theories, catalogue six representative definitions of the range and scope of social psychology:

1. "Social psychology is the scientific study of human interaction" (Watson, 1966, p. 1).
2. "Social psychology is a subdiscipline of psychology that especially involves the scientific study of the behavior of individuals as a function of social stimuli" (Jones and Gerard, 1967, p. 1.).
3. "Social psychology: A discipline that attempts to understand, explain, and predict how the thoughts, feelings, and actions of individuals are influenced by the perceived, imagined, or implied thoughts, feelings and actions of others" (Raven and Rubin, 1976, p. 516).
4. "Social psychology is the study of the way in which individuals are affected by social situations" (Worchel and Cooper, 1976, p. 7).
5. "Social psychology is 'the scientific study of the personal and situational factors that affect individual social behavior'" (Shaver, 1977, p. 14).
6. "Social psychology is 'a scientific attempt to understand and explain how the thoughts, feelings, and behavior of individuals are influenced by the actual, imagined, or implied presence of others'" (van der Zanden, 1977, p. 27).

None of these definitions, however, will really do. Four of them emphasise the scientific nature of social psychology and we have seen in the first part of this volume how far short of science in the traditional sense social psychology research falls. Definitions 2, 4, and 5 all beg the question of what is meant by social by tautologically involving the word "social" in the object of the definition. The interactive nature of social behaviour is stressed in definition 1, but this definition leaves out the possibility of individuals being affected by social forces in the things they do and the thoughts they have when alone. Definitions 3 and 6 acknowledge a person's capacity to think and imagine and to carry the imprint of social influences beyond the face-to-face encounter but they do not say what this involves; what exactly it is that is thought and imagined, whether it is a conscious activity, where it is based, and how it influences a person's behaviour.

None of the above definitions, for example, would class gardening as a social activity. A gardener often works alone, yet he or she follows rules and strives towards ends that are collectively defined and upheld. The way a good garden is established is not arbitrary. One must have an idea of what such a garden should look like, what constitutes a weed, when to water plants and so on, and these things are the result of consensus and are passed through the community. The concept of a desirable garden, methods of gardening, and the role of gardener are categories expressive of one fragment of social order within our culture. The products of people's labours, gardens themselves, are shown off, judged, admired, and scorned. They are the source of pride, hope, frustration, and despair. Although gardening is something that is often done alone, it is by no means free of social association.

Is this perhaps casting the net too wide? In allowing a social status for activities such as gardening are we not bound to class all learned human performance as social? If so, there is a danger that our definition will become so encompassing as to be void of meaning on the grounds that there are no other forms of behaviour against which to contrast what we are calling social. It is my aim in this chapter to represent social behaviour and social meaning in such a way as to avoid this difficulty. The definition I offer is closely tied in with the conception of free choice introduced in the previous chapter.

Most modern philosophers and psychologists would agree that social behaviour involves rule-following (see Peters 1958; Winch, 1958; Collett, 1977). Because logically we cannot entertain the notion of rule-following without the possibility of breaking rules, this definition can be turned around to say that behaviour is social in that it contains scope for breaking rules. Rule-breaking in the gardening example is calling yourself a gardener and allowing the grass to grow and the weeds to take hold. But what about the numerous smaller-scale encounters between people that make up so much of everyday life? Hand-shaking—a fairly universal convention—would be classed by most people as a social behaviour. It normally goes quite smoothly but contains the possibility of breaking the rules. The opportunity is always there for a person to decline to take another's hand. The social significance of handshakes is mostly not great. They are normally routinely got out of the way and quickly forgotten. This is not the case though if a handshake is rebuffed. In these circumstances the situation instantly becomes charged with social meaning and surrounded by speculation as to the reason why such a thing should have happened.

My proposal, roughly, is that behaviour should be called social when it involves alternative possible ways of acting and when at least one of these alternatives can be relied on to evoke criticism and require justification. A polite handshake is not especially meaningful but a refusal to take someone's hand is. Behaviour becomes socially meaningful when a counternormal alternative is intentionally chosen and a rule is understood to have been broken; in short, when it involves justification. Let me explain this in more detail.

Choice and Meaning

If a woman shoots dead an intruder in her house whom she catches about to make off with her valuables, she might be called on to justify this action, legally and morally, on the grounds that she used excessive and disproportionate force. If a man shoots dead an intruder because he sees him holding a knife at his wife's throat, the situation is rather different. The second person can justify his action on the grounds that it is considered normal and reasonable for priority to be given to the protection of one's close family and friends. He can argue to some effect that he had "no choice" in the matter. The first person cannot argue that she had no choice. Criticism is more likely and justification more pressing in her case. She is the one who is seen to have stepped out of line most. Hers is the action that is held most accountable. Should she confirm that it was indeed her intention to aim a shot at the intruder—that it was not a mistake or an action taken out of blind panic—hers is shown up as the action most charged with social meaning in the sense that it is most subject to evaluative (mainly critical) comment.

Imagine a second possibility. Two successful merchant bankers decide to change their jobs. The first agrees to become the chairman of a large public company and the second decides to sell all his belongings, give away the proceeds, and join a poor commune to help in the work of growing organically farmed vegetables. Here too the amount of choice with which each of these actions is attributed differs widely. The first man, with the prospects of a better salary and a knighthood, will be understood when he says he really had no choice in the matter. These readily available reasons are more than sufficient to close off all commentary on his decision. The action of the second man, however, is likely to generate a great deal more talk and speculation. Its social implications are much stronger. It is full of significance and is the stuff of gossip and comment.

In both of these examples it makes sense to say that one act, prima facie involves more choice, expresses more commitment, and carries more meaning than the other. One is intrinsically more arresting and commentworthy because it appears as less warrantable than the other.

Clearly, the more automatic an action is the less thinking, planning and justifying there is associated with it. Automatic and habitual actions are therefore not particularly meaningful, or social, in the sense intended here because they tend to be accounted for on the basis of causal influences rather than in terms of reasons and justifications. The distinction between reasons and causes has been the subject of a great deal of philosophical debate (Davidson, 1980). Locke and Pennington (1982) see it as a more hopeful basis for interpreting many of the findings of attribution theory research than the ambiguous internal–external distinction. For our purpose, it is sufficient to note that normally in everyday life reasons and justifications are not called for in circumstances where behaviour is represented as automatic and caused.

Yet we talk about good and bad habits and condemn people for activities like nose-picking which have a kind of social (or "anti-social") connotation but which seem to take place almost unconsciously. But when we are criticising a person for a bad habit we are not criticising any one episode; any one particular twist of the finger inside the nose. Instances of a habit are automatic in the same way that subroutines under the control of a master programme are. Our criticism is of the master programme itself: of the person for allowing an undesirable behaviour to become automatic. Specific instances, if explained at all, tend to be accounted for causally.

It is unlikely that a person, when criticised, would try to justify a bad habit. But this might happen, in which case the nature of the performance is immediately transformed. It changes from a habit to an act because the criticism that is levied and countered by justification, has the effect of infusing the behaviour (or in this case, the person's failure to check the behaviour) with choice and meaning. Someone who responds, "Why shouldn't I pick my nose?" is challenging the moral assumption of his critics and attacking the social world they are serving up. As soon as justification and debate surround a piece of behaviour that behaviour becomes charged with socialness.

Public Accountability and Private Commitment

One could be forgiven for thinking these comments somewhat bland. Indeed, if they were the whole story they would hardly be worth setting down. However, the bond between action and cognition that has been the main focus of the social psychology theories of the past 30 years, and which was discussed in detail in the previous chapter, points to another, more interesting, consequence of actions charged with choice and meaning in this sense. These theories suggest that an actor, through being a member of the same speech community as those who comment on and assess his or her action—because actor and community are to some extent players of the same language games—is liable to draw similar inferences from reflecting on and talking about his or her own action as they do. Put extremely crudely, in default of being able to point to convincing, arguable, mitigating, "external" circumstances for shooting dead a petty thief, the reckless householder, confronted with her own action as a fait accompli, is unable to escape the ultimate "internal" explanation, "I must have done it because I'm that sort of person." The essential and highly significant discovery of these theories is that under conditions of freely attributed action the mask really does become the man.

In the same vein, the decision by a merchant banker to join a vegetarian commune is likely to be construed as high on personal motivation. But the same line of social psychology theory tells us that actions located in volitional rhetoric are psychologically forming; they augur more enduring commitment. In the terminology of cognitive dissonance theory they are the conditions of attitude change, in that of self-perception theory they are the source of a people's labellings of their own behaviour, and in that of attribution theory they are the starting point of cognitive change mediated by an internal attributional set.

The two preceding examples relate to rather extreme decisions and actions. I have chosen these for the sake of ease of communication because sometimes a point is most clearly made by focusing on extremes. But there is plenty to show that the same mechanism—that of freely attributed action as the carrier of social meaning in both the public (comment-provoking) and the private (cognitively forming) domain—is at work in a less dramatic fashion in people's daily lives. If you want to become a city business executive, you can start, even before you apply for a job, by taking the *Financial Times* and choosing a pin-striped suit. If you want to avoid falling in love but know there is a danger of this happening, the thing to do is force yourself not to make that telephone call or send those flowers. Romantic love, in fact, provides a very good illustration of this point. The ritual of romantic courtship in medieval England and France required that the aspiring lover "prove" his love by electing to undertake a difficult and dangerous task such as embarking on a long journey or fighting in a war. The more difficult and hazardous the task underwritten, the greater the presumed demonstration of affection. A similar phenomenon, the *Romeo and Juliet effect,* is described by Driscoll, Davis, and Lipitz, (1972) in American teenagers. These authors studied parental attitudes to children's courtship and concluded that attempts by parents to block or oppose an attachment actually had the effect of intensifying it. Common to both these cases is a special social environment in which the cost, and therefore the significance, of the choices made and the actions taken is augmented and the strength of the resultant commitment enhanced correspondingly. Actions become more oppositional in character. In the medieval example, the mechanism for enhancement is built into a cultural ritual. In the American example, it is a paradoxical accident which turns out to have exactly the opposite effect to the one intended.

As was seen in the previous chapter, techniques used in real life to manipulate people psychologically also seem to be based on the intuition that commitment and meaning are a function of the degree of choice with which a person's action is attributed. Cult evangelists, as in the old forced-compliance experiments, use hidden social pressures to cajole a person into enacting some seemingly innocuous performance, like reading out loud a passage of text, but afterwards work to construe the performance as deliberate ("well read," "spoken from the heart," etc.). The Unification Church ("Moonies"), in their recruiting campaigns, rely on the powerful pressures that can be generated in a group of people to make a recruit do things that are only done in that community—apparently "neutral" things like the ritual chanting by everyone of "Choo-choo-choo." Not to join in what seems like a harmless piece of fun can easily be made to appear churlish.

As in forced-compliance experiments, the source of the person's involvement is ambiguous. One's participation is engineered by social pressures, but actions are retrospectively construed as volitional in talk such as, "Well you didn't have to join in," "Nobody forces anyone to do anything they don't want to here." Once again the oldest trick in the world is being worked. The rhetoric of free choice is being sold to the recruit so as to draw him or her inside the system, to be stamped with its aims and ideals. Confronted with what he or she has done or said in a nominally free or unconstrained context (although I have argued in the previous chapter that the metaphysics of attribution theory has it that the "nominally" here can effectively be dropped), the recruit is brought mentally one step inside the world of the provocators. The "deprogramming" of the victims of such indoctrination follows a precisely similar path to that of indoctrination itself, with emphasis on contriving internally attributed actions. This time though, it is actions that are considered more in line with the social constitution of the "real" world.

Professional interrogators too are aware of the importance of getting their subjects to perform small, initial actions, like accepting a cigarette or engaging in conversational small talk. Through the same psychological mechanism seemingly trivial commitments, retrospectively cast as self-initiated, open the door to a favourable attitude towards the interrogator and the system he or she represents and so are the first steps toward the psychological capitulation that is the goal of the procedure. The idea of freely chosen, or freely attributed, action as the source of social meaning and psychological commitment, as well as finding support in social psychological theory, also has plenty of sinister everyday counterparts. The most common of all are advertising and sales techniques aimed at eliciting an initial "no strings attached" small commitment: just send off for details, or just test drive the new model "with no obligation".

I have begun the new definition of social behaviour which I want to develop with the proposal that we should reserve the descriptions "social" and "socially meaningful" for actions and decisions that involve attributed choice and justification. If the arguments of the last chapter are correct, we can say that free choice is the same thing as attributed free choice and that an action can be genuinely free even when it can be cast as, or "proved to be," caused. The conviction of freedom and the conviction of determinacy do not clash because they are the products of different incommensurable rhetorics: alternative language games. To the extent that reasons and justifications are not invoked in the description of an action that action can be said to be relatively unremarkable and to contain a relatively low amount of social meaning. Another way of putting this is to say that actions not embedded in a justificatory framework are definitionally actions low on social "information" in the information theory sense (Shannon and Weaver, 1949). Socially meaningful behaviour is therefore to be contrasted with unjustified, unplanned behaviour; behaviour of a normal, habitual kind; behaviour that does not attract evaluative commentary, either by the individual or by others in the community. Social behaviour can therefore be defined quite simply as justified action.

Societies as Multifarious

It cannot be denied that an action that for one person is routine and habitual and is executed without further thought may for another represent the height of daring and cause one to be caught up in a vortex of introspective justification. However, such differences between people and between the social worlds in which they move furnish exactly the condition that makes choice and commitment possible. Imagine a society whose members are so socially harmonious as to have reached complete agreement over the rules of conduct. They are continually in unanimous accord over matters of convention, belief, morality, style, and so on. In such an "ideal" society there would be no scope for choice and no role for justification because nothing would ever be in dispute and no alternative ways of acting would ever present themselves. People would conduct themselves like—indeed would effectively *be*—automata. Actions would be truly meaningless. Social meaning would simply not arise because reasons for actions would never need to be given. In these circumstances there could be no social behaviour.

There are, of course, more or less universally accessible interpretations of actions within a community of same-language speakers. Rommetveit (1980), following Smedslund, calls such uncontroversial ascriptions, whose meaning is exhausted in a standard, boring description of the action itself ("mowing the lawn", "changing jobs", etc.), "public trivial minima." These are the least-meaningful types of action descriptions. More meaningful descriptions are achieved when interpretations with stronger evaluative or justificatory overtones are ventured and the way is open to more idiosyncratic, contentious, divisive accounts. Action descriptions can be pictured in the form of a tree, with public shared minima as the trunk and the proliferation of branches representing successively more private, meaningful interpretations on the one hand and successively smaller-scale social orders on the other. The public categories at the trunk are little more than universal conventions of speech; the neutral descriptions everyone uses and understands; the language games that everyone plays. Branching out from these general, shared categories are progressively more esoteric (and if it does not happen to be your particular scene, alien) interpretations and the more rarified vocabularies and conversational styles in whose terms these more cliquish accounts are drafted. As Rommetveit (1980) puts it:

> As we expand the scope of accounts vertically, from the lowest possible level towards some superordinate "meaning of life", we discover that our *public* trivial minimum branches off into different, yet in some sense, successively more meaningful, *private* entities. And self-accounts will at all levels tend to differ in characteristic ways from those offered by outside observers. What from the outside may appear as a routine in some public game will often, from the position of the agent himself within his own private world, be imbued with intrinsic motivation or intention. We may thus at times be willing to make sense of *the acts of other people* by considering them as robot-like beings, yet protest violently against such accounts of *our own personal acts.* (p. 124)

Communities of speakers of the same tongue are thus both united and fragmented. They are united and cohered through the forms of speech representing that part of social reality that is universally shared: trivially

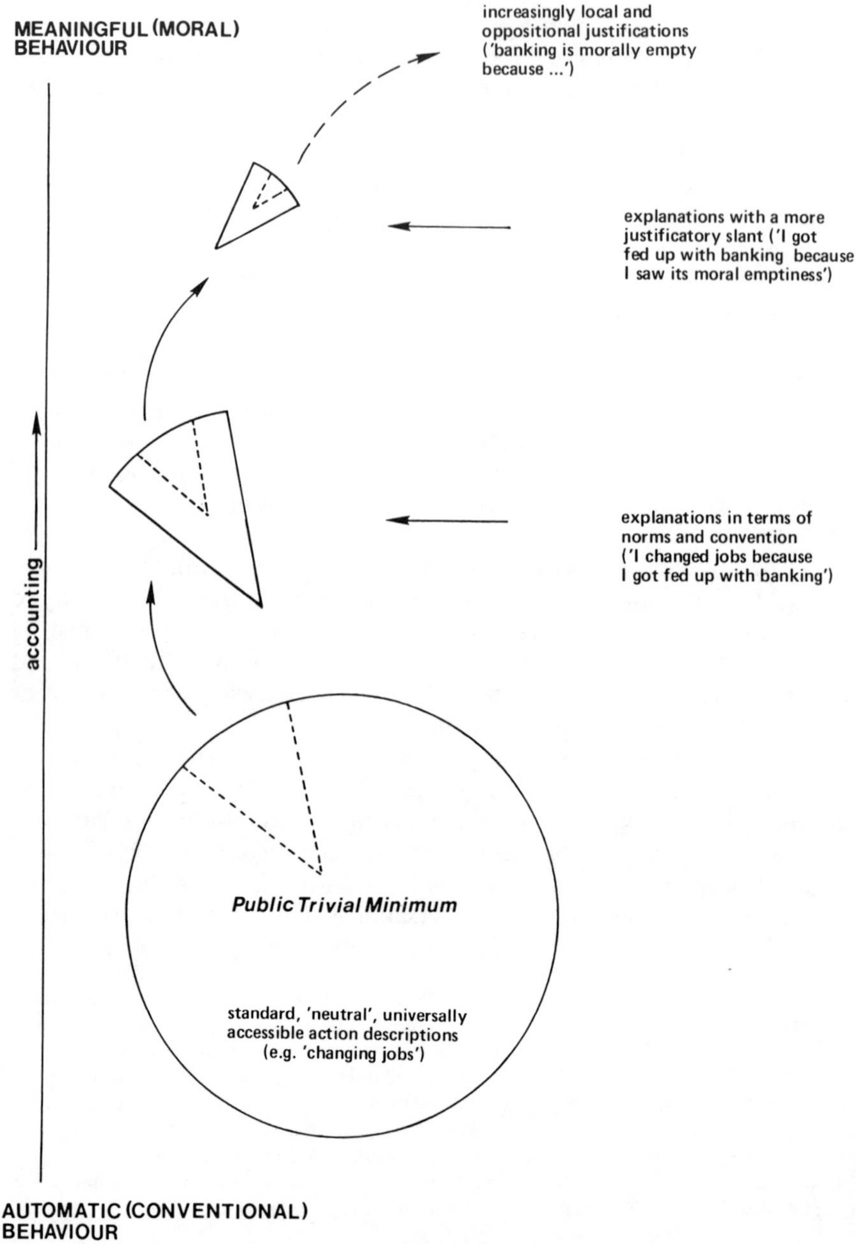

Figure 4.1 The public and private nature of action.

uncontroversial descriptions—Rommetveit's public shared minima. And they are fragmented through the divergent, often dissenting, styles of talk that overlay these universals and that are the basis of more local realities and unions within the overall community. Figure 4.1 is an attempt to illustrate this. Although at various points in this book discourses and language games are referred to as the "source of" social cohesion and so forth, I do not consider the question of whether groups and communities are caused by discourses, or whether it is the other way round and discourses are the product of groups and communities, to be of very much importance. For our purpose it is more helpful to take the two as sufficiently interdependent to each be expressions of what is essentially the same constitution.

Reasons and justifications, and the "languages" in which they are composed, can thus be represented as the hallmark of the socialness of behaviour. The kaleidoscopic array of different, only partially commensurable, styles of talk is the richest expression of the divisions within our societies and the richest source of social meaning. There is a precedent, in ethnomethodology and ethogenics, for not drawing a line between acting and planning and justifying an action. Planning and justifying endow an action with meaning without which it is no more than a conditioned reflex or a habit. The foremost condition of meaning is opposition, and that of social meaning is the inherently differentiated nature of all macro-societies: the oppositions, boundaries, and incommensurabilities that distance groups of people from one another and find expression in, among other things, class, gender, role, profession, cult, club, clique, reference group, and style.

It must be made clear at this point that while I am arguing that the distinctions and oppositions between relatively coherent groupings of people are necessary for the generation of social meaning, I do not want to be construed as championing any one particular source of social division—class or gender for example—on these grounds. My point is that division of *some* kind is a precondition of social meaning, justified choice, and conversation. Whether our existing institutions are the best vehicles for this or whether they are anachronistic and morally inappropriate to contemporary life is a matter for politicians and ideologists. What seems clear from a psychologist's perspective, however, is that the more uniformly conformist a macrosociety is, the less scope it contains for meaningful, or justified, action.

The Exclusive Character of Action

Wittgenstein, discussing propositions in logic, made the simple but important observation that the sense of a logical proposition is entirely represented in an exhaustive list of the propositions it shuts out. The same can be said, albeit less formally, of individual actions. A person embarking on a decision confronts a finite number of alternative courses of action from which one must be chosen. Performance of the action itself is the cementing of one's choice. It marks the point at which the decision becomes publicly accessible and forward planning turns into retrospective accounting. Planning is an attempt to anticipate the way justification will look and to pre-empt criticism and derision once alternative choices have been excluded. While the meaning of an action can thus be represented in terms of the course that is selected, it can equally (following Wittgenstein's argument) be represented in terms of the alternative courses that, as a result of the performance, are shut out.

The construal of action as the closing off of possibilities, while in one sense no more than a technical move, enables a fresh insight into the nature of choosing. For in the act of committing oneself to one course and thereby pragmatically excluding others, an individual is in effect limiting the scope of his or her justification. At the planning stage, before a decision is taken, alternative actions are contemplated and various strategies of justification are assessed. By the post-decisional stage nearly all of these have been eliminated. It may be that before his or her mind is finally made up the person feels it is possible to justify more than one course of action and so chooses almost arbitrarily. But the same principle still holds true: I can do these justifications, therefore I will do the action. The point is that in the necessity of acting some justifications are banished, and along with them the language games in which these justifications are ritualistically embedded.

Central to the main arguments of this book is the assumption that the psychological glue that bonds people together into social categories is the discourse in which justifications are expressed: the web of talk into which reasons for actions are woven. This is a version of the Goffman–Harré thesis having historical links with Saussure's and Wittgenstein's accounts of the nature of language. It is also a view that has traditionally found support among French structuralist philosophers and one that is fundamental to modern semiotic approaches to social anthroplogy and linguistics.

In a book entitled *Language and Social Identity* (1982), Gumperz and his colleagues discuss a programme of sociolinguistic research based on a very similar premise. They argue that the complex communicative nature of the modern world has turned the basis of cohesiveness away from geographical location and that social identity and ethnicity are in large part established and maintained through language.

> Language use creates a social identity for the user. . . . The process is a reflexive one. Language as speaking practice creates and identifies social group membership. Through shared communicative conventions, individuals treat each other as part of their own

> social group. It is this that enables them to acquire knowledge and experience which reinforce the social group and sharedness. (Jupp, Roberts, and Cook-Gumperz, 1982, p. 239)

Research on speech communities consists in analysing tracts of talk and attempting to unravel those stylistic features that identify a particular community (e.g., Gumperz, 1982; Romaine, 1982). That social correspondences between individuals are supported on the basis of similarities in their vocabularies and styles of talk also gets more mundane backing from everyday comments like "I couldn't get on with her because I just couldn't talk to her" and "We don't speak the same language."

How right is it to tie in justification with conversation in general? Clearly there are forms of conversation, greetings, exchanges about the weather, and so forth—seemingly straightforward passages of information—that do not appear to carry the evaluative overtones one associates with the process of justification. Certainly, criticisms of others must be linked with planning and justifying one's own behaviour because in criticising a person one is making a public commitment to exclude a particular class of act, or attitude, or style from one's own repetoire. By the same token, publicly praising someone, or endorsing his or her action, is a little like acting oneself in that it commits you to one moral course at the exclusion of others (see Sabani and Silver, 1982).

In fact, a good deal of people's conversational talk is given over to the criticism or endorsement of others, or of other, past selves, not always in head-on expressions of approval or disapproval but in the many oblique, insinuating ways people have of assessing, condoning, and deriding others. Listening to people talk, more time seems to be spent in criticising others than in praising them. Perhaps criticism and the rejection of social forms that it implies is psychologically more economical than praise and acceptance as a means of establishing and maintaining one's own social identity.

It is true that respect and derision are communicated in gestures as well as in speech. But gestures often have to be explained and it is difficult to think of any deliberate gesture than cannot be described in words. One of the basic assumptions of Searle's (1969) theory of speech acts is that anything that can be meant can also be said. Words are the medium of justification, in the broad sense in that I have defined it, and conversation is turned to this end in an enormous number of often very subtle ways. Evaluative commentary as indirect personal justification is psychologically inseparable from the business of choosing and acting itself. Through his or her praise and admiration, mockery and contempt, advice, censorship, goadings and enjoinders, as well as in his or her own choices and actions, the individual becomes the person he or she is.

Just how far the identification of conversation with justification can be taken probably is more a matter of taste than anything else. Even miniscule exchanges between people (e.g., *A:* "I'll make the beds," *B:* "Put the kettle on first, will you?" can have a host of social categorials and prescriptions read into them. The successful management of the interchange can itself be construed as a commitment to keep alternative worlds at bay. To say that all conversation is justification is to court accusations of emptiness. But the idea of different (although intersecting) species of conversational talk with their divergent vocabularies, styles, and rhythms as the delimiters of different fields of justificatory possibilities and thus as the ultimate anchors of local social order, is both intuitively and empirically supportable.

If it can be said that pockets of social order are sustained through the talk that is done within them, then what an individual does in choosing and committing himself or herself to a particular course of action is, effectively, to limit his or her own social horizons by restricting the range of discoursive possibilities. In choosing and acting, the individual is excluding other choices and other actions. But more significantly, in setting out on one particular justificatory course he or she is shutting off a range of alternative justifications and hence becoming distanced from the language games to which these justifications belong. In cementing a choice in action and in going firmly on a course of justification of that action, the individual thereby implicitly rejects the institutions that go with the excluded alternatives.

Action can thus be thought of as psychologically limiting. An individual, before embarking on an action, "thinks about it". Thinking about it involves exploring a range of potential justifications for alternative courses of action and maybe trying these out on imaginary audiences. The point of choice and commitment comes when certain justifications, and the audiences to which they are matched, are shut out in favour of a particular justificatory strategy: a particular act. Justifications stand like signposts at the boundaries of the different social orders that make up a socially pluralistic society.

Work as Justification

At the beginning of this chapter I criticised textbook definitions of social psychology on the grounds that they all seem to require the presence of other people, real or imagined, for behaviour to be called social. Gardening was given as an example of an activity that, although often done alone, is socially constituted. Is there not a contradiction here if social behaviour is to be equated with justified behaviour? Activities like gardening, writing, painting, and composing are often carried on by solitary individuals who do not spend much of their time with other people. Where is the justification in these activities if it is not, as I have depicted it, in the discourse?

It has been said that the planning and deliberation that precede an intentional act should not be regarded as independent of the justification that follows it because planning an action involves the exploration of various possible justificatory strategies and the rejection of most of those in favour of one or two. Forward planning and retrospective accounting each fulfil the same psychological function; that of contextualising an action in order either to pre-empt criticism and derision or to win prestige in the eyes of those one wishes to impress. Something along the same lines can be said of work. The accomplishment of a piece of skilled work means having a set goal and maintaining a focused effort so as to avoid errors that would jeopardise the attainment of this goal. Work undertaken in isolation tends to be work of a "creative" nature, work towards an envisioned end-product which will later be held up to be criticised or admired. The attention to detail that goes into work of this kind is rather like the planning stage of acting. It's aim is the exclusion of alternative forms to the particular ideal the worker has in mind. Like acting, this sort of work represents the closing off of possibilities and the selection of one from a number of possible forms. The planning and the myriad of decisions made during the accomplishment of skilled and creative work thus has something in common with the planning of an accountable action. Both are characterised by the exclusion of alternatives in favour of a particular intended, socially grounded, end-product.

The same cannot be said of work of a routine kind. In the repetitive work of the production line there is little scope for the exclusion of alternatives—the outlawing of unwanted forms—and hence little opportunity for meaningful choice and action. The contrast between meaningful (justified) and non-meaningful (unjustified) action is mirrored in the contrast between routine and creative performance. Justified action and creative work both involve effort spent deliberately in the appraisal of alternative forms and their exclusion from the scheme. Unjustified action and routine work can be characterised by the poverty of alternative forms available for exclusion, and correspondingly, the absence of meaning and lack of involvement of the individual. This is another contrast which is perhaps best appreciated by looking at extremes. Compare the infinite number of potential forms that an artist or novelist must exclude in order to achieve his or her objective with the possibilities facing a production-line worker whose job it is to spot and reject faulty components.

One does not necessarily have to speak to engage in that psychological aspect of language that carries an indissoluble social involvement. Saussure's distinction between *la langue* and *parole,* and the parallel distinction that Chomsky makes between the competence performance aspects of a language, help the argument. It is *la langue*—the competence element—which lies at the root of social behaviour. This can be active even if nothing is ever spoken as it is carried around in a person's thoughts and is implicit in the concept of action.

The justification of work of a skilled or creative nature, therefore, is in the work itself—in the form and detail that make it good or bad, original or mundane when stood up against other enterprises in the same category. Personal judgments of the quality of creative work are subjective, and there is perhaps as much scope for variation here as there is in the taking of moral decisions. To be successful, work must be seen to be good. "Good" is a matter of consensus and someone who insists his or her work is good in the absence of corroboration from others is likely to be assessed dismissively as insane or delusional.

For the moment, the consideration of psychological defense must be left on one side. In Chapter 8 we return to the idea of delusional defenses as propping up ailing systems of justification in the absence of a supportive consensus. It can be turned into an empirical hypothesis on the assumption that social meaning, achieved through justification, is necessary for health and survival. On the psychosomatic model which is developed we are led to predict, for example, that individuals cannot survive conversationally isolated from other individuals and stay sane *without* engaging in work of a skilled or creative kind.

In his theory of the means of production in industrial societies Marx was acutely aware of the social origins of work and, the other side of this coin, of the powerful forming influence on individual consciousness of the social and economic networks that support work. However, as Harré has pointed out, "work" in Marx's practical, life supporting sense, is not the only preoccupation of twentieth-century men and women:

> Marx said that it was in the nature of man to work. Not at least as the human race is presently constituted. It is in the nature of men to slip off to the pub to display their *machismo,* and of women to exchange anecdotes about the prowess of their children. (1979, p. 8)

For Harré, the practical order with which Marx was so concerned is not nearly as important as the "expressive" order, at least in modern developed societies; the constant striving for honour; the need to gain respect from others and to avoid their contempt. Most of our efforts, Harré argues, go into expressive projects and not into the mechanics of supporting life and maintaining production. Harré's philosophy is a working out of the universal social mechanisms behind the ritual markings of respect and contempt.

Harré's concern over system and science in social psychology leads him to want to represent social life as a succession of social "episodes," analysed as if they were taking place on a stage and as if the participants were actors in a scripted drama. How people's accounts produced in this way can tell us more than can be learned through just talking with them, or through good journalism or sensitive plays and novels, is not clear. Nevertheless, the winning of respect and the avoidance of contempt from others is probably a fair summary of what much of social life is about although the payoff—what in the actor's mind counts as success—I believe to be a more subtle and complex matter than the posturing that Goffman and Harré see as the electricity behind situational episodes. Vocational commitments and creative projects carried on in isolation are two cases in point.

For our purpose it is not especially important whether a sharp line is drawn between the practical and expressive social orders. Both, as Marx and Harré have stressed, represent absorbing social projects. Both, to the extent that they involve justification and the shutting off of alternative forms, are forming of the consciousness and character of the individual. This much we can extract from psychological theories of action.

Explanation versus Justification

What I have been trying to do in this chapter and the previous one is to review the central theoretical advances in social psychology in such a way as to uncover the main assumptions and historical influences that lie beneath them. The previous chapter showed how theories of individual action have become progressively less self-conscious about taking as their point of departure people's own explanations. The work of Rommetveit (1980) and others leads us to suppose that reasons given for an action range from the uncontroversial statement of an intention purely to make an action intelligible ("He is mowing the lawn" or "I crossed the street to get some groceries") to the more loaded business of justifying or warranting. A neutral reason is little more than a description of a commonplace practice—a public minimum, a universal language game. Explaining at this level is a trivial form of justification. Justifying becomes less trivial when a given reason is deemed out of context and challenged. Suppose instead the reason given for crossing the street was "to proposition that pretty girl." Now this might lead to the counter-challenge, "You, a married man!" or "But she's only about 15!" Subsequent to the giving of a reason, any extension of the conversation serves to explicate the respective moral positions of each of the protagonists by establishing a provisional moral opposition. Imagine how it might go:

George. What were you doing over on the other side of the street?
Ben. I was going to try my chances with that girl but she gave me the slip.
George. Don't be crazy! She's only about 15. What on earth would your wife say?
Ben. For Christ's sake, there's nothing you can teach a 15-year-old these days! Anyway Sarah's at her mother's.
George. But you're over 40 and almost bald! You can't prance around like Don Juan every time her back's turned.
Ben. You're so stuffy George! Don't tell me you've never had it off with another girl since you got married?
George. As a matter of fact I haven't. Couldn't handle the angst. Think how you'd feel if Sarah found out!
Ben. She wouldn't mind. Besides, bruises heal. I think you were born middle-aged, George. Life's for living you know!
George. At least I'm not stuck on adolescence. When are you going to grow up?

In exchanges like this respective views are aired in a friendly way and the episode is probably concluded with one of a number of bland devices for agreeing to differ ("It takes all sorts."etc.). Not much reconciliation of views is achieved or even attempted. Each party uses the declarations made to the other to cement his own position. Ben will go away thinking of himself as not stuffy, not boring and not middle-aged and George will think of himself as not reckless, not insensitive and not inconsiderate.

It takes a good playwright or novelist to portray characters in coversational talk. The power of good plays and novels is a demonstration of how literal and stylistic continuities in a person's speech do afford a kind of direct, impressionist insight into the life of that person and the pattern of meanings on which that life is based.

Some philosophers have wanted to preserve a clear boundary between explanation and justification, and between constitutive and regulative rules, while others are suspicious of the separation (see Collett, 1977, for a discussion of this issue). Following Rommetveit (1980), I prefer to treat the two kinds of accounts as occupying different zones on the same conversational continuum. The difference between rendering an action intelligible and rendering it warrantable, I shall say, corresponds simply to the amount of discussion, or work, that is entered into as a postscript to the action in question. Any prolongation of discussion or work consists in an elaboration of the process of exclusion and so relocates the action further along the continuum in the direction of justification.

The Systems Analogy

With the concept of justification at the centre of the stage in our analysis and with the role of choice and action cast as the selection of one from a number of potential justificatory courses, it is now possible to recapitulate the main argument of this chapter using the concepts of system and entropy. The idea of a system has a very wide appeal. It is used in mathematics, information theory, cybernetics, computer science, macro-economics, sociology, political science, and biology to name but a few subjects. In fact, it is difficult to think of any area of discussion, academic or otherwise, in which it does not crop up in some form. Such universality is both good and bad; bad because of the danger that nothing and everything is at risk of being treated as a system, and good because of the concept's obvious intuitive richness. A good analysis of the concept and the way in which it can be exploited in social science is provided by Kuhn (1976), who wisely points out: "Whether something is viewed as system or nonsystem is determined by the investigator with reference to his purpose; it is not determined by the nature of the thing investigated" (p. 24).

There are a few necessary properties of systems that need to be stated before proceeding. The most basic of these is that systems exhibit some degree of stability, or constancy. If they did not it would not be possible to identify them as the same system over time. A system may be closed, which means that it is a self-contained, self-regulating entity that is insulated from, and does not interact with, other systems. Or, it may be open, or interactive. For open systems to be stable they must exhibit equilibrium through negative, or compensating, feedback, because if they do not, their form would change and the necessary property of stability over time would be lost. The "hunting" of servo-mechanisms and the homeostasis of vegetative biological functions in animals are examples of open systems maintaining equilibrium through negative feedback.

The individual's psychological resources for coping with the social world—what we call in everyday terms the person—can be construed as a system in this sense. Analogies with systems in the social sciences usually concentrate on the behaviour of thermodynamic systems. The second law of thermodynamics states that all closed systems are subject to increasing entropy. The entropy of a system is the measure of unavailable energy; energy that still exists but which is lost for the purpose of doing work. In thermodynamics, of course, the energy referred to is heat and the law can be roughly understood as the idea that all (hot and cold) material within a thermally insulated area will eventually come to have the same temperature. The more general version of this principle is that all closed systems are subject to loss of differentiation. A correspondence has been established between the entropy of a system and the loss of information in that system in the sense of information theory (Buckley, 1968). So, this principle can also be taken to mean that the information in a closed system diminishes over time.

Schrodinger, applying the concept of entropy to living organisms, writes: "Thus a living organism continually increases its entropy—or, as you might say, produces positive entropy—and thus tends to approach the dangerous state of maximum entropy, which is death. It can only keep aloof from it, i.e., alive, by continually drawing from its environment negative entropy" (1968, p. 145).

A closed system, in thermodynamics or biology or whatever, like the concept of infinity in mathematics, is an ideal or pure state, unreal when applied to the physical world. But although closed systems are probably never perfectly realised in practice, the pure concept serves as a useful anchor for theories in the study of material things. The same is true of the concept of system applied to the social world. Consider, for instance the "ideal" but incredible notion of a person as a closed system, completely insulated from other systems, from the rest of the community. Such insulation would take the form of never talking with anyone and never doing anything (doing, that is, in the sense of acting and choosing as non-automatic, non-habitual justified performance). Borrowing from the thermodynamics analogy, one of the properties of such a closed person-system would be its increasing entropy; the gradual decline in the harnessable energy, or differentiation, or information, within it.

The raw material of the social psychologist is not energy or information but meaning. So, we might say that the increase in entropy, or loss of information in the system corresponds to a loss of meaning in the person under such improbable totally closed conditions.

The analogy I am trying to draw is really a contrast between two different states of the person-system. This is illustrated in Figure 4.2. Imagine the same individual, first, at a point in time *A* and then at a later point in time *B*. At *A* let us suppose there has just been an injection of negative entropy resulting from a burst of freely chosen (or freely attributed) action. From this point on, assume it happens that little or no choice is involved in the activities of the individual; that his or her life is consistently mundane and he or she does not talk with anyone. In other words, assume from *A* onward the system is more or less closed. Being closed, it is subject to entropy. Through repeated stereotyped performance, actions become automatic, commitment becomes routine, and social behaviour degenerates into habit. There is a general loss of information, differentiation, and meaning within

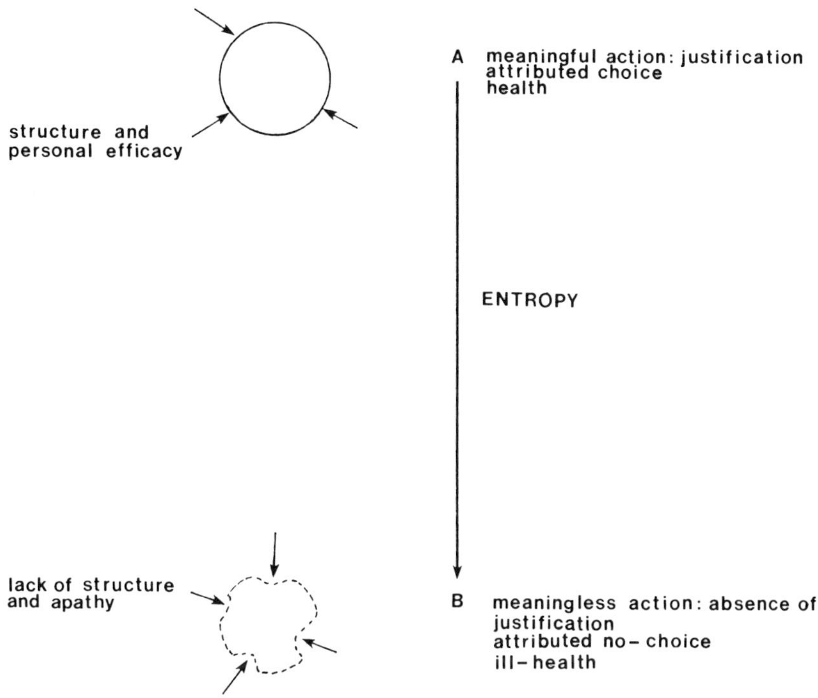

Figure 4.2 The person as a closed system.

the system. This is also marked in another way. At *A* behaviour tends to be explained in terms of reasons; at *B*, in terms of causes.

In subsequent chapters I assess the proposal that it is impossible for a person-system to be totally closed, in a social sense, and to survive biologically. Recent theories and descriptive research on the psychological and social conditions of health and survival suggest that the chronic loss of differentiation and meaning which this entails is associated with illness and death. But it is equally impossible for a living person-system to be totally open, as this would mean lack of any kind of structure and the absence of a prescriptive basis for acting. In such circumstances the condition of stability of the system over time would be lost.

In a social world that is constantly changing person-systems need to strike a balance between the one extreme of closure and stagnation through entropy and the other of openness to the extent of complete plasticity. The key to this balance, and to social life itself, I shall argue, is the process of justification. Its oppositional character—its constant working to shut out alternative forms—makes justification the generator of information, or negative entropy, in the system. As such, it is essentially a force towards equilibrium; equilibrium, that is, between the disastrous extreme of total closedness and the impossible one of complete openness of the system. Both these extremes can be linked to the failure of justification.

Occasionally, people make huge choices, like the decision to forsake merchant banking to live in a poor commune. Decisions like these can be pictured as a massive injection of information, or negative entropy, into the system and a substantial restructuring and differentiation of its contents. Sometimes, on the other hand, as is drawn in Figure 4.2, people drift into ruts. The system stagnates and closes, entropy creeps in, meaning drains away, and the person becomes bored and listless. It is interesting that this is often just the circumstance in which radical choices and commitments are made, almost, as it were, calculatedly to court negative entropy.

A note needs to be added here about the nature of the "meaning" that I have associated with negative entropy, information, and differentiation of the system. How does the concept of meaning, so defined, bear on our use of the term in ordinary discourse when we say, "he lives a very meaningful existence", or, "my life no longer seems to have any meaning"? The answer, I believe, although difficult to argue, is that there is quite a close link between our ordinary use of the term and its tying in with negative entropy in a person-system. Something has meaning when it stands for, or signifies, something else, usually something less tangible and less available for comment than the signifier. Justification as the exclusion of alternatives is what gives action and choice meaning because it stands for, or signifies, identification of the individual with a particular fragment of social order through the implied rejection of other orders predicated on alternative justificatory schemes. The zest with which a particular line of justification is pursued signifies the strength of the individual's commitment to and identification with the particular language games, and hence social institutions, in which that line of justification is traditionally done.

In saying that doing a particular justification signifies the individual's desire to participate in a particular social order, it might seem that we are in danger of falling into the old psychologist's trap of basing a theory on an arbitrary need, want, instinct, or desire. The knock-down challenge to drive-based theories is, of course, "Where does the need or desire come from—heredity, upbringing, out of the psychologist's head?" The reason we do not have to face this challenge is found in the relativistic conception of action that was extracted from modern psychological theory and traced in the previous chapter: the plausibility of regarding the same action as simultaneously both free and caused. This allows us to search for the source of people's individual choices and commitments in the causal influences acting on them without in any way undermining their story of why they did what they did. It was shown that these two seemingly opposed construals do not conflict so long as they are regarded as the products of independent discoursive perspectives.

The grounding of the scheme here is therefore not in terms of the ad hoc needs, desires, or instincts invented by psychologists but in terms of the Saussurian notion of language as capable of dividing the spectrum of conceptual possibilities in a flexible, arbitrary way and the Wittgensteinian idea of the different orders that make up our social world as reflected in different speaking practices.

Part III

5

Health, Stress, and Illness

The Aims of Social Psychology

Why has a concern with health and illness recently crept into the foreground in social psychology? For it certainly has, not only through interest in attribution theory and its implications for therapy, but in research and theory on stressful life events: experiences in people's lives that threaten survival by exposing them to risk of physical and psychiatric illness. The answer is not hard to find. If the hopes of social psychology are pinned on anything, it is a compassionate wish to establish some of the conditions under which individuals can live together in communities successfully, without destructive conflict and without the scope for individual choice being too far compromised. I have already pointed to what I believe is a fundamental flaw in ideologies that press for a unifying and homogenous moral order. Some partitioning and opposition within the broader community is a necessary condition of personal choice and action. Historians who argue that conflict is the natural state of mankind and that periods of peace represent fundamentally unstable episodes can take some pessimistic solace from the psychological thesis that in an "ideal" society where consensus is pure, there could never be any meaningful choice or genuinely social behaviour.

Contentment, self-esteem, adequacy, a sense of meaning, personal fulfillment, a sense of control, and feelings of satisfaction and achievement are some of the dozens of descriptions to be found in the psychological literature as contenders for the utopia of individual consciousness. But there is no pleasure without pain, no hope without disappointment, and no joy without sadness. A world without these complementary emotions would be oddly incomplete.

The so-called crisis in social psychology reflects a growing feeling of disquiet about the sort of research that sets out to establish empirical links between two or more "variables" of social life. Rarely, if ever, do these "variables" turn out to be free of cultural bias and normative assumptions. So, how are we to get round this impasse by anchoring our hypotheses and investigations in something more tangible and universal? One distinction that we can say with confidence is recognised in all societies and in this sense is free of cultural bias, is the distinction between life and death—the physical survival or non-survival of the individual. Can individual survival be related to social forces in any way? I believe it can and that research concerned with the social conditions that distinguish those who are alive and well from those who become ill and die, while not always free of the criticisms of empirical studies that try to interrelate purely social "variables," is generally more soundly based that such studies.

In this chapter I discuss recent developments in this research from the perspective of the model of social behaviour developed in the previous chapter. In rough summary, my conclusion is that there is an essential link between health and socialness. People stay healthy by being social; by engaging in justified action. Justifications and the rhetoric that carries them are health-protecting through being, simultaneously, public and private. They are the umbilical cord between the individual and the collective. A person is at risk if he or she becomes isolated from the community. But the distance separating the psychosomatically at-risk individual from the community or a section of it is not a physical distance but a symbolic or semiotic one. His or her isolation consists in the exile from any shared system of justification.

I want to suggest, in line with current thinking in social psychology, that vulnerability to illness provides a working index of when the relation between the individual and the collective goes bad. By the same token (it is the opposite side of the same coin), healthy, adaptive functioning is a measure of when this relation is good. Before we can explore this idea further we must look in some detail at the link that is claimed between social life and health. Can we be sure this is genuine?

Research on Stress and Illness

Enormous practical difficulties have been experienced by those wanting to present the stress–illness connection in the form that seems most acceptable to the medical and scientific professions: data from experiments. In animal research it is possible to prove the link conclusively by giving electric shocks, or by making living conditions crowded or cramped and watching for a increase in the rate of death or disease in an artificially controlled setting. With humans, or course, it is not. Even in a society in which human beings were expendable and available for this kind of experimentation, it would be difficult to know where to begin; the stresses of the laboratory are not the stresses of everyday life. Administering regimens of electric shock and noting the consequences in an arbitrary way would add little to our knowledge of naturally arising life crises.

The researcher in this field has to make do with methods and procedures that are inherently ambiguous. Ideal controlled experimentation in which the findings of one study lead on systematically to the design of the next—even if one grants that this is an adequate method for studying people in any circumstance, which, from the arguments in the first part of this book, it is clear I do not—is simply not possible in relation to the stress–illness hypothesis. The task is much more complex. It involves sifting through a jungle of epidemiological and sociological surveys, anthropological descriptions, psychological experiments, and clinical case studies, and distilling from these some kind of overall account. While there are many thousands of studies of people in each of these categories, probably not one single piece of research on its own offers conclusive proof of a causal link between stress and illness. Sklar and Anisman (1981), in a very thorough review of research concerned with the effects of stress on cancer, conclude that human studies do support an association between tumour growth and psychological state, but that is is not possible to infer a causal relation. The majority of studies are descriptive and correlational, and of those that involve the prediction of illness from psychological assessments, most are retrospective; they take as their subjects people who are already ill, and work back, trying to uncover precipitating events in their recent lives.

Prospective studies are more genuinely predictive; a population is followed over an extended period of time and differential illness or death rates are forecast from psychological scales. The past few years have seen the completion of a useful number of these. But even their results are not free from ambiguity. Quite apart from the issue of the objectivity of the psychological measures themselves, it is possible to attribute the differences recorded to concurrent changes in patterns of physical exercise, sleeping, diet, drinking, or smoking. Some technical grounds for dismissing individual findings can always, at a stretch, be found.

Some of the most challenging facts come from descriptive and epidemiological studies: comparative surveys of the distribution of diseases in different cultures and social settings. In the past, epidemiological studies have led to the discovery of a link between fatty foods and heart disease and between smoking and both lung cancer and heart disease. This style of study is beginning to play an increasingly important part in investigations of the social conditions of illness. Marmot (1983) provides an illustration of how epidemiological data can narrow the choice between hypotheses. Coronary heart disease is less common in Japan than in the United States. The Japanese culture is characterised by a high degree of social support. To investigate the possibility of a causal link between social support and freedom from heart disease, rates among Japanese–Americans were studied, and much lower rates were recorded among men who stayed with the Japanese ethnic group than among those who became Americanized. This difference could not be explained by differences in smoking, plasma cholesterol, blood pressure, relative weight, blood sugar, or diet—all traditional risk factors for coronary heart disease. In this way, by a process of elimination, the psychological hypothesis gets some tentative support.

Reductionism

There is still some residual prejudice among natural scientists against the idea that psychosocial stress can result in illness and death. This is often found in association with the reductionist belief that only one form of model—that dealing with neurochemical interactions—is admissible in a discussion of the individual as a treatable entity. This is rather like saying that only one style of model—that dealing with the electronic hardware—is admissible in the diagnosis of a computer fault. In real life, at least in the initial stages, diagnosis of a fault on a complex machine rarely concerns itself directly with circuitry and circuit diagrams. Fault-finding first proceeds in the very different language of operating systems, programmes, and hierarchies of operations. This is the language of software. It is quite consistent with, though different from, hardware talk—talk about circuitry and components—but it is nonetheless an equally valid way of representing what goes on. Alternative styles of models are used in other branches of science, for example, chemical, structural, and mathematical models of chemical compounds, and there is no reason to place special a priori restrictions on ways of talking about people, even when the point of the discussion is whether or not they get ill (see Boden, 1981). The conditions of illness can be modelled as a physical malfunction but they can also be modelled, as I try to show in this chapter, in terms of a loss of social meaning.

If no single study of stress and illness with humans among the huge number that have been done can be called definitive, the consensus that emerges from looking at them en masse is impressive. In my previous book, *Social Causes of Illness,* (1979b), I reviewed some of this research and concluded that by far the most striking general observation is that the stresses that undermine health in the twentieth-century are predominantly stresses of social origin. More recent studies and reviews reinforce this opinion.

Bereavement and Loss

One of the most reliably reported findings of research is that unusually high rates of illness and death follow bereavement. Two major review articles firmly support this conclusion (Rowland, 1977; Stroebe W., Strobe M. S., Gergen K. J., and Gergen M., 1982). Parkes, Benjamin, and Fitzgerald (1969) were responsible for some major pioneer research in this field. They studied 4500 widowers and discovered a significant rise in cardiovascular death during the period following the wife's death. In another well-known study, Engel (1971) found that out of 177 cases of sudden death, nearly half of the individuals had experienced a personal loss prior to their death.

There are, of course, other reasons besides psychological ones why recently bereaved people might be at risk of becoming ill. They may not be eating or sleeping properly, they may not be getting enough exercise, they may for years have been sharing unhealthy living conditions with their spouse. Stroebe et al. (1982), in a carefully reasoned discussion of the effects of bereavement on mortality, discuss at length these and other alternative (nonpsychological) explanations, and while conceding that these cannot always be ruled out, tentatively conclude that none of them explains all the facts as well as the idea of a sustained and eventually pathological neuroendocrine reaction provoked by the psychological impact of the loss. Moreover, this effect cannot be dismissed as marginal or insignificant. Stroebe et al. quote figures from a survey of deaths from all causes in England and Wales for the year 1974. These show that widowed males in the 20–24 age bracket are 17 times more likely to die than their married counterparts. The ratio for widowed females of the same age is 10 to 1. This excess rate "slowly declines until the later years when the ratio becomes less than 2 to 1" (p. 528).

The same pattern is repeated in studies approaching the problem the other way round—focusing in the first instance on death and illness rather than on a selected stressful event. Cottington, Matthews, Talbott, and Kuller (1980), studying sudden cardiac death in women, found that compared with matched healthy controls those who had died were six times as likely to have had someone close to them die in the previous 6 months. The review by Stroebe et al. is particularly interesting because longitudinal studies of bereavement and mortality are discussed alongside cross-sectional epidemiological data. The longitudinal studies generally agree that the period of increased risk of death is concentrated in the first 6 months of bereavement. Heart disease is the main cause of death and is also the condition that accounts for most of the excess in death rate. But other forms of death in which psychological state is more directly implicated, including suicide, death from homicide, and (in men) liver cirrhosis, are also more prominent among the recently bereaved. Stroebe et al. (p. 537) conclude:

> Despite the lack of reliable or detailed research on causes of death among the widowed, taken together the analyses reported above seem to point towards an interpretation of the bereavement—mortality relationship which emphasises the role of psychological factors. The widowed in general, but particularly the recently widowed, appear to be vulnerable to those specific types of mortality which are affected by psychological variables.
>
> Support comes not only from the pattern of highly excessive death rates from heart diseases in the recently bereaved, but also from such diseases as liver cirrhosis, cancer, and from suicide, in which (either directly or indirectly) psychological factors can affect the etiology to a far greater extent than is possible, for example, in the case of leukemia and aleukemia. Reprinted by permission from W. Stroebe, M. S. Stroebe, K. J. Gergen, and M. Gergen, "The effects of bereavement on mortality: a social psychological analysis." In J. R. Eiser (Ed.) *Social Psychology and Behavioral Medicine.* © 1982, John Wiley & Sons, Ltd.

Studies of illness in relation to other forms of loss, such as divorce, job loss, "object loss," and "role loss" are generally considered less conclusive than studies of bereavement, although the majority do in fact support the loss–disease hypothesis (Ackerman, Manaker, and Cohen, 1981, Totman, 1979b). Clearly, the circumstances of a divorce, or of losing one's job are all important in determining the event's psychological impact. Neither divorce nor job loss, nor any of the other forms of loss that authors have chosen to research, can be expected to be as universally distressing as bereavement. Correspondingly, the findings of what is mainly statistical research might be expected to show better agreement in respect of bereavement.

Their lack of concern with the meaning of stressful life events to individuals provides an explanation of why checklist measures such as the Holmes–Rahe Schedule of Recent Experience (Rahe, 1972) have their greatest success in predicting small statistical variations in large populations. There is a growing feeling among those involved in human stress research that progress can only be made in the quest for a theory of stress through the development of more sensitive measures of life events based on some kind of personal biography and taking into account the context in which events occur (e.g., Brown, 1974; Brown and Harris, in press; Byrne and Whyte, 1980; McQueen and Siegrist, 1982; Stahl, Grim, Donald, and Neikirk, 1975; Stroebe et al., 1982; Young, 1980). The foresaking of statistical assessments of people using standard tests in favour of more descriptive profiles can perhaps be seen as part of a more general movement in social psychology.

For a time in the 1950s and the 1960s, it was fashionable among psychiatrists and some physicians to publish detailed clinical case histories of the course of symptoms in their patients. Notwithstanding their unpopularity among the behaviourist and cognitivist schools, which dominated psychology at this time, these case histories of sick people often contained considerable biographical and contextual detail and were accompanied by a shrewd commentary. Many also traced the course of symptoms over time in relation to changing circumstances in the patient's life.

One particularly interesting theme recurs in the psychosomatic journals. Several clinicians describe a cyclical pattern in which physical symptoms of an illness initially appear in the wake of a separation, disappear on re-establishment of the lost person or the arrival of a substitute, and reappear again on a second separation or its imminent threat (Chambers and Reiser, 1953; Flarscheim, 1958; Green and Miller, 1958; McClary, Meyer, and Weitzman, 1955; Miller, Lief, and Mittelman, 1955; Philippopolous, Wittkaver, and Cousineau, 1958). In some cases, the doctor comes to act as a substitute for the lost person. There are accounts of symptoms improving during regular contact between doctor and patient, worsening when the patient is discharged, and improving again on renewed contact, the oscillation in health being apparently independent of the effects of medication (Adler and Hammett, 1973; Chambers and Reiser, 1953; Engel, 1955). Health, in these cases, appears directly geared to a specific social contact.

Perhaps the best way to consider these case histories is in conjunction with the other descriptive research that has been done. The review articles by Rowland (1977) and Stroebe et al. (1982) make it clear that the risk of illness and death is statistically raised among the recently bereaved. But most people who suffer a bereavement do not get ill and die, so we cannot conclude that it is bereavement per se that is responsible. If we are to hold onto any form of the loss–disease hypothesis, we must ask what it is that the sick and the non-survivors lose following a bereavement that the fit survivors do not. Schmale and Iker (1966) and Engel (1978) concur with many other authors in identifying a sense of hopelessness as characteristic of those most at risk. Others have commented variously on a "loss of security", a "difficulty in adjusting to the event", and an "erosion of self-esteem." In a detailed following of the course of symptoms in three pulmonary tuberculosis patients, Flarscheim (1958) writes that the "loss of a loved object per se was not necessarily associated with the onset of respiratory symptoms" (p. 481). He describes the key factor in terms of the loss of a significant relationship that had enabled them to sustain conformity of behaviour and self-esteem. Much later, Stroebe et al. (1982), discussing possible interpretations of the loss–illness effect, say more or less the same thing, albeit in the very different language of behavioural-cognitive psychology: "A person who has just lost his or her partner will find over and over again that response sequences cannot be completed because completion would require some action or reaction from the lost partner" (p. 545).

The idea of incapacitated action as a result of circumstances that appear uncontrollable is also expressed in Seligman's much-discussed learned helplessness model of depression, at least in its original form (Seligman, 1975). Inability to initiate actions is one of the core symptoms in the diagnosis of clinical depression. That we might expect to find the same psychological antecedents in depression as in physical illness is perhaps not surprising in view of the two now-acknowledged facts: (1) depression itself is correlated with increased illness risk (Shekelle, et al., 1981; Wolcott, Wellisch, Robertson, and Arthur, 1981) and (2) those circumstances most often cited as the onset conditions for depression are also those most often associated with the onset of illness. Bereavement itself is a prime example (Maddison and Viola, 1968; Maddison and Walker, 1967; Parkes and Brown, 1972).

Personality and Vulnerability

The main problem with research on personality is that psychologists are anything but agreed on how individual characteristics should be measured, and indeed on the nature of personality and emotion and how they should be conceived in theory. Sometimes the person is assessed psychoanalytically, sometimes according to self and ego theories, sometimes in terms of the scales of classic trait theory, but most often by an ad hoc measure devised specially for one individual piece of research. If there is no quorum for how stressful life events should be conceived and measured, the situation is even worse in the study of personality. The first systematic attempt to correlate particular personality traits with particular symptom-complexes was a 14-year programme of research, begun in 1951 by Alexander and his associates, working within the framework of psychoanalytic theory (Alexander, French, and Pollack, 1968). Symptoms were said to be the symbolic expressions of unresolved unconscious conflicts and dependency needs. Some success was claimed for *specificity theory,* as it was known, but the findings of Alexander and his colleagues were not generally considered strong enough to sustain interest in this approach. A jungle of experimental, clinical, and anecdotal descriptions of the personalities of patients with specific complaints has grown up since.

Cancer and the Blocking of Emotion

In the 1960s, a series of controversial studies were published by Kissen and his associates (Kissen, 1966) allegedly showing that the lung cancer patient is characterised by a poor and restricted outlet of emotions. The idea was taken up and extended by the Bahnsons, who produced data supporting their theory that the extreme repression and denial of the cancer patient acts to block the outward expression of negative emotions. It was suggested that these impulses find expression somatically, through "internal discharge mechanisms" (Bahnson and Bahnson, 1969). The idea that the failure to act out one's emotions, especially anger, may be maladaptive and associated with a greater-than-normal risk of cancer has subsequently been supported in several studies (Abse, et al., 1974; Greeer and Morris, 1975; Morris, Greer, Pettingale, and Watson, 1981; see also the review, *Stress and Cancer,* by Sklar and Anisman, 1981). The same finding has been reported in connection with childhood asthma (Straker and Tamerin, 1974) and hypertension (Holroyd and Gorkin, 1983; Scotch and Geiger, 1963; see also the discussion on "Ventilation of feelings" by Silver and Wortman, 1980).

The problem of disentangling the emotional impact of a worrying diagnosis from the measure of personality itself leads to some difficulty in interpreting these findings, especially when the diagnosis is itself emotive, as is the case with cancer. In those studies where the assessment of personality was made shortly after a diagnosis of cancer, it could reasonably be argued (as it was) that defensiveness and repression are natural reactions to the alarming news. The same can be said of the many studies that have reported "negative emotions" in conjunction with raised risk of illness; emotions such as resentment, frustration, depression, anxiety, and helplessness (e.g., Luborsky, Docherty, and Penick, 1973).

However, the association of vulnerability with blocked expression of emotion holds up in prospective studies as well; malignancies have with some success been predicted from psychological data in suspected cases before the clinical diagnosis has been made. In Greer and Morris' study (1975) diagnoses of breast cancer were successfully predicted on the basis of a characteristic abnormal release of anger—mainly extreme suppression. Pre-biopsy identification of breat cancer cases was also made by Wirsching, Stierlin, Hoffman, Weber, and Wirsching, (1982) from a composite psychological measure which included among its sub-scales "emotional suppression with sudden outbursts." Blumberg, West, and Ellis, (1954) were able to predict 2-year survival of cancer patients on the basis of MMPI personality scores. Those who died over this time had low neurotic-outlet scores and very low acting out scores. Furthermore, Grossarth-Maticek, Siegrist, and Vetter (1982), in a 10-year follow-up study of the inhabitants of a small town in Yugoslavia, reported that being a "passive receiver of repression," where "repression" means the restrictive interference of others, predicted incidence of cancer of all kinds. Emotional blocking as characteristic of cancer patients is a relationship that is much repeated in the research literature. How is it to be explained in terms of action and justification?

Expressions of emotion are performances. When a person gets angry he or she is usually angered *by* something and the angry outburst is a concentrated stand *against* the provoking agent. In this sense, the psychological effect of getting angry is very like that of acting in that it commits the individual to a particular moral position: a position identified by the criticism and implicit rejection of an incompatible position (or its spokesperson) which is the object of the anger. Like acting, being angry can also be construed as psychologically forming, or entropy reducing, because it helps construct the person's justificatory scheme and so define for him or her a place in the community. Insofar as restrictions placed on a person's actions by others and the suppression of emotional expression by the self both entail a thwarting of the processes of action and justification, they might be expected to carry the same consequences for social identity and health as occasions of action paralysis arising from stressful events such as bereavement and loss.

The Type-A Person and Vulnerability to Heart Disease

The link between cancer and the blocking of emotion is one of two findings in research on personality that are now generally considered to be well established. The other concerns the risk of heart disease and the Type-A personality. Type-A individuals, contrasted with Type-B's, are characterised by strong achievement motivation, addiction to work, a pervading sense of deadlines and working against the clock, and impatience and hostility when interrupted (Rosenman and Friedman, 1974).

Jenkins, in a classic two-part review of the evidence accumulated prior to 1976 on psychosocial factors and proneness to heart disease, concludes that the strongest evidence for a connection comes, in fact, from studies using the Type-A profile to predict illness. More recent discussions of the Type-A pattern cast it as a style of behaving that is not necessarily maladaptive on its own, but which tends to be so in the wake of challenging environmental situations. The interactive model, which concentrates neither on stressful life events nor on personality in isolation but on their mutual interplay in a person's life; that is, on the person's ability to *cope* with stresses, has won general acceptance in modern discussions of the conditions of illness. Glass (1977), for example, has interpreted the Type-A pattern in the language of Seligman's model of learned helplessness as a developmentally acquired style of coping with the world; essentially an exaggerated need to control the environment. Situations are stressful when they are perceived as uncontrollable and therefore pose the threat of failure. Initially, Type-A's react to such situations by vigorously stepping up their efforts. But they give up more quickly than the more plodding Type-B's, and become subject to a state of helplessness allegedly similar to that observed by Seligman in dogs pretrained in the laboratory on a helplessness schedule involving noncontingency between stimulus and response. *Learned helplessness,* as Seligman called this condition, is theoretically associated with a species of clinical depression (Abramson et al., 1978; Garber and Seligman, 1980; Seligman, 1975) and, according to Glass, underlies the Type-A pattern and proneness to heart disease. A review of research on the Type-A pattern and heart disease is provided by Dembroski and MacDougall (1982). Most of the evidence on the structure of the Type-A profile has been obtained in precisely the kind of laboratory experiment that has come under attack for its bastardisation of the social situations and naturally arising life events it is presumed to emulate. The assumption that real-life problems can be modelled in laboratory tasks like solving anagrams, turning off white noise, and throwing hoops onto pegs, in the presence of an "experimenter," is certainly not to be accepted uncritically. However, there is also a body of clinical and field work linking Type-A behaviour with proneness to heart disease. The task now confronted is to further define the Type-A pattern and to explore more fully theoretical possibilities for its association with vulnerability.

The study of Type-A, or *coronary-prone behaviour,* as it is often now called, has become a fairly fashionable pursuit, both in the eyes of researchers and in those of journal editors. Such a situation not infrequently engenders a certain narrowness of focus in the spectrum of research possibilities. I conclude this section with two suggestions: (1) that the Type-A pattern has not been fully explicated and, in fact, represents just one instance of a more general (maladaptive) coping strategy and (2) that this more general style is not only associated with vulnerability to heart disease but with vulnerability to other diseases as well. Neither of these possibilities denies the specific association that has been established between Type-A and heart disease. The point I want to make is that to concentrate too shortsightedly on this relation may be to miss a more general relation.

Other Characteristics of the Coronary-Prone Person

Proneness to heart disease has been associated in research with certain other characteristics besides Type-A behaviour, but because these studies do not quite fit into the Type-A/heart disease slot there has been a tendency for them to be neglected in discussions and reviews. Most notably, the coronary-prone person tends to feel dissatisfied with his or her achievements (Bruhn, Paredes, Adsett, and Wolf, 1974; Caffrey, 1967; Howard, Cunningham, and Rechnitzer, 1977; Romo, Siltanen, Theorell, and Rahe, 1974; Siltanen, et al. 1975). Satisfaction with one's lot in life, especially with one's job, is traditionally linked with health in the psychosomatic literature (e.g., Hinkle, 1974; Burchfield et al., 1981). The Type-A profile is primarily that of a workoholic, but at least two authors have remarked on a tendency for heart patients also to be overcommitted to their social and leisure pursuits (Russek, 1958; Thiel, Parker, and Bruce, 1973). Minc (1965) describes a tendency for heart patients to be overly concerned with propriety and doing the socially correct thing. Other characteristics that have been said to differentiate heart patients from healthy controls include a very strong sense of duty (Mertens and Segers, 1971), rigidity and scrupulousness (Liesse, van Imschoot, Mertens, and Lauwers, 1974), obsessional tendencies, and, as seems to be the case with cancer victims, a tendency to overcontrol emotions and self-expression (Bonami and Rimé, 1972; Dongier, 1974; Rimé and Bonami, 1973; Thomas and Greenstreet, 1973). Therefore, the possibility needs to be examined that the Type-A pattern is just one example of a more general disposition that includes but extends beyond work attitudes, and concerns the excessive and rigid nature of the personal goals the individual sets.

Overperformance and Non-coronary Illness

Rigid and obsessional characteristics, some of which come close to Type-A traits, have also been ascribed to groups of non-coronary patients. Again, because these studies do not fit into the Type-A/coronary-prone behaviour series they have not received as much publicity as those that do. References to the rigidity and conventionalism of cancer sufferers and to "a tendency to check and recheck work to assure oneself of accuracy" appear in several studies (Bahnson, 1969; Booth, 1965; Le Shan, 1966). Moos (1964), reviewing findings concerned with rheumatoid arthritis, found general agreement that arthritic patients tend to be self-sacrificing, perfectionist, and overly conscientious. Solomon (1982) sums up his own and other people's experience of patients prone to autoimmune diseases in the following way: "People who are prone to such diseases are described generally as quiet, introverted, reliable, conscientious, restricted in the expression of emotion (particularly anger), conforming, self-sacrificing, tending to allow themselves to be imposed upon, sensitive to criticism, distant, overactive and busy, pseudo-independent to deny dependency, stubborn, rigid and controlling" (p. 4).

His extensive studies of ulcerative colitis patients have led Engel (1955) to characterise this group as indecisive and as holding obsessively rigid standards of orderliness, neatness, conscientiousness, punctuality, and morality in general. Hinkle (1974) echoes the comments of many authors when he concludes from his research on the general health of telephone operators that those most prone to illness see their jobs as less satisfying than healthy controls.

These findings certainly caution against too blinkered a reading of the Type-A literature, and too restricted a focus in research. There seems little doubt that the Type-A style and the hyperactivity that it involves does correlate specifically with raised risk of heart disease. Perhaps this has something to do with the erratic physical demands this kind of behaviour places on the heart. But there may also be a more general factor, of which Type-A is a subsidiary, which correlates with raised risk for illness in general.

Type-A and the Failure of Justification

How can we account for these findings and the possibility of a more general, theoretically unexplored, individual vulnerability factor on the model of social behaviour developed in the previous chapter? The nature of this more general factor seems to have to do with the level of self-set standards and how much effort must go into actions and projects for a person to feel pleased with his or her performance. In the most extreme cases, it is almost as if no conceivable standard of performance will bring satisfaction. Type-B individuals and people relatively free of these other forms of obsessive perfectionism are content with a more modest amount of effort and concern, and have perhaps a more realistic image of their own limitations than Type-A's. This seems to be the case both in their work and in their leisure activities. Reports that the Type-A person seldom feels satisfied with his or her achievements provide an important clue in the explanation of these phenomena.

The model of action that I have presented has at its centre the idea that justification is the individual's passport to membership of the social world. To justify an action or a series of actions is to participate in a particular social, or moral, order by adopting the line of talk that is peculiar to that order. Such exclusive talk, I have tried to argue, is what constitutes a social order and what distinguishes it from other incommensurable orders. So far as individual consciousness is concerned, justification is a way of injecting negative entropy into the system. Now, an individual for whom, perhaps as a result of early experience, the license to justify rests only in a superhuman level of effort and achievement, neatness, punctuality, self-sacrifice, or whatever, (and sometimes not even in this) is clearly handicapped as a candidate for social identity. The reason for the disadvantage is that such a person's tie with the collective—his or her socialness—is that much more expensive in terms of effort and achievement than for a more easy-going person. To qualify as a social being the Type-A and the other varieties of overperformers have to feed in an exceptionally large amount of grist to the justificatory mill. The risk of such a person remaining alienated and detached from the community—not physically but *symbolically,* or psychologically—is therefore correspondingly higher.

In that our sense of personhood itself is intimately tied in with the language and social practices of a culture (see Harré, 1983), one might expect the state of symbolic isolation that I associate with increased vulnerability to go hand in hand with a sense of failure, hopelessness, self-abasement, and lack of self-esteem. Many times these and similar self-deprecatory attitudes have been mentioned as typical of Type-A's and of studied populations of patients with non-coronary diseases (Abse et al., 1974; Bonfils and de M'uzan, 1974; Burchfield et al., 1981; Flarscheim, 1958; Hagburg and Malmquist, 1974; Jacobs, Silken, Norman, and Anderson, 1970; Liesse et al., 1974; Luborsky et al., 1973; Parens, McConville, and Kaplan, 1966; Romo, Siltanen, Theorell, and Rahe, 1974; Siltanen et al., 1975; Solomon, 1981; Van Dijl, 1975). A sense of personal worthlessness is so much a part of depression and grief that the many studies linking these states to increased risk of illness and death can be included in the corpus of evidence supporting this general relation.

Social Support

The presence of social support has been consistently linked through research to low relative risk of many forms of physical and psychiatric illness, and to favourable prognosis. The absence of social support, on the other hand, can itself constitute a risk factor for poor health. In addition, supportive systems appear to cushion the individual against the potentially harmful physiological consequences of stress in a person's life. The presence of support may also reduce the likelihood of a crisis occurring.

These statements summarise the conclusions from what is now a sizeable literature on the role of social support. Useful general reviews of the concept and of the effects of support on health are provided by Caplan (1981), Cobb (1976), Hammer (1983), Leavy (1983), and McQueen and Celentano (1982). Examples of research showing an effect on health of the presence or absence of social support per se are provided by Pilisuk and Froland (1978) and Funch and Marshall (1983). In Pilisuk and Froland's study, absence or loss of support was shown to have a detrimental effect on general health status. Funch and Marshall traced 208 women with diagnosed breast cancer over a 20-year period and found that social support was predictive of survival. Demonstrations of the role of support in protecting the individual against work stress are given in studies by LaRocco, House, and French, (1980) and Winnubst, Marcelissen, and Kleber, (1982). Brown and Harris (1978), in their studies of depressed London women, found that having at least one close friend or confidant reduced risk of depression by a factor of four. Evidence that the presence of support may itself reduce the likelihood of a crisis occurring is presented in a study by Ensel, Simeone, and Kuo, (1979).

Authors of studies of social support have different ideas about the critical ingredients of support, and their different conceptions are reflected in the different ways in which level of support has been assessed. The literature contains dozens of definitions. Those in the caring professions not unnaturally emphasise the importance of instrumental aid. The more biologically inclined researchers emphasise the practical advantage of attachments and the survival value of pooled resources (Bowlby, 1979; Henderson and Byrne, 1977; Wilson, 1975). Researchers with a psychological or psychoanalytic training often place emphasis on the provision of emotional support. In times of stress, others can help strengthen the individual's defenses by giving supportive advice and moral encouragement (see Caplan, 1981). Social support, in this sense, is seen as an aid to the coping resources of the individual.

The more sociologically inclined authors (e.g., Cobb, 1976; Lin et al., 1979; Moss, 1973) have concentrated more on the information-providing nature of the supportive individual or community. The social network contains prescriptions for normal and morally proper behaviour in the structure of roles and rules involving reciprocal obligations. Insofar as the person has good access to this information and to confidants who help him or her decide between difficult options in times of conflicting information, he or she is protected from uncertainty and the inability to act. Whereas "emotional support" has to do with warranting the individual's actions and decisions, support as the provision of information is concerned with the individual's ability to construe the social world.

In fact, these alternative conceptualisations are a good deal more intertwined and overlapping than I make them seem. Most modern discussions of social support acknowledge its multi-faceted nature and treat the various alternative approaches as complementary (see the review by House, 1981). Antonovsky's theory of health and coping (1979), based on the idea of a "sense of coherence" goes some way toward integrating them into a single concept. The sense of coherence is theoretically linked with health and is defined as: "a gobal orientation that expresses the extent to which one has a pervasive, enduring though dynamic feeling of confidence that one's internal and external environments are predictable and that there is a high probability that things will work out as well as can reasonably be expected" (1979, p. 123).

The different emphases have expressed themselves in different research programmes and it is perhaps surprising, in view of the lack of a common theoretical base, that studies show such consistently good agreement. But the literature is full of confirmations of the health-protecting consequences of social support in relation to a very large number of illnesses including psychiatric disturbance, hypertension, infections, heart disease, and cancer. The recurring conclusion is that people well supported have a better chance of staying healthy and surviving than those poorly supported. It is worth adding that the belief that the health of the individual depends upon a harmonious relation between him or her and the community is commonplace among primitive societies and is by tradition an integral part of their healing practices (Sterling and Eyer, 1981).

A caution must be added at this stage concerning the provisional status of the concepts of stress, social support, life events, and coping. It has been said many times that one person's stress is another's pleasure. Similarly, what counts as social support for one individual may represent an intolerable level of meddling interference to another. For discussions to proceed at all it seems we must make use of these concepts, however provisional their definitions. But living with this ambiguity carries with it an inherent danger. The very fact that these terms are used so extensively in academic discussions can lead one to take it for granted that they denote objective and universal characteristics. As Young (1980) has warned, the danger lies in the generalisation from local (i.e., Western academic) intuitions about, for example, what it is to be stressed and supported. Behind the desire to objectify these notions lurks the assumption that waiting to be discovered in research is a standard set of life crises, contexts, and reactions that reliably produce maladaptive consequences independently of culture and history. Once again, in reviewing psychological research and uncovering the assumptions on which it is based we are brought back to a problem that is raised many times in this book. How is it possible to represent someone else's world in terms that are alien to that world and the property of a very different one without corrupting it by confounding its categories with our own? Psychologists, like everyone else, are social creatures, and neither they nor the world in which they move can escape the considerations that they apply to the community at large. The arguments of this book are built on the assumptions that the identity and constitution of a group inhere in its exclusive talk and that human social phenomena are to be discovered in this talk. If this is correct, then any attempt to define stress and social support according to what we as self-styled scientists agree between ourselves is stressful and supportive is not likely to be impartial or "objective" at all but quite value laden and idealistic (see Marmot, 1983). Is it not a precondition of impartiality that social investigators include themselves and their activities in the social world that is the object of their investigations?

An example helps to illustrate this point. The mechanism of social support is widely assumed, by those who study it, to involve the physical presence of at least one other person. Physical isolation is taken as virtually synonymous with lack of support. But the assumption that it is not good for people to be alone, handed down to us from the traditions of structural fuctionalism and symbolic interactionism - is not borne out in an investigation by Hughes and Gove (1981). These authors found no evidence that unmarried people living by themselves are in any worse mental health than unmarried people living with others. Living alone in and of itself does not necessarily appear to be problematic. Hughes and Gove's conclusion is consistent with the position argued in the previous chapter—that for behaviour to be social, it does not have to take place in interaction with, or even in the presence of, other people. Recall the example of the recluse gardener or the composer. Insofar as either of these follows culturally derived rules in the work they do (this condition, in effect, being contained in the concept of work), he or she can be said to be engaging in fully fledged social behaviour and participating richly in the supportive structures that make up the social order.

Studies of social support may show good agreement, but in the absence of any general, large-scale theory of the individual as a social entity, our definitions are bound to remain ad hoc and as such narrowly dependent on our own culture and experience.

Social Structure and Supportive Networks

Overlapping and complementing psychological studies of stress and coping is a voluminous demographic literature from the disciplines of anthropology, epidemiology, and sociology. This deals principally with comparative illness and death rates in different populations. Findings are correlational in nature—descriptive rather than empirical—and their interpretation is therefore always a controversial matter. Nevertheless, a wide reading of this research leaves one with considerably more than a hint of what kind of society or community promotes the good health and longevity of its members. The health of the individual appears almost universally to be better if he or she lives in a relatively stable, cohesive, traditional, non-industrialised society than if he or she lives in a social environment where there is constant pressure for change and "development" and in which the structure of roles and rules is uncertain. The debate continues over whether this relation can be put down to social forces per se or whether it is due to physical factors that go hand in hand with the different life-styles of the communities being compared; differences in body weight, eating habits, salt consumption, exercise, drinking, and smoking are a few much-discussed examples.

It has to be admitted that it is extremely difficult in descriptive research of this kind to rule out alternative (non-psychological) explanations. Some have actually been confirmed. Economic modernisation is indeed correlated with increase in body weight and salt and alcohol consumption—all factors that are statistically related to hypertension and risk of heart disease (McQueen and Celentano, 1982; Waldron et al., 1982). But apart from proven physical associations, the hypothesis that the psychological stress of cultural disruption constitutes an additional and independent risk factor for various illnesses is well supported. The breaking up of cooperative social relations and the undermining of traditionally held beliefs and customs by themselves appear to exert a highly destructive influence. The classic summing-up remarks of Henry and Cassel in 1969, arrived at from a systematic review of 18 world-wide studies of blood pressure levels in different cultural groups, still hold true and have been reinforced by the research that has been done since. Henry and Cassel concluded that in general, blood pressure levels were healthier where the culture is stable, traditional forms are honored, and the group members are adapted to them by early experience (see also Waldron et al., 1982). Brenner and his colleagues (Brenner, 1979; Brenner and Mooney, 1982) have produced evidence that economic change itself, whether this means growth or recession, has an important influence on the health status of occupational groups and their families. Multiple and to some extent counterbalancing influences can be identified, but in the long run the net effects of economic growth are beneficial and those of recession are detrimental to health and survival (see also the review by Colledge, 1982).

Henry and Cassel's remarks are consistent with those of Leaf (1973) who made a study of remotely situated, isolated rural communities in which it appears the members enjoy unusual longevity and comparative freedom from illness. Leaf (1973) writes:

> It is characteristic of each of the areas I visited that the old people continue to be contributing, productive members of their society. The economy in all three areas is agrarian, there is no fixed retirement age and the elderly make themselves useful doing many necessary tasks around the farm or the home. . . People who no longer have a necessary role to play in the social and economic life of their society generally deteriorate rapidly. (p. 50)

Sociological comparisons of different groups within a community of same-language speakers have produced very similar findings and conclusions. For example, Berkman and Syme (1979), in a 9-year follow-up study of all the residents of Alameda County, California, showed that those who lacked social and community ties were more susceptible to illness and premature death than those with extensive social contacts. There was evidence that poor health reduced socialising but also evidence for a more powerful effect in the other direction. With initial health status taken into account, people with few social contacts still were exposed to a higher risk of death than those with many.

In a detailed discussion of possible explanations of the correlation between supportive social networks and health, Hammer sums up the current consensus:

> Such an association does not appear to be adequately accounted for by a deleterious effect of illness on social contact, nor by the role of social networks in mediating health-related practices or in buffering the effects of stress. Thus the proposition is tentatively warranted that the social network is more directly and causally involved in health outcomes—perhaps through the impact of social feedback as mediated by the network. Reprinted with permission from M. Hammer, "'Core' and 'extended' networks in relation to health and illness." *Social Science and Medicine, 17, p. 405. © 1983, Pergamon Press.*

Religious communities are a good example of social networks constituted and sustained through special systems of talk. It is known that people holding religious beliefs and regular church-goers enjoy better health than non-believers and non-attenders (Caplan, 1981; Comstock and Partridge, 1972). Moreover, this relation seems valid even when some of the more obvious non-psychological explanations, such as differences in socioeconomic status and smoking and drinking habits are taken into account.

If sharp changes in the social environment are associated with a threat to health, one might expect moving to a new home sometimes to have deleterious effects, especially when the move is to a culturally dissimilar setting. Schulz (1978), summarising the extensive literature on relocation of the elderly and its effects on health and survival, concludes

> Elderly people who are forced to relocate for reasons such as urban renewal, debilitating physical decline, or decreased financial resources are often stressed by the loss of a familiar and supportive environment and by the demands of coping with a new set of stimuli in an unfamiliar setting. The predominant finding is that relocation has negative effects on the elderly. Many researchers have claimed that the psychological and physical well-being of the sick and elderly are adversely affected by abrupt or severe changes in their living environment. The adverse effects are typically assessed by measures of mortality, depression and activity level. (p. 120)

More severe changes (e.g., from home to institution) have worse effects than less severe changes (e.g., from institution to institution). Furthermore, whether or not the individual has a choice in the move seems to matter too. Having a choice results in improved health and increased longevity (Schulz and Brenner, 1977).

Studies of immigrant communities, on the surface, present a less cogent picture. Using the social stress hypothesis, one might expect immigrants to be more prone to ill health and premature death than non-immigrants. Generally this is so (Gallagher, 1980). But it is not always the case. It is important to keep in mind that a considerable number of these studies were done in America in the 1950s and 1960s. Marks, reviewing the research on immigration that had been completed prior to 1967 (Marks, 1967), points out that for convenience of sampling, most of the individuals studied were people coming to live in ghettos where many of the old customs were continued. There is a hint from some studies that the children of immigrants suffer more than immigrants themselves, presumably because they have to make the biggest adaptation; the switch from the locally upheld old traditions of their parents to those of contemporary young America (Marks, 1967). In Syme's (1967) terminology, they are the most culturally mobile. In Moss's (1973), they are the most alienated and consequently the most uncertain. In Antonovsky's (1979) terms, they lack a sense of coherence. In the language of social learning theory (Bandura, 1977), they face alternative and frequently conflicting social models. Consistent with the latter explanation is evidence that heart disease is especially prevalent among people whose parents belong to different religious denominations (Lehr, Messinger, and Rosenman, 1973), and evidence that rheumatoid arthritis is prevalent among women whose parents are not of the same social class (Cobb, Schull, Harbur, and Kasl, 1969). Mental health too is poor among socially mobile people (Kleiner and Parker, 1969). In line with Moss's theory is a study of Chinese–American immigrants by Kuo (1976). This showed those aspects of immigration most strongly associated with poor mental health to be social isolation and poor adjustment to the American way of life.

None of these models and studies are, however, really conflicting. Their differences, for the most part, are differences in emphasis and expression rather than reflections of deep-rooted theoretical alternatives. How might the separate approaches be incorporated? The ethnographic investigations of Gumperz and Cook-Gumperz and their colleagues lead them to a hypothesis that has much in common with the position taken in the present book. Jupp, Roberts, and Cook-Gumperz (1982) analyse the problems faced both by first- and second-generation immigrants in terms of an unfamiliarity with established systems of interactive discourse. Their analysis, however, goes far beyond the straightforward learning of a language. It is concerned with the signalling of personhood and social position that is done in the artifacts of speech. Misperceptions of inflexion and other aspects of speaking style lead to misreadings of intentions and, in due course, to socially destructive stereotypes like "they never seem to come to the point" and "they understand when they want to." Jupp et al. believe these difficulties can be rectified by training people to appreciate each other's speaking styles with the use of recorded conversations.

On a smaller scale, other researchers have looked at the structure of the family unit. Lack of cohesion and an absence of positive attitudes among family members appears to be related to enhanced risk of several illnesses, including cancer (e.g., Grossarth-Maticek et al., 1982; Thomas and Duszynski, 1974; Wolcott et al., 1981). Jacobs and Charles (1980) recorded a higher incidence of stressful life events over the year prior to the onset of symptoms among the parents of children with cancer than among parents of non-cancerous children. If family disturbances are a cause of illness, then there is a logical case, at least in respect of close-knit families, for practitioners to take the family as the unit of diagnosis and treatment rather than administering to each of its members separately. This possibility is discussed in detail by Schwenk and Hughes (1983).

Small work groups are a little like families. In an interesting but neglected study of small groups of shift-workers, Cassel (1964) recorded higher levels of serum cholesterol—a major risk factor for heart disease—in men working on shifts whose personnel varied than in men whose shifts always included the same group of people.

It would be possible to continue almost ad infinitum quoting studies and research reviews with broadly the same findings as those summarised here. There is now so much of this research that in spite of the difficulties in interpreting individual correlations, the conclusion is clearly warranted that a strong association exists between social structure and physical and mental well-being. The cohesion of a community, the familiarity and precision of the rules and roles within that community, and the relative temporal stability of the macro-structure are all factors that have a favourable effect on health and longevity (Henry, 1982; Waldron et al., 1981).

Animal Studies

Some parallel conclusions have been reached in laboratory studies in which colonies of animals are allowed for a while to develop naturally. Mice, the unfortunate principal victims of this research, are social creatures. Left alone to breed and interact freely, a community will evolve with a definite organisation involving hierarchies of individual dominance, cooperative nursing, and other reciprocal and mutually beneficial arrangements. Should this natural organisation be artificially disrupted by physical restraint, spatial restriction, or a technique known as "force breeding" (involving the regular removal of newborn pups), an acceleration in the death rate and physiological pathology will result. Physical deterioration of individuals follows close on the breakdown of the social order. The same phenomenon has been observed in other social species (Calhoun, 1973; Henry, 1982; Henry and Stephens, 1977).

Conclusion

There is an obvious correspondence between descriptions of the social environment in these artifically interfered with "animal cities" and descriptions of the social milieu of the human individual in times of enhanced risk of illness and death. In both cases, ambiguity in the social structure leaves the individual isolated—without direction—deprived of an opportunity to act and thereby to relate to the collective in a socially meaningful way. In the case of humans, we have seen that this psychological condition can result from the loss of social sources through death or separation, from unfamiliarity with rituals and social conventions, from absence of goals in life and work, from conflicting social models, and from suddenly imposed ferocious changes in the structure of the social system itself. The common denominator of these situations is the powerlessness of the individual to engage in socially sanctioned (i.e., goal-directed) pursuits and his or her consequent exile from any of the moral orders that make up a complex society. To reiterate Wittgenstein's phrase, this state of exile is a disqualification from the language games in which the rules and institutions of socialness (hence personhood) reside.

6

Physiology and the Biological Significance of Social Stress

The documented experiences of those researching in this field add up to a strong case for a link between mental state and life-threatening physical conditions. Some of the best data have come from descriptive studies. Assuming there is such a link, the question logically arises as to the bodily mechanisms involved. Do the physiological channels of communication exist through which activity in the higher regions of the neocortex—those regions responsible for our handling of meaningful information and our socialness—could be transformed into the good and bad states of organs and tissues that we associate with health and illness?

In the early years, psychosomatic research dealt almost exclusively with a small group of "nervous" conditions: headache, migraine, asthma, low back pain, sinus trouble, and certain skin disorders. Selye was responsible for much of the pioneering work on the biological alarm reactions that are mediated by the sympathetic nervous system—the *general adaptation syndrome,* as this came to be known. He produced evidence that visceral damage occurred from excessive and prolonged stimulation of the pituitary–adrenal-cortical axis by an environmental stressor (Selye, 1956). Ulcers were therefore added to the list, and the possibility was opened up that a wider range of conditions might also be affected by neuroendocrine responses to environmental stressors. Diseases in this category included hypertension and cardiovascular disease and, tentatively, some autoimmune conditions.

In recent years, research on possible physiological mediators of stress effects has mushroomed and there have been several important changes in the field. Fundamental among these is the distinction between the amygdaloid and hippocampal functional complexes in the limbic brain and their association with, respectively, the sympathetic adrenal–medullary axis and the pituitary–adrenal-cortical axis. As well as the old notion of stress as excessive activation of one or the other system, modern theory emphasises the interactive nature of the two and the necessity of balance and homeostasis in normal healthy neuroendocrine function. In their review, McQueen and Siegrist (1982) discuss evidence for the hypothesis that the simultaneous activation of these two axes is a causal factor in the aetiology of cardiovascular disorders and that hyperactivation of the pituitary–adrenal-cortical system can critically influence the immune system and increase vulnerability to infection and malignancies.

A large number of other possible channels for the communication of stress effects have been enumerated. For example, neuroendocrine imbalance through the actions of ACTH and hydrocortisone, growth hormone, and insulin is known to be a critical influence in the development of atherosclerosis in its early stages (McQueen and Siegrist, 1982).

Psychoneuroimmunology

Recent animal studies and human in vitro studies have undermined the traditional assumption that the immune system enjoys autonomous status. Immune competence has been shown to be affected by central nervous system lesions, hypothalamic stimulation, and changes in the levels of neuroendocrine secretions, especially those produced by experimental stressors. Both acute physical challenge and chronic social disruption can lead to a depletion of brain dopamine and norepinephrine levels and a corresponding enhancement in the growth of transplanted tumour in mice. Effects of neuroendocrine changes have been detected on antibody formation, lymphocyte response to mitogens, and graft versus host reactions (see Riley, 1981; and *Psychoneuroimmunology,* edited by Ader, 1981, for reviews of this research). Bereaved people are known to show immunosupression during the period of grieving (Bartrop, Lazarus, Luckhurst, and Kiloh, 1977). Ader and his colleagues (Ader and Cohen, 1981) have demonstrated that it is possible to classically condition humoral and cell-mediated immune responses in mice. Totman, Kiff, Reed, and Craig, (1980) successfully predicted titres of rhinovirus in 52 experimentally challenged human volunteers from measures of recent life change and personality. The psychological assessments in this study were made before the virus inoculation was administered, and virus titrations were carried out by independent staff members who were unaware of the subjects' psychological scores. These predictions were therefore genuinely prospective and remained good when the effect of initial antibody to the viruses used was statistically controlled. Contrary to what might be expected on an infection communication model, introverts, as assessed by the Eysenck Personality Inventory, were significantly more vulnerable to colds than extraverts.

Lymphocytes themselves have been found to bear receptors for a variety of hormonal and neuroendocrine substances. More speculative but intensively investigated possibilities exist in immunosurveillance mechanisms. For example, natural killer (NK) cells—white blood cells not yet assigned to any of the defined leukocyte classes—circulate in the blood and are thought to have a policing function. They become hostile to target cells, especially tumour cells, without prior sensitisation. Little is yet known, however, about the signalling mechanisms involved, although some evidence suggests that interferon may be necessary for NK cell activity (Lipinski, Virelizier, Tursz, and Griscelli, 1980). Interferon production is known to be supressed by stress and high levels of glucocorticoids (Amkraut and Solomon, 1975). Pavlidis and Chirigos (1980) have also presented evidence that the tumour-destroying function of macrophages can be impaired by stress and corticosteroids. The general theory that tumour cells arise naturally in the healthy body but that their concentration is controlled by immunosurveillance mechanisms that are in turn the subject of neuroendocrine influence can no longer be dismissed as mere speculation (see also Hanna and Fidler, 1980).

To the traditional list of stress hormones—ACTH, the corticosteroids, and the catecholamines—must therefore be added a new list of pituitary hormones such as prolactin, growth hormone, and vasopressin. Yet another set of possibilities concerns the thymus itself. Thymus and bone marrow are richly innervated, although the significance of this is not yet understood. It has been suggested that there exists a bidirectional network of communication between the thymus and the neuroendocrine system (Fabris, 1983). Humoral factors are released from the thymus, which confer immune competence on extra-thymic lymphoid cells (Kook and Trainin, 1974). It is possible that growth hormone and steroid hormones interact with thymic factors to control the maturation and differentiation of lymphocytes (Solomon and Amkraut, 1979). Recent research furthermore suggests that a newly discovered group of neuropeptides, the endorphins, may also play a critical role in thymus and immune system regulation (Monjan, 1983).

There is also strong evidence from current research that the immune response to antigenic stimulation itself brings about changes in the hypothalamic–pituitary–adrenal-cortical axis, perhaps via the action of thymosin peptides and interleukins (Hall, McGillis, Vahouny, and Goldstein, 1983). The fact that the targets for stress hormones, neurotransmitters, and neuropeptides are not just restricted to peripheral organs and organ-systems but include the brain itself raises the possibility of a highly sophisticated, complex pattern of self-regulatory control through neuromodulatory feedback. Aging has been theoretically linked to genetically programmed, centrally controlled neuroendocrine changes that have immunosupressive and cancer-disinhibiting effects and are accompanied by psychological depression (Dilman, 1981).

As this briefest of overviews indicates, the new discipline of psychoneuroimmunology is one of enormous potential and vast complexity. To give any kind of thorough summary of the research is quite outside the scope of this book. However, reviews exist in respect of cardiovascular disease and differences in physiology between Type-A and Type-B individuals (Dembroski and MacDougall, 1982; McQueen and Siegrist, 1982), and there is an extensive and growing literature on immunomodulation (e.g., Ader, 1981; Riley, 1981; Solomon and Amkraut, 1981) and on psychoneuroendocrine mechanisms in the aetiology and development of cancers (e.g., Sklar and Anisman, 1981; Cox and Mackay, 1982).

In concluding this section on physiological mechanisms, it can be said that the main question to be asked is no longer whether or not physiological channels of communication exist by which activity in the neocortex can be transformed into positive or negative effects on organs and organ-systems and hence into consequences for health and survival, but how powerful and extensive this influence is. To answer this question using biochemical techniques, however, will not be easy. In vivo assays are notoriously insensitive and in vitro assays are often criticised as artificial because of the dissociation of their subject matter from its naturally rich neuroendocrine environment. There is more precision in in vitro studies, but their effects are not always reproducible in vivo (see Ader, 1982). Certainly, we can say from the present state of knowledge that no organ of the body, including the brain, is impervious to influence by neurohormones, neurotransmitters, and neuropeptides, and hence the effects of psychological stress. This means, of course, that no category of illness, including psychiatric disorders, can be excluded from the possibility of partial social psychological control. Investigation of the modulation of immune responses is clearly one of the most significant developments in recent biochemical research, especially as it is becoming clear that the immune system is involved in the onset conditions of a very large number of pathological states, including malignancies. Although much of this research is still only nascent and many of the interactions glossed here remain strictly hypothetical, evidence for the physiological possibility of psychosocial influence on health is a case of *embarras de richesses.*

Stress as a Breakdown in Social Adaptation

Turning again to social and psychological research, this, especially research done in the last decade, leaves little doubt that social forces play a crucial part in affecting people's health and their chance of survival. Most life-threatening illnesses are now reckoned to be multifactorial in origin and social stress can be numbered with other major risk factors in the aetiology of almost all of these. If it is difficult for a physiologist to unravel the biochemistry of stress, it is equally difficult for a psychologist to gauge how profound the influence of stress is compared with the influence of other known contributory factors such as genetic predisposition, diet, and exercise. It is comparatively easy to measure the amount of animal fats in the diet or the amount of regular exercise that is taken. To quantify social stress is more problematic.

The main reason, of course, is that we do not have a proper theory-based definition of social stress. Existing definitions are either vague and confessedly provisional ("tension," "strain," "cognitive overload," etc.) or highly specific to a particular experimental design ("crowding," "conflict," "helplessness," etc.). What is needed, as so many writers concerned with these matters have said, is an integrative theory of social stress that will itself constitute a definition. I have argued that such a theory cannot exist independently of a theory of normal, adaptive, healthy social living.

As well as confirming a general relation between social stress and illness, recent research also supports certain more specific relationships. The link between Type-A behaviour and heart disease and the connection between the denial and suppression of emotions and cancer are the two strongest examples. The specificity of these associations is itself interesting. But I do not believe it is as consequential for an integrative theory, at least at the present stage of knowledge, as the observation that similar psychological circumstances are implicated in the aetiology of a wide range of different illnesses. No contradiction resides in saying, on the one hand, that there is a general relation between social stress and life-threatening illness and, on the other, that this affects different individuals in different ways resulting in different physical symptoms. A causal connection between personality and diagnosis cannot, of course, necessarily be inferred from a simple association of the two. It may be that a third factor, such as heredity or upbringing, or the two in combination, results in a particular personality style and also a specific physiological vulnerability. The immediate task for social psychology theory, however, is to come up with an overall definition of the general form that social stress takes.

It is most significant that the hazards of social stress are not limited to physical and psychiatric illness. Other forms of death and disability also appear to be brought on by the same social contingencies. Durkheim's famous studies of suicides led him to the conclusion that a state of alienation, which he called *anomie,* often precedes the suicide act and appears to figure in its causation. Durkheim's account of anomie bears a strong resemblance to the symbolic rift between individual and collective which I have proposed is a common denominator of the social stress leading up to illness (Durkheim, 1952; Merton, 1957; see also Mestrovic and Glassner's application of Durkheim's theory to the concept of social stress, 1983). Stroebe et al. (1982), in their discussion of statistics on bereavement and mortality, quote figures showing that the suicide rate for widows and widowers is excessive compared with that among married people. There is a legendary and undisputed association between social stress and heavy drinking. Very heavy drinking is known to raise the risk of high blood pressure, alcoholic hepatitis, pancreatitis, certain cancers, alcoholic cardiomyopathy and other cardiac disorders, as well as malnutrition and psychosis in extreme cases. McQueen and Celentano (1982), in a detailed discussion of the relation between elevated blood pressure and heavy drinking, represent each as a response to the same class of social stressor and each as critically influenced by level of social support.

It is also interesting that the risk of death from homicide is increased in widows and widowers compared with married people. In a sample that included the entire U.S. population between the years 1959 and 1961, the chance of widowers dying in this manner was found to be 2.69 times that for married males (Stroebe et al., 1982). Even the death rate from accidents is elevated in widows and widowers. On its own each of these statistics is open to various interpretations. But together with the statistics on death through chronic illness, they take on a more coherent, theoretically more provocative look.

In *The Psychopathology of Everyday Life,* Freud suggested that accidents may be unconsciously precipitated. Tabachnick (1973), in a book entitled *Accident or Suicide? Destruction by Automobile,* catalogues an impressive body of findings supporting the hypothesis of accident-proneness: that there is a class of individuals who are inherently more likely than others to become the victims of accidents. Holinger and Klemen (1982) review the evidence that accidents and homicide, as well as suicide, represent self-destructive tendencies. Using all the death statistics available in the United States from 1900 to 1975, which from 1933 to 1975 include records for the entire population, they show that national mortality rates from suicide, homicide, and motor accidents tend to be parallel over time; that is, suicide rate increases are in synchrony with accident rate increases, and so on. Unemployment is associated with generally high mortality (Brenner, 1979), and a strong negative relation is known to exist between the mortality rate and cycles of economic activity (Colledge, 1982). Holinger and Klemen point to an increase in accidents of all kinds in the depression of the early 1930s and a decrease in suicide, homicide, and motor accidents in World War II.

These data and reviews are generally consistent with the hypothesis that the same psychosocial predicament can lead to psychiatric illness, life-threatening physical illness, suicide, accident proneness, and one's chances of being the victim of a homicide attack. Cassel makes more or less the same point: "A remarkably similar set of social circumstances characterizes people who develop tuberculosis and schizophrenia, alcoholics, victims of multiple accidents, and suicides. Common to all these people is a marginal status in society" (1974, p. 474).

Each of the various research initiatives I have mentioned is admittedly incomplete. Nonetheless, their findings foreshadow the enormous scope of a general theory of stress and coping; a scope even wider than that suggested by studies of neuroendocrine imbalance and illness. Stress seems to be in the background whenever there is a breakdown in adaptation. Research and theory on stress converge on the idea that if the relation between the individual and the social world is not right, his or her chances of survival are reduced through illness, suicide, drug abuse, accidents and so on. Encompassing though it sounds, "stress and illness" may actually reflect quite a narrow focus in a theoretical scheme which, it seems, can only be complete if it is expanded into a thoroughgoing analysis of the nature of human socialness.

Sociobiology

Altruism and Cooperation

A contingent link between social stress and raised risk of death, or, conversely, between social well-being and survival, has an obvious Darwinian flavour. Biologists have for a long time recognised the adaptive advantage of social organisation: level of evolutionary development is often guaged from the degree of division of labour and social cooperation that is found in a species. Wilson (1975), in his book *Sociobiology: The New Synthesis,* identifies four "pinnacles of social evolution": the colonial invertebrates, the social insects, the non-human mammals, and humans. Insects are believed to be among the first animals to colonise land about 400 million years ago. They have had plenty of time to evolve communities in which there is a high degree of specialisation, particularly in relation to the distribution of food and the defense of territory. Ants are among the most "social" of insects in this sense. Almost all of their activities are run on a cooperative basis. Many ant species "farm" aphids, constructing pens where they feed and milk them for the nutritious honey that the aphids secrete. South American leaf-cutting ants even have a kind of horticulture, cultivating and harvesting fungi on a mixture of chewed leaves and faeces.

Arrangements between individuals involving cooperation and mutual obligation are common among monkeys and chimpanzees. Long-lasting cliques and partnerships have been described among the females in troops of rhesus monkeys and among the males in troops of anubis baboons. A male baboon will enlist the help of another in gaining access to a female and can later be called upon to return the favour (Packer, 1977; Sade, 1980). Biologists call this *reciprocal altruism.* Packer has made it clear that the friendships and loyalties that spring up are not restricted to kin.

In animals other than humans there is a stereotypy about these mutual behaviours that suggests they are instinctual, the result of fairly rigid genetic pre-programming. Our social organisation, because of language and a greatly enhanced capacity for learning, is more flexible and much more complex than that of the other three of Wilson's groups. Nevertheless, it is widely believed that, like these other species, a propensity to organise ourselves into structured, labour-sharing communities is one of mankind's most important aids to survival (see Averill, 1979; Bowlby, 1969; Wilson, 1975). The same general rule can be said to hold good for all social species: a cooperative order insures that the survival potential of the group as a whole is greater then the sum of the isolated survival potentials of each of its constituent members. In human societies reciprocity and altruistic deeds are commonplace. So too are self-sacrificial acts: acts that have no chance of benifiting the actor by ever being repayed. Indeed, such acts are generally held in the highest esteem. Every culture has its legendary heroes—men and women who have risked their own safety and comfort to protect others, or who have died gloriously in the defense of a cause.

I believe that self-sacrifice for the sake of an ideal is no more difficult to account for in Darwinian terms than the various forms of pre-programmed altruism found in non-human social species. The social consequences of martyrdom are in fact extremely potent. Language insures that such acts are not quickly forgotten. On the contrary, a martyr comes to be the very symbol of an ideal: a figurehead of social unity. The death of a single, honored individual serves to underline the goals and values of the remaining members of the community and so strengthen its moral effectiveness. The group is revitalised at what in utilitarian terms is very low cost. The crucifixion of Christ, which has unified millions of people, is an outstanding example. It is true that wars are fought in the name of Christianity, but the theme that antipathy to outsiders is a condition of the internal form and cohesiveness of a group is one to which I have alluded in the idea of the oppositional structure of justifications, and one to which we shall return.

Self-sacrifice and Murder

In considering the evolutionary history of any social species, the mechanisms of individual survival must be distinguished from those of group survival. The interests of the individual and those of the group are not commensurable and are not always compatible. In the highly developed but nonetheless hard-wired social specialisation of the insect world, the individual is cheap and expendable in the interests of the community as a whole. Self-sacrifice and murder can be as instinctual as mutualism and cooperation. Honeybee males die after mating and drones are regularly killed off by the females in the autumn when food starts to get scarce. Unproductive males in some ant colonies, unable to get food for themselves, are starved to death by the workers.

Among eagles, pre-programmed murder of siblings by the first-born is necessary because there is only enough food available to support one offspring. The second-born is merely a standby in case the first-born fails to survive (Brown, 1970; Wilson, 1975). Instances of the group turning against the individual are also to be found in non-human mammals. Goodall (1971) has observed that disabled and deformed monkeys attempting to return to their group are not cared for by their former allies but are reacted to with fear and treated as outcasts.

Humans, it could be said, are different from all other species in the human capacity for reflexivity and compassion. To what extent compassionate feelings are learned or inherited is a question that may be quite difficult to answer. But it is clear that any comparison of human with non-human societies must proceed cautiously. On the other hand, it would be wrong to ignore mankind's phylogenetic history. Comparisons of our socialness with that of other species reveal some intruiging parallels and lead to some interesting speculations. In human societies too, what perpetuates the group is not necessarily what helps the individual to survive.

Trivers (1971) is among those biologists who emphasise the adaptive value of altruism and self-sacrifice among unrelated friends. To the strict Darwinist, however, altruistic and self-sacrificial deeds can only be made sense of if they are somehow related to kin selection. Self-sacrifice among kinfolk is explained as serving the purpose of genetic egoism. By forfeiting her life to protect two or more of her children, the mother has effected a net egoistic gain, where the "ego" is a set of genes (Dawkins, 1976). Wilson's (1975) controversial book has done much to reopen this debate. He defines *sociobiology* as "the systematic study of the biological basis of all social behaviour" (pp. 3–4). One of the main concerns of the book is with how to explain unselfish behaviour.

Wilson's recasting of sociobiology is an attempt to broaden the scope of evolutionary biology to encompass ecology, demography, population genetics, and the social sciences. Many regard this as an overly ambitious aim. Nevertheless, Wilson's ideas have stimulated much debate and have injected new life into discussions about the functional significance of social behaviour. With few exceptions, organised mammalian societies do not consist only of kin. Sociobiologists in the new mould argue that kin-selection theory imposes too narrow limits on the discussion of altruistic and self-sacrificial behaviours. It cannot be denied that kin relations afford scant protection to the individual when "higher" group selection interests are at stake (Breuer, 1982).

Colony or Organism?

Of the four pinnacles of social evolution to which Wilson (1975) refers, the colonial invertebrates are considered by him to have reached the most advanced level of socialness, where this is defined in terms of division of labour and the specialisation of individual members of the colony. Several species are included in this class. In some species the individuals exhibit such unity that a community could easily be mistaken for a single multicellular individual. Slime moulds are the most social single-celled organisms. They are formed of amoeba, thousands of which come together when food is scarce. The amoeba coalesce into a single physical mass which thereafter behaves as if it were a single entity. Once together, individual cells quickly take on different functions. In 2 weeks the colony transforms into a fruiting body with some amoeba forming a base, some forming a stalk and those at the top taking on a spore-bearing function. Not all individuals thereby get to reproduce. Those forming the base and the stalk forfeit their reproductive capability so that at least some members of the colony have progeny.

Other species of colonial invertebrate in which the adaptive and reproductive functions of the community are shared between members include sponges, corals, and the siphonophores. The siphonophores—free-floating colonies such as the Portuguese man-of-war—have evolved a very sophisticated system of division of labour. A single individual at the top serves as a buoyant balloon to keep the colony afloat while beneath there are other individuals, nectophores, functioning like little motors, or pumps, to propell the colony. Each propellant nectophore has its own nervous system but nerve strands connect it with other nectophores so that the motion of the colony can be coordinated.

These, and many other intriguing examples of individual members of a species coming together, specialising, and cooperating in the interests of collective survival are described by Breuer (1982). Breuer concludes his discussion by saying that the distinction between an organism and a society is not as sharp as biologists have in the past assumed it to be. The fact that we are able to observe the formation of the colony convinces us that what we are dealing with is in fact a pseudo-organism. But without this historical information it would be very difficult to tell some such colonies apart from single multicellular organisms.

Cohesion and Social Survival

Cooperative societies are adaptive because they enable reproduction to take place that might otherwise be impossible. Many colonising species, especially the colonial invertebrates, rely on a proportion of individuals in the colony who do not themselves get to reproduce but who aid the reproduction of others. Generally, the genes of the individuals who reproduce are very similar to the genes of those that do not, so cooperative behaviour can be explained as perpetuating the same gene pool if not actually the same genes. Fruiting slime moulds have, however, been produced in the laboratory from amoeba with different genetic properties, although whether this happens naturally remains unknown. Studies of some species of ants and bees have also shown that the genetic material shared by workers and reproducers is often much lower than would be predicted on a strict criterion of kin-selection (Harvey et al., 1980).

Breuer is also among those biologists who believe that kin-selection theory does not sufficiently explain the facts and who see in sociobiology's extension of the Darwinian model to the evolution of social behaviours a constructive and discussion-provoking set of ideas. Whole colonies of a social species can be wiped out in a single misadventure. It is a reasonable assumption that some colonies and groups will be better equipped to survive than others.

As a general rule, the more cohesive the cooperative structure is within a group of social animals the more aggressive this group will be against other similar conspecific groups (Markl, 1976). Colonies of ants are known to war against other colonies of ants of the same species to the extent that one group may completely destroy the other (Wilson, 1975). The same level of warring activity has been observed in chimpanzees (Goodall, 1979) and, of course, in humans. The two general observations (1) that the dividing line between a unitary organism and a cooperative agglomerate is not a straightforward matter, either conceptually or physiologically and (2) that some cooperatives are better at surviving than others, add up to support for the claim of sociobiologists that it is essential to countenance mechanisms of natural selection at the level of the collective as well as at the level of the individual genotype.

It is worth adding that cooperative and mutually adaptive arrangements are not the exclusive right of conspecifics. *Symbiosis,* meaning the living together of organisms from different species, is quite a common phenomenon. One organism has its habitat in or around the body of another. The host may be inconvenienced by the arrangement (parasitism), unaffected by it (commensalism), or may even benefit from it (mutualism). Many bacteria in the human gut feed on undigested food and some produce B vitamins that are absorbed and used by the body. Nitrogen-fixing bacteria in the roots of legumes are another example of mutualism. In exchange for food from the host they transform nitrogen compounds that are used by the host to synthesize proteins. Some symbiotic relationships involve such highly developed forms of mutual dependence that one organism is unable to survive without the other. Lichens are a symbiotic combination of a fungus and an alga. The alga can exist independently, but the fungus is never found on its own. Interdependencies of this kind may involve complex adaptations of structure and function of one or both species. Mutual symbiotic relationships provide an extreme example of how the survival and spread of one organism can depend on a chance meeting with, and subsequent reliance on, another genetically unrelated organism.

It therefore makes sense to talk about adaptation and natural selection both with regard to individuals and, in the case of social and symbiotic species, with regard to communities and combinations of individuals. In non-social species, and up to a point in social species too, an organism's independent powers of self-defense and self-preservation are plainly all important. But in social species the whole is stronger than the sum of the parts and individuals are ultimately expendable in the interests of the group. The adaptiveness of any group is clearly related to its cohesion. Groups that are inefficient through the failure of their consituent members to take on clearly differentiated mutual roles are "weaker" in a biological sense than well-structured groups. Well-organised armies of ants or people are easy victors against a rabble.

In social species then, strong cohesive groups with a clear structure of roles have a better chance of surviving than weak groups in which the roles are blurred. This is well illustrated in studies of mice colonies that are artificially forced to increase in size until there are too many animals for too few roles. The consequence is a catastrophic deterioration in the social order simultaneous with an epidemic of degenerative physical conditions (Calhoun, 1973; Henry and Stephens, 1977).

The Individual "Outsider"

What does this mean for the individual genotype? Natural selection will favour genes for mutualism and role occupancy. Individuals possessing such genes will presumably, by virtue of their combinative strength with other similar individuals, be better equipped to survive than "stragglers"—those with only a weak disposition to participate in cooperative enterprises. This is so because these individuals will unite into strong, effective groups. Mechanisms of genetic egoism and kin-selection, important as they are in the evolutionary scheme, are not the only considerations. In social species they may not even be the prime movers. Selection for cooperative behaviours may have originated in the days when groups were principally kin, but whether or not this is so, the functional significance of social organization has to be acknowledged as an important factor in its own right (see Henderson and Byrne, 1977; Henry, 1982).

In the remainder of this chapter I discuss mechanisms of natural selection in humans which favour their survival as a social or cooperative species. My main purpose is to outline the argument that illness, victimization, and self-destructive tendencies are compatible with the workings of a natural selection and can be represented as an evolutionary asset. A genetically based contingent link between social stress and illness, where social stress implies a rift between the individual and the collective, protects the integrity of the group and so favours those groups that are most cohesive, most effective, and thereby best fitted to survive.

Social Opposition and Individual Participation

I am concerned at this stage to re-emphasise the nature of our own societies as multifarious, and in particular, to develop the argument that paradoxically, small-scale social divisions play an important part in nurturing and sustaining the larger social order. Markl's correlation between intra-group cooperation and inter-group conflict is nowhere more appropriate than when applied to ourselves. Humans are believed to have lived as social animals for at least 2 million years, most of this time in hunter-gatherer groups of between 20 and 50 individuals. Goffman (1969) and Harré (1979) have both stressed that in modern affluent cultures and in some primitive cultures where food is plentiful and shelter easily come by, people's daily lives are determined more by expressive interests—the achieving of honour and respect—than by the practical business of staying alive. Where either practical or expressive needs are prepotent, but perhaps especially in settings where expressive interests dominate, it is easy to see how the common purpose is helped, indeed defined, by its being stood up against the competing and opposing interests of other alien social orders. The last few thousand years do not leave us short of examples of forms that this antipathy can take. Men and women have clubbed together and paraded opposite one another in the name of territory, kin, race, tribe, clan, class, gender, religion, ideology, profession, and dress, to take just a few instances. The clearest illustration of Markl's principle applied to people is the sense of solidarity and unison of purpose that unites and energises a nation in times of war. Put very roughly, if you are human it would seem you cannot unite unless there is something to unite *against.*

If, as I suggest, human groups get their identity and internal cohesion by being in a state of contradistinction to other groups, this arrangement will have little use for individuals who are members of no group at all. Practically or expressively such individuals are a drain on the community's resources and a threat to its integrity. Virtually all social species have evolved ways of killing off these "drones." We have seen that in humans, life-threatening illness, suicide, and other self-destructive tendencies become more likely precisely in those circumstances in which the individual finds himself or herself alone, without ties to any collective. This opens up the possibility that chronic illness has evolved along the same lines as genetically pre-programmed self-destructive and murderous contingencies in other social species. A genetic programme under which normal healthy patterns of neuroendocrine, neurotransmitter, and neuropeptide activity are disrupted in times of (centrally mediated) social stress so as to raise the risk of illness and death serves the interests of resource conservation and thus can be represented as a functionally adaptive mechanism.

The circumstances in which the self-destruct option is engaged in humans are, of course, considerably more complex than the parallel circumstances for other social species. This is because the nature of human socialness is itself much more complex. The facility for language and the consequent handling of socialness in ways not necessarily involving physical proximity and hand-to-hand cooperation mean that the state of detachment from the collective must be more subtly represented than for other species. The bond between the individual and the collective is expressed and maintained symbolically, through action and its context of justification and through conversation itself. Human collectives inhere not primarily in the kind of behavioural reciprocity that we see in ants and monkeys but in the systems of shared justification that make up ordinary talk. Unlike all other social species, the social nature of humans is not just represented in the individual's physical dealings with others. People carry their socialness around with them in the words they speak and the thoughts they think.

Markl's rule lends credibility to the proposal that it is advantageous for the overall social structure to be diversified and to contain within it oppositions. It is also highly consistent with the thesis that the scope for action and choice, and the sense of meaning and commitment that comes from human liasons, derive from the antipathy between opposed elements in the macro-community. Uniting to defend a piece of territory makes no sense unless that piece of territory has borders beyond which the terrain is foreign. "Our patch" has to be contrasted with "theirs".

But the primary group in modern man is a semiotic one. What its members jointly own is not a piece of land but a common metaphysics—an agreed code of truth and value—the potency of which reflects the clearness of the relation in which that group stands to semiotically contrasting groups. Because local human communities are built on talk and gossip, the Saussurian model adopted by structural linguists—of languages as relational networks—is replicated in the organisation of societies. The identity of any single group is a function of its place in the overall macro-structure of the culture and its standing vis-à-vis its social neighbours. (The meaning of any one concept in a language is a function of its place in the macro-structure of *la langue* and its standing vis-à-vis its semiotic neighbours.) Social groupings of individuals mutually fluoresce in the deliberately exclusive nature of the activities and talk—the justifications—that are done within them. Within the larger community of speakers of the same language, social oppositions generate meanings that could not arise in a semiotically uniform society. The most basic and also perhaps the most powerful argument for pluralism and opposition as sustaining attributes of human societies is the implausible vision of social uniformity: the idea of one single, large, agreed community. The latter would simply not contain the scope for the choice and action that we associate with social being and individual morality.

If we take language to be an inherent part of our human socialness and the different kinds of language games (on which alternative edifices of truth and justification are built) that different kinds of people play to be the basis of the pluralism which exists in our societies, there will be no place in this scheme for individuals who are players of no language games at all. The efficacy of the macro-societal structure depends upon the elements that comprise it standing in a clear oppositional relation to one another. This, in turn, relies on groups of individuals continuing their particular local projects of justification and moral criticism.

This discussion of human socialness, and in particular the necessity of the threefold distinction between the individual, the primary group, and the society (or macro-culture), gives rise to a double ambiguity as to what counts as the organism from the perspective of a sociobiological commentary. The idea of institutions created and sustained on a semiotic basis, primarily through language, leads logically to an application of the functional model at a third level. Not only can it be applied to the survival of the individual and the primary group, it also becomes relevant to the survival of complex societies and perhaps even whole civilizations. If a functional analysis taking colonies or groups of individuals as the unit of survival is possible and if in the case of humans we allow the idea of large groups formed of oppositional networks of smaller groups, at what stage is it appropriate to stop reapplying the principles of natural selection? Why should the same analytic principles be any less relevant to large composite groups of people than they are to small collectives of individuals both in human and non-human species? The analysis of humans has to be unique and peculiar because the capacity for representation in language is itself unique.

At what point in history human utterances acquired a grammar sufficiently rich to affect the ordering of groups and societies is not clear (for a discussion of the evolution of language see Schilcher and Tennant, 1984). The human limbic system is known to have extensive cortical connections and to be involved with emotion and social behaviour. One suggestion is that a quantum development of the limbic system took place some 2 million years ago resulting in a greatly increased capacity for symbolic representation and a corresponding revolution in social behaviour and communication through speech (Henderson and Byrne, 1977; Vilensky, Van Hoesen, and Damasio, 1981).

To sum up the main argument, the presence of a self-destruct gene such that the individual's chances of survival are diminished when he or she is not part of a social structure functions in a general way to promote the group as the principal unit of adaptation. In humans, a contingent link between life-threatening illness (or suicide, drug addiction, accident proneness, or victimisation) and social uninvolvement acts in favour of the articulation of individuals into cooperative and competitive units. Warring tribes sometimes destroy one another, but such a state of affairs, favouring the better-organised opponent and thus in a general way promoting genes for collectivism, may in fact be conducive to macro-societal stability and species survival. Supporting this interpretation is the mass of evidence confirming that risk of death is increased when an individual is not symbolically attached to any collective by virtue of sharing with others a common justificatory scheme (see Chapter 5).

The same evidence gives some clues as to the psychological expression of this genetic programme. The depressed state that accompanies social detachment probably interferes with cognitive and perceptual skills, making the individual more prone to accidents. It may make him or her less tolerant and a more likely target for other people's hostility. It certainly plays on the emotions and makes some people think about suicide. It probably even renders the individual physically and socially less attractive and therefore less likely to find companionship and a sexual partner.

The physiological expression of the gene for collectivism, returning again to our main concern—the conditions of human organic pathology—is the central modulation of endogenous degenerative factors. An example is the failure of immune surveillance mechanisms in their normal task of recognising and killing circulating cancer cells. The role of the hypothalamic–pituitary sex-steroid axis, as this is described by Henry (1982), is quite consistent with a Darwinian interpretation of the link between social stress and illness. Henry comments that testosterone enables aggression, drive, and persistence and that it is important in determining social status, reproductive success, and quality of parental care and protection. Low levels of testosterone may combine destructively with the high corticoids that accompany life stress and dejection.

The Disinhibition Theory of Illness and Death

Research on stress, recent discoveries in psychoneuroimmunology, and contemporary ideas in the field of sociobiology add up to what can be called the *disinhibition theory of illness.* This centres on the notion that the potential for organic pathology is genetically pre-programmed and endemic in every healthy individual. Disease is at least in part the consequence of a disturbance in natural bodily processes that work to keep potential pathogens at "managable" (i.e., non-toxic) levels. Fifty years ago, under the influence of germ theory, illness was understood by the scientific community entirely as a passive yielding of the organism to challenges from outside. Today with our better knowledge of the body's chemistry, internal, self-regulating mechanisms are credited with a much more active role in the determination of health status. It is significant that many micro-organisms responsible for infectious diseases, for example, *streptococcus,* are now catalogued among the natural fauna of the healthy body.

The two main causes of death in modern developed countries are cardiovascular disease and cancer. In the year 1900, before antibiotics were discovered, influenza, pneumonia, and tuberculosis were the main killers. Malignancies were relatively uncommon. All of these fatal illnesses, however, are conditions in which endogenous states such as immune competence play a crucial role in the onset and course of the pathology. Average life expectancy in the year 1900 was, of course, much lower than it is now. But the figures show that this difference is mainly due to the high mortality rate among children before the age of 15 years. Life expectancy for older people has not changed much in the last 100 years (Schulz, 1978). As Schulz puts it, "while we are not living much longer than people did 100 years ago, a greater proportion of us are attaining old age" (p. 42).

These observations imply a ceiling on longevity that seems resistant to advances in medical treatment. Antibiotics, preventive vaccination, and stipulated levels of hygiene mean that more people survive the earlier years of life than was the case a century ago. But these medicines do not seem able to extend the life expectancy of, for example, 65-year-olds, a great deal. As the old causes of death become treatable or avoidable, new, previously uncommon forms of illness proliferate and seem almost to take over from their now obsolete predecessors as the main threats to life.

Medical treatment may not be able to raise the ceiling of old age, but style of life, it would seem, can. In the three remotely situated agrarian communities studied by Leaf (1975), enough documentation was available to show that the incidence of centenarians was far in excess of that in the United States.

That longevity should be relatively unaffected by medical measures, and that new fatal illnesses take over from old ones when the old ones become curable or preventable, is what would be expected on a functional model of illness such as the one put forward in this chapter. These facts are consistent with the hypothesis that aging and health are under the control of a semi-flexible genetic programme whose course is linked in with the individual's success as a social entity. Gerontologists do not make a sharp distinction between the mechanisms of aging and the mechanisms of chronic degenerative illness. Some authors have reasoned that the harmful consequences of social stress are not due to fresh illnesses but in fact represent an accelerated deterioration of an already malfunctioning, or genetically weak, organ system (Engel, 1978; Fredrick, 1976). Solomon has speculated that aging itself and the diminished immune competence and increased incidence of autoimmune phenomena and cancer that go with it may be the cumulative product of life stresses (Solomon, 1982).

The disinhibition theory of illness is also broadly in line with two major theories of social gerontology. *Disengagement theory* (Cumming and Henry, 1961) casts aging as a process of mutual withdrawal of individual and society. The individual necessarily withdraws because of his or her reduced abilities; society withdraws so that younger people can fill the vacant roles. *Activity theory* (Lemon, Bengtson, and Peterson, 1972) says something similar in proposing that a person's level of activity, which diminishes with age, correlates with life satisfaction, health, and longevity. On my model, aging is characterised rather differently as the progressive unavailability of shared systems of justification.

It is perhaps necessary to point out that in all of this there is no assumption that the individual necessarily *wishes* to self-destruct to protect the integrity of the group any more than it could be said a worker honeybee wishes to sacrifice itself in delivering its mortal sting. On the contrary, health services are set up and hospitals are built specifically because there is wide agreement on the ethical propriety of caring for the sick and elderly. But men and women also die in millions for their religions, their countries, and their ideals, and what I have been trying to describe in this chapter is not a consciously held, intentional need (except of course in the special case of the self-styled martyr) but a genetically based tendency that is fixed and works its way into our lives in many different ways. In the next chapter, we turn to the relation in which this tendency stands to the human capacity for moral consciousness and reason.

7

Opposition and Negotiation

It is not my purpose in this book to ideologise and prescribe but rather to place research on psychosocial stress in the context of contemporary discussions in the fields of social psychology, sociolinguistics, physiology, medicine, and sociobiology. A theory does not have to be nice to be right, and the issue of the palatability of the ideas that spin off from this aim should be kept separate from the ideas themselves.

Nevertheless, extrapolating from psychological research on action and attitudes and borrowing from ideas in sociolinguistics, I have represented small-scale social orders according to the conventions and moralities that they shut out and large-scale ones as inherently containing oppositional elements. It cannot be denied that the picture of our world that this involves—a world forever partitioned and factioned, and never fully reconcilable—presents, on the surface, a somewhat gloomy prospect. Many political and ideological groups, it could be argued, are explicitly based on an ethic of equality and openness. But has any such group in the history of mankind ever existed other than in contradistinction to opposed forms? It is my thesis that it is not possible for such ideologies to exist in isolation. Like every other social union, ideologies are states of contradistinction. They arise as reactions against an attributed despotic order. As for the openness and ease of entry that ideological movements sometimes profess, it may nominally be the case that anyone can join, but lurking in the peculiar language games and styles that are the ritual markings of the movement are strong conditions of membership. It is often in the most boastfully libertarian factions that the most extreme forms of exclusiveness lie.

That the divisiveness endemic in our societies may have a biologic basis might seem the ultimate in nihilistic speculations, especially in the light of the destructive arsenals that the major world powers now control. But does the plurality of social life in fact mean that mankind is headed on an unstoppable course of mutual destruction?

There are two separate issues here. The first is whether mutual antagonism is actually an inevitable ingredient of a pluralistic system, and the second is the extent to which humans as reasoning beings can impose counterbalancing, conciliatory influences on an oppositional social world. We will consider the former of these first. Is it possible for the opposition that is entailed in our social life to exist in simple, neutral, non-competitive juxtapositions between groups of persons? Is the condition of fragmentation of the macro-community met simply by having alternative, incommensurable subsections of the community that are not constitutionally *against* one another in any way? In other words, cannot sets of people just agree to differ without having to judge, condemn, and kill one another all the time? Communities are extensively divided according to the different jobs and career structures within them. Outside their work, some people are interested in sports and others in fashion or gardening. Do these different interests have to contain an emotive, conflictual component?

Personal Commitment in a Pluralistic World

Social psychology may have an answer to this question. The conclusion toward which it draws us is that a "neutral," non-competitive, non-evaluative society is only possible in practice if the roles within it are rotated between individuals. The message of the main theories of action and attitudes reviewed in Chapter 3 is that freely chosen—or rather, freely attributed—actions form the person. An individual's attitudes, values, and styles are crystallised, reaffirmed, and changed according to the things he or she does and the explanatory schemes in which actions are embedded. These theories assert that in a very real sense, you become what you do, especially if you do it consistently over any length of time and especially if you attribute your actions to volitional, or *internal* causes. This can be watched in the gradual adoption of the attitudes and styles characteristic of their trades and professions by men and women who work at the same job for any length of time. To an extent, the person "becomes" a secretary, a salesman, a nurse, a miner, and so on. It would be comforting to construe this becoming as a neutral process, but psychology and natural observation concur that it is not. Action, choice, and personal commitment, as I have tried to demonstrate, are action, choice, and personal commitment *against* alternatives. A secretary who attributes his or her line of work to personal choice comes eventually to despise lack of organisation and inefficiency in a way that extends beyond the office. Someone who by choice and training has become an experienced carpenter is bound to come to look at other people's joinery with a critical eye. Role occupancy, by its very nature, when extended over a period of time, carries with it a degree of fixedness and mild prejudice: a certain entropy-reducing gel of attitudes and opinions.

In reality, we know there is a great deal of backbiting and prejudice among different trades and professions. The more closely related vocational interests are, the stronger this tends to be. Soldiers and sailors enjoy a mutual animosity which goes back centuries. A traditional disdain of architects is widespread among manual workers in the building trade. Regrettably, psychologists and sociologists are rarely to be found speaking to one another. Friction between doctors and pharmacists and between doctors and social workers is commonplace. There is downright hostility among physicians toward the derogatively named "fringe" medical practitioners.

The same pattern is repeated in nonvocational spheres. Oxford football fans hold a particular hatred for Swindon fans because Oxford is near Swindon (Marsh et al., 1978). Mudslinging is not unknown even between different charitable organisations with similar interests. Clashes between rival gangs of teenagers, such as the Mods and Rockers of the early 1960s, often take place apparently on no other grounds than that of style of dress. Yet, neither side would dream of ganging up against, for example, city business executives, whose dress represents a far greater stylistic distance from either group than that which exists between them.

Parties with widely different constitutions and interests seem able to tolerate one another more easily. Again, we must look for the reason for this in the arena of action and choice. The choices and possibilities for personal commitment presented by an unfamilar social order are in a sense not *real* choices and possibilities. That is, they are not anchorable in the representations of the world that we, as a result of the partiality of our own cultural exposure, possess. Personal experiences and dealings prevent any single individual from encompassing in a balanced manner all existing cultural forms. The pure openmindedness this would entail is psychologically impossible because such a condition would negate the possibility of action.

Given that personal partiality is an inescapable part of being social, some communities are bound to appear more threatening to the individual than others because of the rivalry they present as alternative bases for the organisation of planned action. A committed high Anglican is more suspicious and contemptuous of the Low Church than of Hindu practices because the defense of the high service involves keeping low influences at bay. To practice a thing committedly is actively to police and defend local boundaries.

The most impressive evidence for the non-neutrality of different vocational and non-vocational interests is the vast lexicon of critical and evaluative words and phrases and their extensive deployment in everyday talk. Even the commonplace words "nice" and "good" carry an implied disdain for "nasty" and "bad" alternatives. Theoretically, it might seem possible to "neutralise" roles, to wash away their self-imposed status and mutual enmity, but in practice this seldom seems to happen. In practice, opposition and evaluation seem to be the lifeblood of our complex social world.

The Conditions of Neutral Roles

With these insights, gained with the help of social psychological theory, into social life such as it is—partitioned and oppositional—it is an interesting exercise, if nothing more, to derive from the same theory the conditions of a more ideal social world—one made up of less fractious communities. How could this alternative be realised? For an individual to be equally favourably disposed to the different roles in a community, he or she would need to be equivalently personally committed to each of those roles. Personal commitment, as we have seen, comes from freely attributed action, so we might say that in a society in which the roles were rotated between individuals so that there is no permanent role occupancy, the person-forming consequences of action would, so to speak, balance out across the different roles. A person might prefer one task to another but no one would end up with a greater psychological commitment to the artifacts of that task—to the role itself—than to any other. Individuals and roles would not merge in the way they do when the person becomes the role. More to the point, the impartiality of his or her actions would ensure that no individual would end up set against any other cultural form. Such a system, in which each person takes a turn at each of the various tasks within a community, is the basis of kibbutz life and stands in sharp contrast to the ethic of specialisation.

Leaving aside the impracticality of applying this recipe to any extent in modern societies, there is a darker reason for doubting the efficacy of role-sharing as a general basis for social life. This has to do with the relation between justified action and health. The core of my argument concerning the social conditions of illness is that an individual remains cognitively "differentiated"—low on entropy—and hence, healthy, precisely through his or her actions and the justificatory scheme in which they are embedded. Moreover, Markl's principle (see p. 126) is echoed in the logic of justification itself: the potency of any one justificatory scheme is a function of the sharpness of its contrast with other schemes. This very proposal seems to deny that a network of neutral, reciprocal role relations is compatible with a society of healthy individuals. For a start, such a situation would banish the tension that we know as moral choice and committed action and along with it the spice and interest of conversation. People living in a kibbutz in which all the work is shared evenly between individuals may be healthy without being set against one another. But it must be remembered that kibbutz life is not the order of the day in the wider world and that the members of the kibbutz are all knowingly members of a small splinter group whose solidarity is itself at least in part a reaction against more standard ways of western living. If the whole world worked like a kibbutz, then the situation would be very different. Under these circumstances we might speculate that the community spirit would fall away along with the local system of justification that fires it.

Enmity as a Psychological Principle

I believe there is no getting away from the necessity of opposition and a degree of mutual antagonism within the macro-community. Sociobiology and common sense suggest that viability in a social species depends on clear and mutually effective differentiation of roles. In animals, the stronger the cohesion within a group the greater would seem to be that group's aggressive inclination toward other groups. Social psychological theory on action and attitudes confirms that this latter principle has a strong counterpart in humans. But most importantly, the logic of the justification process and the empirical link between potency of justification and the health and survival of the individual means that in human societies it is necessary for the overall social structure not only to be differentiated but for its divisions to embody a degree of mutual enmity. It is worth adding that there is nothing in this proposal to suggest that this enmity must inevitably express itself in physical violence. Because humans are unique in their ability to manipulate symbols, especially in language, mutual animosity can be given expression, at least provisionally, in talk and ritual.

I do not personally desire the conclusion that opposition and mutual enmity are as indispensible in human life as health itself. Indeed I wish it were not so. But I do believe that no politics or ideology can succeed unless it is underpinned by a sound social psychology. If divisiveness is a fact of social life, as I believe it is shown to be, it cannot be ignored by policymakers. Some provision for opposition is built into the rituals and traditions of every society in the competitive pastimes that are encouraged. Succeeding at work, winning at sports, being "good" at something are institutionalised ways in which the individual can achieve a crude social identity. In democratic countries, of course, this vital state of opposition is represented in the parliamentary constitution itself.

Prejudice and Tolerance

I have used the word *prejudice* in connection with the personal commitment that follows from freely attributed action. This might seem a little strange because it bears the implication that the more a person acts and chooses in a particular direction the more prejudiced he or she becomes. In its ordinary sense the word prejudice refers to a rigidly held (probably negative) attitude to a class of people or things. One is usually prejudiced *against* a stereotype of some kind. It is important to be aware of the norm-bound quality of the word as it arises in ordinary usage. Talk of prejudice is related to time and place. It would not make much sense, for example, to describe someone in the 1980s as prejudiced against the horse and cart as a means of transport. It would be a curious and not exactly appropriate use of the language to accuse an eighteenth-century slave trader of racial prejudice. The men of rural Greece who traditionally drink together in all-male tavernas while their wives work at home would treat an accusation of chauvinism with amused contempt. Prejudiced opinion in its ordinary sense is what the consensus of the time cares to call prejudiced opinion. Invariably, it carries the connotation of morally reprehensible opinion. The forms it takes therefore change, as does morality, with the times.

The prejudice that comes from committed action, however, is a psychologically universal phenomenon. It is neither ethnocentric nor chronocentric but a condition of being a person. To act and to choose is to exclude alternative possibilities, and to act and to choose at all consistently is to consistently exclude them. A person free of prejudice is a person without structure, a fully entropised person—in fact, no person at all. Total absence of prejudice is precisely the circumstance I have associated with illness and death.

Does it therefore follow that the more prejudiced one is, in this psychologically necessary sense, the healthier one will be? The answer is a heavily qualified yes. I have referred to wars as great uniters of nations. One way of accounting for the solidarity and national euphoria that are seen in times of war is in terms of the prejudice that the state of war licences. In fighting a war, it helps if the enemy is caricatured as evil and therefore expendable. The point of the dehumanising labels that are used ("Hun," "Jap," etc.) is to underline the us–them distinction and facilitate physical aggression. The theory of illness that I have put forward predicts that the rate of illness and maladjustment in communities at war will be less than that in peacetime, with the obvious exception of the casualties of the fighting itself, because of the availability of a strong, shared, unifying system of justification. Unfortunately, this prediction is difficult to test. Even if, as reports suggest, civilian hospitals and psychiatric clinics were comparatively empty during the two world wars, this may have been due to changed patterns of presenting and referral.

Some accounts by those directly involved in active service are more informative. Not only do British soldiers who fought in the Falklands war speak and write eulogistically of their feelings of unity and comradeship, there is more than a hint in their reports of a state of super-health. The following are verbatim extracts from interviews with two servicemen.

> Then I wasn't frightened any more. It was an adrenalin high. You saw all these bullets flying about but you never thought you would be hit. It was a real high. I just thought "This is it, what an experience." It was the first time I had been under fire. (Shirley, 1983, p. 20.)

> It was a pleasure to fight in the Falklands with "42." There was a fantastic spirit. The professionalism came out in those 18-year-olds. I think I was reliving a cycle of my own life, because I could remember how I came up. You became like a fox—the sight, the smell, the ear, everything's there. (p. 21)

And this is what a journalist who accompanied the troops had to say:

> We had not, when it started, even been friends. To me they were soldiers, bound up in an insular, chauvinist world I found repugnant. To them, I was simply a "hack," anarchic and scruffy. Inevitably, of course, that changed. During 94 days we crossed half the world, went through a small war and, together, came home. In *The Seven Pillars of Wisdom,* T. E. Lawrence wrote of his Arabs: "We were fond together." It has become a little like that in the Falklands. (p. 18)

These are representative statements, and they are certainly not the accounts of depressed or ill people (although they could in one sense be described as people under stress). But we do not need to turn to anything as extreme as war for examples of physical and mental well-being associated with strong shared commitment. The charismatic ardour and vitality of champions of minority causes suggests that good health is almost synonymous with committed campaigning against an oppressor. Family life itself is built on an unshakeable us–them distinction: blind loyalty and priority to your own. On the other hand, the health of originators of new forms—men and women whose work by its nature is isolationist and innovatory, who, as it were, choose to take on the whole world—is notoriously poor. The myth of the mad genius, like most myths of its kind, is propped up by a certain amount of fact. The biographies of famous artists and musicians in particular attest to the unusually high incidence of illness, suicide, alcoholism, and psychiatric disorders among these men and women.

The prejudice that arises in wars and in charismatic movements is a public affair. Far from being alone, the individual glories in a shared commitment. The prejudiced viewpoint is supported and legitimated through consensus. The person cannot be described as "closed"; his or her point of view is constantly aired with others in a ferment of conversation and agreement. It is just that the cultural conditions of the time and place set clear and narrow limits on the nature of this conversation so that everyone involved (in wartime this means virtually the entire nation) becomes sucked into a common language game predicated on justifications against a common oppressor.

But there is another kind of prejudice, of a more private and insular kind, seen most clearly in the senile and the paranoid, where the individual rigidly clings to attitudes and ideas that are not shared and not negotiable. On the systems-theory analogy, this isolationist prejudice approximates a closed state of the system. The opposite state—total openness—is the absence of any prejudice at all; the "ideal" but psychologically impossible condition of total tolerance. This contrast is diagramatically represented in Figure 7.1 as the two opposite ends of a continuum. The figure summarises many of the ideas of this book. Both ends of the continuum are associated with symbolic isolation of the individual from the community due to the failure of justification. Both are therefore associated with life-threatening illness and non-survival. The left-hand extreme encompasses the sort of aloneness that may be experienced following the loss of someone very close, or the loss of an all-absorbing job, and the corresponding loss of a psychologically sustaining system of justification. The right-hand extreme marks the second kind of isolation: the idealised openness and self-criticism that logically disqualifies the individual from any title to justification and hence from membership of any moral order. Social support is drawn as a force pushing toward the centre point, this central area representing the domain of shared oppositional structures that make up a pluralistic society and that support the health and normality of its individual members.

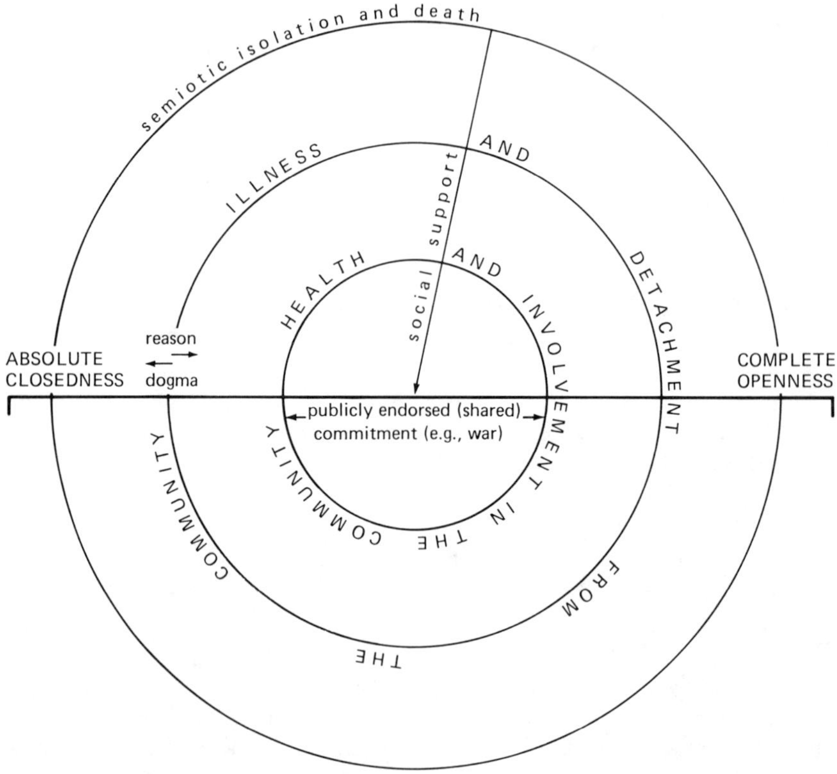

Figure 1 Social domains of life and health and of illness and death.

Reason and Balance

The right-hand half of the continuum, as drawn in Figure 7.1, suggests that there is a tension between health and survival on the one hand and the ideal of open-mindedness and criticism on the other. The dilemma this presents is acute but straightforward. It concerns the association of health, survival, and charismatic energy with what I have called prejudice, or less contentiously perhaps, committed belief, and the linking of depression and illness, and ultimately death, with open-mindedness and self-criticism. Radical openmindedness, according to this representation, must be bought at the expense of psychological and physical well-being. I have tried to show that no-one can achieve personhood without being somewhat prejudiced, without being biased toward certain social orders and ipso facto against others. Personal choice and agency are not otherwise possible. This is one of the main conclusions toward which Tajfel's work led him (Tajfel, 1981). On the other hand, reasoning humans quite properly persist in guarding against the complacency and self-aggrandisement of entrenched prejudice. It is the cornerstone of liberalism that a value is placed on negotiation of opposite positions; the indefinite extension of conversation under conditions of freedom of speech. What research on the psychology of health and illness tells us is that this involves something of a psychological sacrifice on the part of the individual.

The defining of consensus as shared prejudice requires further comment because it can be taken to imply that there is no overall moral progression in human life and that the fresh, apparently liberal ideas of today are destined to become the dogmas and prejudices of tomorrow. It is fair to say that the history of politics is to a large extent the history of action and reaction, nowhere more clearly seen than in the succession of counter-revolutions which typically follow episodes of violent political change. Whether or not the movements that inspire historic changes can be said to form any overall moral progression is a question that is outside the reach of social psychology. The identification of prejudice with consensus is thus neutral with regard to whether civilisations can improve themselves or not, because "improve" requires a different framework of axioms and theories to that on which the present arguments are built. The naive optimist who puts his or her faith in moral growth certainly faces some awkward questions. One of the most awkward is how, on a moral-advancement argument, it is possible to account for the carnage and cruelty of the two world wars, the most recent of which took place less than 50 years ago.

For the individual to strike a balance between the impossible extreme, on the one hand, of pure open-mindedness and the morally bankrupt one, on the other, of blind prejudice, it would seem that he or she too must act and react in a similarly reflexive, revisional fashion. A person's position on the continuum of Figure 7.1 must therefore not be thought of as necessarily fixed and static but as fluctuating around a pivotal point. This pattern, I believe, is familiar to most of us and is the dynamic basis on which our natural prejudices are undermined, replaced, undermined again, and so on. Piaget characterised it as a natural and dynamic equilibrium between the process of assimilation and the process of accommodation. Other writers have expressed it in different ways.

One might speculate that where the pivotal point is set along the continuum is something that varies between individuals. No moralist, however strict, it could be argued, has a right to insist on a person knowingly jeopardising his or her mental well-being and physical health for some arbitrary standard of open-mindedness. On the other hand, it could also be argued that all individuals are morally bound to set this point as far to the right-hand end of the continuum, as this is drawn in Figure 7.1, as is possible *for them.*

But what does this highly abstract and theoretical statement mean in practice? We have already encompassed one way in which a person can actively strive to achieve this end: through the undertaking of not one single monogamous role, but as many different and varied roles as possible. The other related way is through conversation. By the same argument from psychological theories of attitudes and actions, we can say that it is in the interest of tolerance and therefore a good thing morally speaking not to argue habitually from any single, fixed position but rather to role-play, as it were, all kinds of different points of view and even experiment with different styles of talk. A similar logic underlies the therapeutic and occupational use of role-play techniques in which an individual publicly acts out a part or puts forward an argument that is not his or her own and may even go against his or her personal inclination. By role-playing an unfamiliar series of actions or styles, or by expressing a view that is not one's own, the mentally forming and psychologically prejudicing effects of the individual's real-life performances can be, up to a point, mitigated. These procedures may even generate new higher-level perspectives from which previously incongruous and conflictual positions can be reconciled. This view of individual change and growth gives us a psychological counterpart to Hegel's theory of knowledge as based on negation and a continuing sequence of thesis–antithesis–synthesis.

Few individuals, however, are god-like enough to be able to achieve a perfect balance, and in practice all of us must have certain preferred or at least well-oiled personnae and certain habitual forms of talk that are *us.* I do not consider that this, either, is an issue to which social psychology can usefully contribute. Where the balance is struck is a highly private matter answerable only to the morality of the individual and touching on the very nerve of personal freedom and choice.

Negotiation

It is, of course, quite possible for opposing views to be negotiated in conversation and reconciled. Successful negotiation can be put down to the threshing out of a new perspective; a higher-level set of rules tabling which moral courses are fitting in what circumstances. From such productive exchanges meta-language games are evolved which are tolerant of previously opposed systems.

But the process of reconciliation by forging a wider-ranging, or higher-level, justificatory framework has a sting in its tail. The oppositional logic of justifications still applies. Unification of opposed positions can only be achieved providing the essential ingredient of opposition is preserved; that is, providing the new higher-level system itself stands in a state of contradistinction to some other system. The negotiative initiative has its own rhetoric of justification. In this meta-language game the "morality" and "wisdom," for instance, of conciliation contrasts with the "intolerance" and "narrow-mindedness" of logger-headed antagonism. Prejudice is still necessarily present in the meta-system in order for it to have form but it is prejudice against what are dubbed more vulgar forms of prejudice. Battle is still in the air, but the nature of the war has changed and, in a sense, broadened its scope. Forces have combined and the offensive has widened from a local skirmish to a larger-scale campaign.

Does it therefore follow that negotiation and conciliation are inherently as oppositional in their character as the divisions they set out to repair? Is the eventual depressing resting point of these arguments that all attempts at morality are vanity in disguise? I have to answer this by saying I do not know. Words such as "liberty," "freedom,' and "democracy" pose as universal desiderata. But their significance varies enormously according to who is using them and for what purpose. The democracy of the German Democratic Republic is not the same as the democracy boasted by the United States. Communists insist that state control liberates the people, capitalists that only free enterprise paves the way for freedom. The point is that each is correct and ingenuous within its own rhetorical and coercive system.

Nonetheless, one can be quite sure that intelligent men and women will not abandon their efforts at conciliation, at all levels of human and political life. Of great relevance to this overall aim is the knowledge that social psychology can bring to bear; in particular, the caution against absolutism and the caveat that reconciliations by their nature are built on shifting sands because they themselves depend on an oppositional relation. The quest for an absolute universal consensus is almost certainly a vain one but a dynamic of new and constantly transforming structures is conceivable providing the conversation can be kept going and new challenges continue to appear in it.

It must be said that the accumulated psychological wisdom on which these arguments are based makes it seem unlikely that solid and lasting agreement can be reached between protagonists who are themselves styled by their roles as exemplars of opposed moral or political institutions. The reason is that the very roles and rules that enable and guide their actions and speech are derived from an ideology that itself only arises as a state of opposition to the ideology of their negotiating counterparts. For deep reconciliation to be achieved, these reciprocal roles would have to disappear. The problem is at its most acute when the opposite sides of a debate represent institutions that have grown so large as to be virtually all-embracing so that their respective identities are almost reflections of one another. The capitalist and communist worlds have become somewhat like this. The respective delegates, by virtue of their mutual positions as negotiators representing entrenched, antipathetic ideological positions, ipso facto play incommensurable language games. There is thus a strong psychological case for matters of critical importance, such as the reduction in the build-up of nuclear weapons, to be negotiated other than between career politicians. This would remove what at very least is a psychological barrrier to the meta-level of discourse that must be forged for mutual trust to be possible and for agreement to be reached. Recent experience in Britain with disputes between unions and employers tends to confirm that differences are most effectively resolved through the mediation of an independent arbiter.

Social psychology in its most basic form is about transcultural and trans-temporal aspects of human social behaviour (e.g., Semin and Manstead, 1983). It is a meeting point for discussions in biology, physiology, medicine, sociolinguistics, social anthropology, and the philosophy of action. As such, it would be inappropriate for social psychology to address itself directly to political and ideological issues although, as I have tried to show in this section, it does have something to say about the conditions by which any political or ideological scheme is bound. It perhaps would not be too presumptuous to say that the conditions it imposes, while not themselves moral conditions, are the fruits of a meta-commentary, which emerges from the comparison of ideas in these various different fields.

8

Coping and Psychological Defense

This is primarily a book about social psychology, so it is appropriate to end it with some thoughts on the implications that these ideas have for the individual in a social context. As we have seen, modern approaches to stress research emphasise the interactive nature of person and environment. Investigations concentrate not on stressful events or personality traits as independent influences on health and survival but on how the individual copes with upsetting experiences in his or her life. Lazarus (1966) was one of the first exponents of this difference in emphasis.

A great deal has been written about psychoanalytic mechanisms of coping and psychological defense. In this chapter I approach the subject from a general ethogenic standpoint while retaining the functionalist perspective that characterises the main arguments in this book. It is my firm belief that the task of social psychology is neither to produce a theory of illness nor a theory of health, but to encapsulate both in the same account. "Stress" in this scheme is no more or less than life itself, and coping with stress is the business of living.

Coping as a Shared Framework of Justification

Ordinarily, when we ask someone how well he or she is coping we are asking if they are getting things done and achieving objectives that they hold important. Some people can cope with some tasks and eventualities but not others. It is well known that some chronic schizophrenics can cope with quiet jobs in which the tasks are well defined, such as working in a library, but not others involving more decisions and more social contact. Coping would seem to be related in a fundamental way to acting. Those theories that make a distinction between action and behaviour are agreed that actions are goal-directed and that they are given meaning in the social world by being accountable. I have called action accounts *justifications.* The main social psychological theories of the past 30 years have convincingly demonstrated the person-forming quality of freely attributed performance (see Chapter 3, this volume). To justify an action is to ascribe an intention or goal to it and hence implicitly to endorse that part of the social order that upholds this goal and other goals related to it by tradition. In Chapter 4 I try to show how this process has both a social and a psychological differentiating quality about it.

How is coping related to acting? To say that to act is to cope must be wrong because many actions in the course of life are done under duress, and some things that are done, such as murders or compulsive behaviours, we regard as distinctly maladaptive and as signalling the failure of coping. At what point is this failure identifiable? Why is washing the hands again and again maladaptive? What might happen when we ask such a person what he or she is doing?

Y. Why are you washing your hands?
Z. To get them clean.
Y. But why do you keep on washing them?
Z. Because I can't get them clean enough.
Y. But you've washed them 26 times in the last hour .
Z. I know. I wish I could shift this mark. It's like it's etched onto the skin.
Y. What mark? Aren't you being a bit extreme?
Z. I can't seem to get them clean . . .

Here *Y* is asking *Z* for an order of explanation of behaviour which *Z* probably cannot give. The only sort of answer acceptable to *Y* is one grounded in the roles and rules of normal practice. *Y* is trying but failing to elicit an explanatory utterance that he or she can assimilate to a form of talk that is familiar. There *are* answers that would be satisfactory, for example, "Maybe it's silly but I spilt acid on my fingers and it still stings" (the careless car mechanic) or even, "Ha! knew I'd have you fooled, crypto-Freud!" (the practical joker).

The failure of coping cannot be explained simply by the failure of action per se. Rather, it corresponds to the failure of action to take on meaning; in other words, to the failure of justification. Coping in this analysis is synonymous with accountable action. It has an intimate bearing on the individual's social identity—his or her position in the web of social life—because the kind of talk in terms of which a justification is drafted is the passport to a particular moral order. Coping is therefore logically tied in with social support. The more vehement a justification, the more dedicated is the declaration of allegiance with the community or complex of communities laying claim to this justification.

The demands an individual faces are obviously related to time and place. Coping in a foreign town poses special problems for the tourist, not just because of the lack of practical knowledge necessary to survive but also because of the unfamiliarity of local systems of justification and idioms of style. People are naturally jealous of these expressive orders and do not readily admit outsiders to their secret worlds. The reason is straightforward. If cherished local customs were to become public property, their contradistinctive quality would be undermined and their identity lost. There is a sullen inevitability in the regarding of tourists by locals the world over as the lowest of the low.

Psychological Defense

The concept of psychological defense originated in Freudian theory and is common in discussions of psychological stress. Katz, Gallagher, Hellman, Sachar, and Weiner (1969), in a classic series of studies of women awaiting breast biopsies, equate psychological defense with coping. Their research showed that cortisol production was inversely related to the strength of defense. Those women who coped by denial, prayer, or intellectualisation were said to have avoided the unhealthy high cortisol level that was characteristic of women who were poorly defended. Solomon (1982) reaches the same conclusion from his work with autoimmune illness:

> The onset of disease occurs either after a period of psychological stress, such as loss of a significant person, or after the interruption of the ability to maintain previously successful patterns of adaptation and defense. Rapidity of progression of disease, degree of incapacity by disease, and lack of response to treatment in autoimmune disease in our work have all been shown to be related to failure of psychological defenses and concomitant anxiety, depression and alienation. (p. 4)

These remarks summarise the generally agreed status of psychological defenses as offering protection against the potentially destructive impact of stress (see also Cobb, 1974). On the model of social behaviour developed in this book, one class of psychological defenses—those involved with the conscious, active side of life—can be equated with the level of social support and again defined simply as justified action. The person who prays is ritualistically confirming his or her membership of a religious community and psychologically reasserting a right to the world of meanings contained in its doctrinal theories and talk. The person who intellectualises is doing effectively the same thing. The latter, in turning to accredited forms of argument, cements a link with the "rational" community and re-establishes his or her title to the language games and roles that it supports.

Repression and denial, involving the selective exclusion of material from conscious awareness, are forms of psychological defense belonging to a different logical class. For this reason they require a different kind of explanation. The theory of social behaviour that I have developed is essentially a theory of consciously intended action and deliberate talk. As such, it is not directly concerned with the hidden workings of the unconscious mind. The processes of repression and denial are, by definition, not deliberate and mainly not accountable. They imply a level of control beyond the sphere of conscious volition and they must therefore be represented in a different style of theory: one incorporating a model of causes and effects. Freud's theory of repression, while difficult to assign to a particular logical category, relies to some extent on energy-flow and energy-conservation metaphors and involves the workings of unconscious deterministic forces (Peters, 1958). Unconscious mechanisms may supply the process of rational justification and cultural location by, for example, blurring or blotting out memories, but unconscious moves of any kind are by their nature id-like and not reflexive.

Some forms of mental illness, especially those expressing themselves in delusional fantasy, are widely believed to represent exaggerated, out-of-hand versions of normal adaptive defenses. It is possible for an individual to remain in a delusional state for a considerable period of time but nevertheless stay physically healthy. Indeed, it is known that with the notable exception of tuberculosis, schizophrenics are unusually resistant to a wide range of physical illnesses and physical assaults (Huxley, Mayr, Osmond, and Hoffer, 1964). Some authors have even reported a contradictory relation between physical and psychiatric symptoms in their patients. Symptoms of physical illness start to apppar when the psychiatric condition improves, and vice versa (e.g., Appel and Rosen, 1950; Weblin, 1963). It has been suggested that certain psychiatric states can function as a protection against physical illness (Doust, 1952).

I have defined psychological defense and social support broadly in terms of actions endowed with meaning through their context of shared justification. But with whom does the paranoid share his or her delusional world? His or her actions and beliefs are diagnosed as abnormal precisely because they are not part of any consensus. The delusional web that the paranoid weaves is often very elaborate and highly consistent but, to the rest of us, it is not based on fact. The paranoid is alone in the main justification around which his or her life is organised; that he or she is being persecuted or is a special agent of the cosmos. Nobody agrees with the claim, so we say it is false or illusory. It is even possible that the perceptual disorders and hallucinations that sometimes accompany these fantastic schemes compensate for the absence of social support by furnishing the paranoid with what to him or her counts as objective proof of the delusional conviction.

In a sense, psychologically, the paranoid's defensive strategy can be reckoned a success. Within the context of his or her delusion the paranoid achieves a systematic basis for justified action. Except for the fact that his or her main premise is shared by no-one else, the paranoid's beliefs are rational and the actions are meaningful. They support a nest of goals, projects, and ambitions that have a coherent logic about them. It is perfectly sensible for someone who is being poisoned to be wary of food that is offered, or for someone on the receiving end of a beam of X-rays to seek cover and to wear protective clothing.

What above all distinguishes delusional from normal belief systems is their completely non-negotiable quality. No amount of argument or persuasion can talk the committed paranoid out of it. Yet even this is not the whole story because the same can be said of religious fanatics and political extremists. Both these categories of people are at the centre of a magnetic field that repels all opposite charge in the form of negotiative initiatives. Both are shielded by a highly developed insular rhetoric which is esoteric and axiomatically incommensurable with other forms of talk. At the school carol service each year I remember listening attentively to the passage from the beginning of St. John's Gospel in which St. John "unfolds the mystery," hoping that my mind—now 1 year older—would at last give me the key to this important yet baffling explanatory text. I never got what I wanted of course, because the account I sought was of a different order to the rarified doctrinal one I was given. A person can only know what that text means if he or she *is* a Christian in the fullest and most committed sense.

Christians, in common with most religious orders, count on their teachings having some practical application in the world. There is an obligation to cull from the Scriptures a moral code. In this task, academic theologians confront a number of scriptural inconsistencies and moral doctrinal dilemmas. These too are dealt with rhetorically. The most intractable problems are assigned to the category of "mysteries" (e.g., Owen, 1969). Esoteric, non-negotiable categories are the last resort of every committed order when pressed by outside sources to commensurate their concerns with those of other discourses; when asked to explain to others what their theories *mean.* In the case of political extremists, they take the form of those slippery worthies, "freedom," "liberty," and so on. Non-negotiable words are the ultimate in psychological defense. They armour-plate a moral system by making it irrefutable.

But religious and politically extremist explanatory schemes both differ in an important respect from that of the paranoid. Their structures of beliefs, though irrefutable, and their languages, though non-translatable, are not just the property of one solitary individual but are shared by a community of people. Negotiability and consensus can be drawn as the vectors in a 2 by 2 table (see Figure 8.1). In the non-negotiable, non-shared category fall the delusional personality, into which category we might put certain types of messiahs and dictators: the sort convinced of their own uniqueness in having private access to an absolute authority. Their delusional conviction itself supplies a rich justificatory scheme and insulates them from social criticism. St. Joan was able to fly in the face of all her counsellors and advisors by listening to her "voices."

In the non-negotiable category where there is some sharing of beliefs fall evangelists, political extremists, and other entrenched ideologists. Strictly speaking, there may be some negotiation between individual members of these groups, but so far as the rest of the world is concerned, the community is a closed shop. Most social institutions concerned with the practicalities and expressive projects of everyday life, including ordinary conversation, fall into the category of shared–negotiable. Personal creative projects are

	Negotiable	Non-negotiable
Shared	Individuals involved in the practical and expressive projects of everyday life	Religious evangelists Political extremists Entrenched ideologists
Unshared	Artists Creators of new forms	Delusional personalities (Dictators) (Messiahs)

Figure 8.1 Negotiability and consensus in human activity.

included in the category of non-shared and negotiable. The latter are negotiable because they are not independent of history and of other contemporary expressions of a particular form. These projects are also of course negotiable on the more basic level that they set themselves up to be praised or criticised, accepted or rejected, as a result of public consensus.

In the following sections I discuss some practical implications of the ideas developed in this book from the point of view of the individual and from the point of view of social planning. Let me start by restating the main arguments.

Summary of the Main Arguments

Mankind's inherited socialness is the key to health and survival, both as a species and, ipso facto, as individual men and women. The development of language has shifted the axis of this socialness away from hand-to-hand cooperation in physically bounded groups to behaviour of a symbolic nature. I have referred to this symbolic behaviour as made up of acts and actions performed within a context of justification. Included in this category are illocutionary acts. Justified action has a functional role. It serves to locate the individual in the social order and in so doing gives him or her a role and an identity and also a sense of purpose. Justified actions are thus different from habitual actions, or "behaviours," in that they involve accountability to a rule or convention invoked by the community or some part of it. When we talk about an act being "meaningful" we are referring to the extent to which it is held accountable. One can envisage gradations of accountability representing shades of meaning. For example, failing to do the washing up probably will not carry the same meaning as walking out of a board meeting.

Justifications are the property of conversations and conversations the property of discourses. Justifications, conversations, and discourses are the constitution of alliances, groups, and communities. Justifying is necessarily exclusive and oppositional in nature. Its implicit effect is to bind the individual to one moral order by elaborating the boundaries and contradistinctions between this moral order and others.

Systems of Support

From the preceding summary we can deduce that to survive in the jungle of our social world and to live in a reasonably healthy state it is necessary to maintain a certain level of justified action. The stronger the system of justification the more effectively the individual can be said to be coping with life. Figure 8.1 illustrates the point that for a system of justification to be strong it does not necessarily have to be widely shared. The fever of national pride in times of war and the strange theories of religious splinter groups are equally efficacious protective systems. In the first case there are more people to talk to who share the same commitment and in the second, supportive conversational partners are fewer but a greater proportion of time is spent in their company.

On the other hand, highly esoteric supportive systems, their complement of members being small, are less stable than more general ones, and so contain an element of risk that the latter do not. The danger on the horizon for the very locally committed individual lies in the possibility that his or her social source could disappear overnight. The psychological consequences of such a thing happening are clearly more serious for the person whose commitment is singular and all-absorbing than for one with additional, more diversified interests. At its tiniest the "community" can comprise no more than two people—husband and wife perhaps—whose closeness achieves expression in esoteric ways of speaking: the "silly talk" that springs up and is kept incomprehensible to outsiders, exclusive to and defining of the micro-community. Wittgenstein argues convincingly for the impossibility of private (i.e., completely individual) languages. Maybe the closest thing to a private language is to be found in the curious turns of phrase and twists of syntax that characterise the special talk of close living partners.

Two general dimensions of social behaviour, or, as I have called it, justification, can be distinguished, although I think the distinction in the end turns out to be a superficial one: accountable acts involving the physical manipulation of materials, and talk. The individual's belonging to a particular social order (and non-belonging to others) is signified through these.

It was with these thoughts in mind that I made a study at Oxford of 25 men, aged 40–60, who had recently suffered a first myocardial infarction (Totman, 1979a). I was interested in finding out about any changes in the lives of these men during the year preceding the first onset of symptoms that may have affected the enduring goals, projects, ambitions, and social liasons that made up their lives. I wanted to see if their reactions to the things that had happened to them over this period could be characterised as the failure of justification.

A rather free-ranging questioning procedure, loosely based on the semi-structured interview developed by Brown and his colleagues (Brown and Harris, 1978) was used to get an idea of the events that had precipitated changes in the pattern of the men's daily lives over the pre-morbid year. A rough biography of each man's main interests, aspirations, and social contacts was assembled and the significance of every life event that came to light was assessed against this. Specifically, each person was questioned at considerable length to discover the amount of change resulting from a given event in terms of the net amount of time spent (a) actively involved in doing or planning goal-directed activities—projects with a definable (i.e., socially constituted) end, and (b) actively involved in conversation with others.

If the outcome of a particular event was a net drop in amount of time spent in either (a) or (b) this was scored as a minus number corresponding to the number of hours per week decline, on average, as far as this could be gauged from people's accounts. If the outcome was a net increase in either (a) or (b), this was scored as a plus score. The assumption of the study was that these scores were negatively related to the threat to health entailed by the stressful event. Care was taken to account all the changes in routine following a given event. For example, if the individual was a keen gardener and pub-goer and had moved during the year in question he would not only be asked how much more or less gardening and pub-going he did, but also whether he did more or less of other things besides, and whether he spent more or less time than before chatting with others. In this way a kind of diary of life before and after each event was reconstructed, and the event's impact was gauged in terms of the changes in pattern of living which it brought about. Scores arrived at for each event thus represented an overall gain (positive numbers) or an overall loss (negative numbers) of meaningful (i.e., justified) action in a person's life attributable to that event. Scores obtained for all events were arithmetically summed to give a final cumula-

Table 8.1

The 10 Most Negative Scorers in the Myocardial Infarction Group

Individual	Score	Associated life event
Mr. P.	−22.5	Made redundant because of injury to hand
Mr. D.	−17.0	Conclusion of major work project; daughter left home
Mr. H.	−15.5	Returned from overseas
Mr. W.	−15.5	Forced to change jobs
Mr. T.	−13.5	Reorganisation at work—fewer duties; mother died; eldest daughter left home
Mr. N.	−13.0	Major row with wife; friends moved away
Mr. S.	−5.0	Dog died
Mr. S.	−4.0	Sister died
Mr. S.	−4.0	Mother-in-law died
Mr. H.	−3.0	Son left home

tive index of gain or loss of meaning during the pre-morbid year. Laborious though this procedure is, it proved possible to apply it to gain a rough insight into the significance of life events along the dimensions I have identified as theoretically significant for health.

The same procedure was also followed with a group of healthy men of similar age attending the same hospital with minor non-degenerative complaints (polyps, etc). While the average number of "stressful life events" discovered was roughly the same in both groups, their impact appeared to be different in the case of the heart patients than in that of the healthy men. Heart patients showed both a net reduction in the amount of time spent chatting with others and a net reduction in goal-directed activities attributable to the events that they recounted. This was not so for the healthy men. The 10 negative scores in the heart group and the events which gave rise to them are listed in Table 8.1. Most of these events were circumstances over which it can be assumed the individual did not have much direct control. The possibility that the events themselves were the result of pre-clinical morbidity can therefore be largely discounted.

Solitary Social Sources

I do not hold this up to be a particularly good piece of research—even as research of this kind goes. The scoring procedure is very crude. But some interesting biographical detail came from talking to the men which illustrates the danger inherent in solitary sources of social involvement. It was noticeable that several of the high negative scorers (the at-risk men) led rather restrictive lives, having one major preoccupation—usually their job—and comparatively few alternative interests, hobbies and social contacts. The two highest scorers had both been cut off from their work. In the case of Mr. D., a welder employed by a small firm of metal formers, a 5-year contract for the manufacture of heavy doors for use in underground mines, involving regular overtime and working weekends, had come to an end. His firm's order book was not full and the workforce was placed on a normal working week, with little to do even during this time. Mr. D. was single-mindedly committed to his work. Unsolicited, I was shown an album of photographs of the metal structures the firm had produced that he had worked on. He was married, as far as I could make out had no hobbies, and his daughter had recently left home. The surplus time that he found he had was spent doing "nothing in particular;" sleeping more, switching on the T.V., sitting around at work and so forth.

Changes in pattern of exercise, diet, smoking, financial worries, and such may have contributed to the cause of this man's infarction. However, applying Occam's razor, it seems unlikely that any of these possibilities can explain all the cases in Table 8.1 as effectively as loss of meaning, calculated as a drop in the net amount of time spent in justificatory activity.

This example illustrates the hazards of a single, strong commitment. The trouble comes when the opportunity for acting on it suddenly disappears. Antonovsky (1974) says what amounts to the same thing in his proposal that having more than one social role in life contributes to the "resistance resources" of an individual. It is well known that in western developed countries the rate of non-psychotic psychiatric illness is much higher among women than it is among men. The traditional role for women as housewives and minders of children is both very restrictive and also under the cloud of at least partial termination when the children leave home.

Work and Monotony

One particularly important consideration in the design of an adaptive and healthy style of life was not addressed in the study of heart patients just described. This has to do with jobs and roles becoming monotonous. Repetitive and routine activities, exciting at first because of their novelty, can very quickly pall. We tend to say that such tasks lose their meaning, or that they become meaningless. On the social model I have put forward this can be represented as the disintegration of justified action into habit, or mere behaviour. The missing ingredient in a dull and repetitive project is sufficient oppositional structure to enable justification. Over time the socialness—the accountability—of such tasks, if there ever was any, drains away, leaving them void of that quality that supplies psychological well-being and health. Routine work becomes less of an activity than a decisionless, mechanical, virtually unconscious performance.

Kohn (1969, 1976) and Kohn and Schooler (1978), from their research on work conditions, have deduced a relation between the "subjective complexity" of work and a person's "psychological functioning," by which they mean his or her general ability to cope with the world. Their definition of "subjective complexity" as the extent to which work requires thought and independent judgment is similar to my idea of justified action. Kohn regards the individual's orientation at work as a major determinant of his or her sense of self and general bearing. He concludes that subjective complexity is the most important aspect of work. Kohn's theory gets support from other research on work conditions. Alfredsson, Karasek, and Theorell (1982) studied all cases of myocardial infarction in men aged under 65 years who were living in the greater Stockholm area between 1974 and 1976. The work environment of infarction victims was compared with that of healthy men, matched for age and area of residence. Shift work and monotony were both associated with excess risk. Hectic work was not on its own associated with excess risk, but in combination with low decision latitude and/or few possibilities for progression, it was. The authors of ths study state that a link between low decision latitude and heart disease and hypertension has also been established in male American workers.

While studies of work broadly agree about what is important in working conditions, it should be kept in mind that the key concepts, subjective complexity, decision latitude, and monotony, are not free of normative assumptions. What represents a challenging and involving level of complexity for one person may be quite intolerable to another; hence, presumably, the "subjective" in subjective complexity. But how can we assess subjective complexity without asking individuals themselves how they find their work? Being a subjective matter, complexity does not lend itself to standard measurement ipso facto. From an ethogenic perspective, and from the perspective of the arguments in this book, the descriptors subjective complexity, decision latitude, and absence of monotony all come down to the same thing: the extent to which the work itself is embedded in a system of justification; in other words, the extent to which its structure contains oppositional relations making the end product accountable.

Letting People Talk

What further observations can be made about society and social planning with regard to the psychological well-being (and, hence, physical health) of the individual? Starting from the premise that action and talk are integral and inseparable elements of adaptive living, one point that springs to mind is the importance for physically incapacitated people—the sick, the old, and the handicapped—of being able to talk and being listened to. The scope for physical action in such people is limited. For some, the only kinds of acts left open to them are illocutionary ones. In social work with the elderly the value of allowing old people to reminisce and theorize is well recognised (Butler, 1964). Hospices for the terminally ill traditionally welcome visitors and encourage them to stay and chat with residents. The therapeutic effect of visitors to patients undergoing hospital treatment seems to be credited in some hospitals more than others. In the more traditional wards there is still a tendency for visitors to be regarded as an interference with the real business of healing through physical intervention.

Choice and Accountability as Therapy

"Alternative" Treatments

In Chapter 4 an analogy was drawn between a style of life which, through the repetition and stagnation of activities, becomes increasingly monotonous and meaningless and the naturally increasing entropy of a closed system. The way out of this depressing degeneration, it was suggested, is through justified action. From the concepts of choice and justification that were elaborated, it was reckoned that a decision such as that of a successful merchant banker to leave the world of finance and go and subsist on a farm, carries with it a heavy burden of justification and so marks a sharp reduction in the entropy of the "system." In other words, it represents a big decision. Big decisions, it might be supposed, are the appropriate medicine in advanced cases of existential meaninglessness to get a person out of the sort of psychological rut that can end in illness and even death. This principle often seems to be implicit in the practices of "alternative" medicine, especially in those which specifically set out to treat the "mind" rather than the body. The Bristol Cancer Health Centre, recently the subject of a BBC television documentary, is among the few such establishments currently operating in Britain. One of their most successful cases, a women with breast cancer, had this to say on her return to work as a hospital sister:

> I think all my life, really, I've always done what other people wanted me to do. I grew up in an environment where I was brought up really strictly and I went to school where they were very strict and expected me to behave in a certain way which I did, although I didn't agree with it. But I went along with it. And then I grew up and I went nursing and the same thing followed me there. And then I got married and my husband and my children expected me to behave in a certain way. And now I've shed all that and I'm living how *I* wanted to live all my life but never dared to. So I feel free to do that now. . . . I'd rather live the way I do now than I did before. (British Broadcasting Corporation, 1983)

Could this case, along with the findings of research on work and working conditions, be explained in terms of Seligman's theory of loss of control and helplessness? (Abramson et al., 1978; Garber and Seligman, 1980). The concept of helplessness as attributed lack of control certainly captures some of what is going on. But it is not on its own enough. In one sense it is fair to say that the speaker of this passage has exercised control at every stage in her life; control not only over everyday matters—her domestic and hospital work—but control over whether she became a nurse, whether she married, and so on. Similarly, it could be said that a worker standing by a conveyor belt sorting eggs into different sizes has full control over what he or she is doing. Neither of these individuals is properly described as helpless because they are most likely carrying out their respective duties quite effectively. It is not the lack of control per se that is the problem. Control over what? The problem is rather the greyness of the role itself and the lack of oppositional structure in its sanctified tasks. What for one person counts as a crushingly tedious existence may indeed for another be infused with colour and meaning. To know which is the case we must ask the people themselves, listening not for one of a number of pre-ordained categories of "attribution," but for the specialist, rhetorical—i.e., oppositional—talk that is the mark of a prolific system of justification and the lowering of entropy. The alienation of the suburban housewife and the assembly-line operator is ultimately an exile from the *process* of moral accountability.

Interest in alternative treatments would seem to be on the increase. To what extent can we interpret their practices in general terms according to the justification-commitment-involvement argument? It must be remembered that, by definition, none of these alternative practices is "normal" in the West in the sense of being an institution with government and legal backing like physical medicine. Many are not even reckoned by mainstream practitioners to be respectable. The decision on the part of the individual to seek treatment from one of these sources is therefore likely to be a big one. It is not like going to the doctor or being taken to hospital. It constitutes more of an act. In the language of the theory of social life I have put forward this decision is rich in justification and full of meaning. The decision itself may represent a significant injection of negative entropy into the system.

Consider those forms of group therapy in which the individual becomes part of a community of other individuals who have also opted for the same off-beat, perhaps even disapproved, form of treatment. What is being offered in these circumstances is, in a sense, psychologically, the best of all possible worlds: an initial difficult decision pregnant with justification, a programme of ritualised activity to cement the commitment, and a separatist community offering scope for extended justification in joint action and in conversation. The essential ingredient of social belonging—participation in a local community through the justificatory elaboration of its boundaries and oppositional structures—is present under these conditions in good quantity.

In my analysis, it does not matter what form the treatment takes, whether it involves acupuncture, biofeedback, spiritual healing, or whatever. From outside, through, as it were, an anthropologist's eye, the procedure itself is an artifact, a ritual, and like rituals its form is arbitrary (see Harré, 1979). What matters is the change in direction that participation implies and the new supportive network that either explicitly or implicitly is brought to bear. Health is restored, if it is, as the by-product of a new social and psychological identity. Faith healers are sometimes heard to remark that their best results are with non-believers. A much heavier burden of justification hangs on the non-believer's decision to seek spiritual healing than is the case with the believer.

Primitive and Historical Cures

How do primitive and historical cures measure up to this analysis? Their devices seem strange to contemporary scientific men and women, and Shapiro (1959) has pointed out that very few pre-scientific treatments contained any specific organic effect for the condition being treated. Prescientific treatments in Europe cannot be said to offer counter-normal choices in the way that present-day alternative treatments do because there was no such thing as normal, accredited medical practice. But there were a wide variety of cures from which to choose and it is a striking fact that almost universally they were either highly unpleasant or very demanding. Built into every remedy was some kind of difficulty. The sick confronted an alarming array of expensive, time-consuming, painful, disgusting, and downright dangerous administrations (Shapiro, 1959; Totman, 1979). Going on a pilgrimage was one option. This represented no small investment of money, time, and effort, especially when the pilgrims had to travel a long distance to the shrine. Janet in 1925 noted that a long and arduous pilgrimage to Lourdes was reputedly conducive to a cure and that cures were rarely reported among the local inhabitants.

There is a tradition of privation in tribal medicine too, stemming from the belief in a connection between the potency of a cure and the violence associated with it. One common belief was that the strength of a wild animal could be transfered to a sick person in medicines containing parts of the animal. Shamans often demanded sacrifices and harsh penances from the patient or his or her kin, the most extreme example being cures that required a human sacrifice. It is not overstating the case to say that where there were choices in historical and tribal treatments, the options could not have been better designed to maximise the level of commitment and potential justification of the would-be patient.

I am suggesting that the psychological principle on which therapies with no specific organic effect are based is the same. All of them are geared to reintegrating the individual within the community by involving him or her in action with a heavy overlay of justification.

Horwitz (1982), on the other hand, following a line of argument charted by Reiff (1966) and Scheff (1966, 1974), draws a sharp distinction between group and individualistically styled therapies. He argues from the general premise that the style of therapy that is prevalent in a community reflects the dominant ideological persuasion of that community. Therapy is seen as institutionalised social control. Therapy in tribal groups often takes place in the presence of the family and maybe other members of the community and is surrounded by ritual emphasising the ascendancy of the collective and the subjugation of the individual. Psychoanalysis, on the other hand, Horowitz argues, stresses the private, unique nature of the individual. In the one-to-one confidentiality of the consulting room all moral censors are removed:

> Finally, the therapeutic process itself becomes a private relationship between the patient and the therapist that is an oasis from the social world, rather than a communal affair mobilizing the energies of the community. . . . psychoanalytic therapy reflects the development of an individualistic society and the liberation of the individual from the ties of the communal group. (Horwitz, 1982, p. 170)

Horowitz believes that psychoanalysis has flourished in America because modern American society is a paradigm of individualism. Its achievement, in direct contrast with tribal therapy, is the freeing of the individual, finally, from the shackles of the community.

Adequate though this distinction may be as a description of different cultural practices, I do not consider it is of much psychological importance. For individualism is itself a cult and its proponents, along with the proponents of every other strong cause, are to be heard shouting those old perennials—liberty, freedom, and independence—from the rooftops. The following passage gives the lie to the distinction: "The goal of analytic therapy is to achieve autonomy for patients and to allow them to regulate their lives by norms of their own choosing. In dramatic contrast with communal therapy, analytic therapy affirms no values beyond the self, but only the value of personal independence" (Horwitz, 1982, p. 173).

In "choosing the norms" by which to "regulate his life," Horwitz's patient, just like the recipient of the communal therapy he contrasts, moves from a state of normlessness, or non-belonging, to a state of affiliation, or integration. Horwitz's mistake is in failing to realise that the end result of analytic therapy is exactly the same as that of the tribal shamanism that he sees as having been superceded. Both, if they are successful, in fact work by reintegrating the individual back into the social community. The only difference between the two is the nature of the community and the form of the ritual by which this is done. Symbolism and sorcery are the ritual of tribal methods; attributed choice is the ritual of analytic ones. His own stake in the American way of life holds Horwitz within the rhetorical scheme he is attempting to analyse and compare.

Group Therapy

Therapy groups, encounter groups, and training groups (better known as T-groups) have become increasingly popular in recent years. The differently named groups have different emphases but all of them rely on a small number of individuals allowing themselves to be closeted together for a fixed period of time. Talking freely and openly, even aggressively, is encouraged. Kovel (p. 218) sums up what is involved:

> When one is enmeshed in group life, the outside world fades away, the constraints of reality vanish, and less adulterated forms of our inner selves clamber on to the stage. Loyalties reminiscent of groups in war, whose members would unhesitatingly die for one another; raptures comparable to those of the monastery; jealousies forgotten since age four; power plays worthy of a Borgia; tender intimacy one could never muster with one's spouse—it can all be summoned up within the group. (Reprinted with permission from J. Kovel, *A Complete Guide to Therapy*. © 1981, Pantheon Books, a Division of Random House, Inc.)

Groups of this kind are by their nature exclusive and the talk that is done in them has a ready-made us–them, insider–outsider quality about it. They represent a closed order within which the negotiation of individual accounts is encouraged and a common perspective sometimes forged. The members may not from the start agree to agree with each other but, almost as a condition of membership, they do agree to play the same language games for the duration. These are displayed in the emergence of cliquish personal references and in the common rhetorical ground that develops as the sessions wear on. In this way the group behaves rather like an incipient social organism. Those that have had experience of such groups are impressed by the powerful forces that develop in them and the sense of oneness and belonging that the group can bring. Individuals often express a strong sense of personal loss when the group is dissolved.

The Self-sufficient Person

Active participation in a group, be it formally convened like a T-group or informally constituted like the family, has a health-protecting function. In Antonovsky's terms it helps foster a sense of coherence (Antonovsky, 1979). Doing things together, whether in talk or in manipulative action, creates and maintains a local social order. But this is not the only way in which the individual can affirm his or her social identity. The theory I have put forward must also be able to accommodate the loner; the individual who lives most of the time physically and verbally isolated from other people. My argument is predicated on the notion that a person's socialness is the key to his or her health and survival. Where then does the socialness of the recluse lie? The answer I would venture is that it lies in the things he or she does: in action. In my hypothesis, it would not be possible for a recluse to survive completely apart from other people without an absorbing project of some kind. Moreover, there are grounds for supposing that the solitary activities that fill the recluse's life are activities whose value is widely endorsed, like gardening, painting, or worshipping. In other words, the systems of justification exploited in sustained solitary activity have to be strong and firmly rooted in culturally historic practices. The justification of an artist working alone, for example, consists at least in part in a dedicated reaction against what are perceived as stale conservative forms. His or her system of social support is the body of opinion that recognises and respects art as a dynamic and innovative enterprise.

Social Change

Finally, and perhaps the most difficult of all issues to address from the perspective of social policymaking, is the condition of opposition within the global social structure. I have tried to show that this condition is both a psychological and a biological necessity, for opposition is the key to justification and justification the key to health and survival. How can we even entertain the possibility of building this condition into policy decisions without an abiding moral contradiction?

One uncontroversial statement that can be made about the social world is that it does not stand still. Categories, moralities, roles, and styles are constantly changing and the transformations that change brings about themselves generate oppositional structure within the macro-community (new versus old, modern versus old-fashioned, fresh versus stale, revolutionary versus reactionary, etc.). In a sense, social change can be thought of as the ultimate and the only ever-present source of new justificatory schemes. So, can we look for some kind of meta social order, even for a superordinate morality, tied to the idea of change itself?

Obviously, the roles and rules of a society must not be so plastic that they are unrecognisable from one day to the next. There must be continuity and a degree of stability. Once again, it is a matter of balance and an optimum rate of change. What counts as an optimum rate of change itself depends on a variety of factors, among the most important of which are the scale of social divisions and the speed of dissemination of new forms. Both have grown so fast in mankind's recent history as to radically shift the axes of the criteria for change and opposition. For nearly 2 million years oppositional structure was contained within what are by present-day standards microscopic geographical arenas. In small hunter–gatherer communities it found expression in feuds between neighbouring tribes and in local scales of honour and respect. About 2000 years ago in Europe the emergence (and subsequent demise) of some much larger-scale speech communities was evident. Conflicts between cultures for a time became grander affairs and the hierarchies of roles within these classical civilisations more complex. Today, there is still some scope for local as well as nationalistic opposition in sport and other institutionalised competitive pastimes. But there is a growing and increasingly alarming tendency, at least in the industrially sophisticated world, for it to be funnelled into the global tension that we know as the East–West divide. Perhaps this can be put down to enormously improved lines of travel and communication. Rapid communication means that roles, moralities, and styles *within* each of the huge communities comprising the two sides of this divide are becoming more commensurable across states and even across nations. Capital cities in the West are becoming increasingly cosmopolitan and increasingly similar. All over the West as a result of economic pressure one sees local traditions turned into mere sideshows for tourists. The blame for this wholesale homogenisation must be laid at the doors of the coercive institutions at the centres of each of the respective sides: the state in the East and big business in the West. The political and economic dangers of progressive de-localisation are too well known to require further comment (see Schumacher's prize-winning book *Small Is Beautiful,* 1973). The psychological dangers, I believe, are less well appreciated. Every time two social categories are collapsed into one; every time an act of commensuration is performed under the banners of fairness, equality, liberty, and so on, local oppositional structure is lost and the scope for meaningful (i.e., justified) action at a local level is diminished. This can be watched in the growing feeling of political powerlessness and pawnishness among ordinary voters as well as in the growth of terrorist splinter groups throughout the western world. Politicians are at pains to insist that every individual's vote counts, but of course under present systems of representation it rarely if ever does.

There is one circumstance, however, in which oppositional structure and the scope for justification does not dilute with the collapsing of two social categories into one. This is when the combinatorial act is counter-balanced by a fresh act of division, thereby creating new, morally less repugnant categories simultaneously with the dismantling of old ones.

The Women's Movement provides a good example of this kind of counter-balancing social change. Feminists seek to destroy the historical distinction between men and women as it arises in the literature, art, and speech of most cultures. Their discovery is that biological differences are not a necessary basis for social ones. The success of this movement is its achievement in blurring the old practical and expressive differences and establishing less discriminatory attitudes toward women, especially in respect of work and power. In doing this, however, a new opposition has been set up to replace the old one; namely, the contrast between feminists and traditionalists. The new distinction is apparent in the growth of feminist literature, in feminist art forms, and in new vocabularies and ways of speaking that have quietly entered ordinary conversational talk—in short, in all the innovations of form and style that spin off from the movement. Traditionalists might want to argue that these do not add up to very much and that the whole business is a fad, but it must be remembered that the same is said whenever new ideas pave the way for cultural change and fresh expressive opportunities. It is true there is a great deal of groupiness and band-waggoning in the feminist movement but again this seems to be the case in respect of any new form that is at all well publicised.

The psychologically vital ingredient of opposition within the macro-community is preserved through creative aspects of projects (such as the Women's Movement) that are not solely given over to the collapsing of existing categories but are also involved with the generation of new oppositional forms. The point about social change of this progressive kind is that it supplies new fields of justification as well as knocking down old ones. With the passage of time the new order itself will probably pass into disrepute and provide a springboard for fresh radicalisms and changes. Such a continuing dynamic is the perpetual fons et origo of justification. To stifle it is to stifle meaning, to court entropy and, because of the link there seems to be between socialness and health, literally to go against life itself.

Epilogue

The arguments of this book are based on the by no means original idea that the rules and institutions of human societies inhere in language: in forms of talk that groups of people share. Wittgenstein's insistance on the impossibility of private languages prepares the way for a theory that represents the social world as constructed between individuals through common speaking practices. The role of language emphasised in this approach is not so much as a medium for transmitting information but as the means of establishing, sustaining, and changing social order.

I would not want to claim that talk is all there is to social life. Visual and tactile signals, ignored in this presentation, are clearly of great importance in people's lives. A lot can be said in a silent gesture or a look. Yet I wonder how far these non-verbal forms of signalling would be able to develop in the absence of a linguistic ability. We can often tell when a dog is angry, hurt, or even jealous but there is nothing like the same degree of subtle complexity in the gestures and facial expressions of non-verbal species as there is in humans. It is hard to imagine a dog *intending* something by its expression.

Searle claims that anything that can be meant can be said. His argument, and my own experience of the social world, lead me to suspect that the efficacy of non-verbal signalling of an intention depends on possession of at least the competence if not the performance component of a language—*la langue* of Saussure. Languages contain an enormous repetoire of qualifiers by which the meaning in gestures and facial expressions can be described. There is some empirical backing for the prepotency of language in the fact that script writers can communicate in words to actors nuances of movement and expression every bit as intricate as those of real life.

In saying that human socialness rests on characteristic ways of speaking and strategies of justifying, and in arguing that the social world is composite and its elements incommensurable, I suppose I can be accused of an extreme form of relativism. I do not deny this challenge but would seek to defend the notion of social relativism from its critics. The main criticism is that a thoroughgoing relativism is incompatible with the taking of any kind of a moral stand. Relativist theories of truth can seem repugnant because they seem inherently to imply amorality and to mock the possibility of personal betterment through striving toward moral goals.

It will be clear, I hope, from the arguments in the last two chapters of this book that I do not share this latter view. In fact, I have tried to argue exactly the opposite. The criticism of relativism as amoral rests on the assumption that a moral base is to be found in one particular discoursive framework. It denies that the social world is pluralistic—that there can be equally valid, incommensurable constructions of truth—and relies on the promise of one isolated and immutable set of transcendental rules by which eventually all standards of truth and falsity may come to be judged. Rorty (1980) and Feyerabend (1981), I believe, have convincingly shown that any system claiming transcendental status for itself, be it religion, science, or epistemology, has ended up merely glorifying its own procedures and systematically closing off the possibility of reflexion by propagandising and institutionalising its own rhetoric.

But we like to think of ourselves as moral agents and there is no argument in all this for why we should not do so. Some sociobiologists are claiming that there is an inherited capacity for moral behaviour in human beings. If the expression of morality is to be found anywhere I would suggest it is not in any particular institution but rather in the dynamic of social change itself; in the *process* of negotiation. But to imagine the outcome of successful negotiation to be simply the reconciliation of opposite views is to miss the vital point that creative negotiation itself produces fresh oppositions. The version of morality as a dynamic of constructive change is, I believe, truer than the psychologically impossible (indeed, thoroughly dangerous) idealism of working toward some ultimate commensurability and uniformity.

The champions of any moral order that calls itself absolute would do well to remember that their moral system can itself only arise as a contradistinction. Gods cannot do without devils or science without magic. To shift the argument one meta-level and say that morality lies in the discoursive process itself is to see any particular social order as no more than a provisional stage in this process. The absolutist tries to stand outside the discourse, but the relativist sees himself or herself as part of it.

References

Abelson, R. (1977). *Persons: A Study in Philosophical Psychology*. London: Macmillan.

Abelson, R. P., Aronson, E., McGuire, W. J., Newcomb, T. M., Rosenberg, M. J. and Tannenbaum, P. H. (1968). *Theories of Cognitive Consistency: A Sourcebook*. Chicago: Rand McNally.

Abramson, L. Y., Seligman, M. E. P. and Teasdale, J. D. (1978). Learned helplessness in humans: critique and reformulation. *Journal of Abnormal Psychology,* 87, 49–74.

Abse, D. W., Wilkins, M. M., van de Castle, R. L., Buxton, W. D., Demars, J-P, Brown, R. S., and Kirschner, L. G. (1974). Personality and behavioral characteristics of lung cancer patients. *Journal of Psychosomatic Research,* 18, 101–113.

Ackerman, S. H., Manaker, S. and Cohen, M. I. (1981). Recent separation and the onset of peptic ulcer disease in older children and adolescents. *Psychosomatic Medicine,* 43, 305–310.

Ader, R. (1981). *Psychoneuroimmunology*. New York: Academic Press.

Ader, R. (1983). Psychoneuroimmunology. In *Breakdown in Human Adaptation to Stress. Towards a Multidisciplinary Approach II. Proceedings of the E.E.C. Workshop on Psychoneuroimmunology, Utrecht.* The Hague: Martinus Nijhoff.

Ader, R. and Cohen, N. (1981). Conditioned immunopharmacologic responses. In R. Ader (Ed.) *Psychoneuroimmunology*. New York: Academic Press.

Adler, H. M. and Hammett, V. B. (1973). The doctor–patient relationship revisited. An analysis of the placebo effect. *Annals of Internal Medicine,* 78, 595–598.

Alexander, F., French, T. M. and Pollock, G. H. (1968). *Psychosomatic Specificity.* Chicago: University of Chicago Press.

Alfredsson, L., Karasek, R. and Theorell, T. (1982). Myocardial infarction risk and psychosocial work environment: an analysis of the male Swedish working force. *Social Science and Medicine,* 16, 463–467.

Amkraut, A. and Solomon, G. F. (1975). From the symbolic stimulus to the pathophysiological response: immune mechanisms. *International Journal of Psychiatry in Medicine,* 5, 541–563.

Antaki, C. (Ed.) (1981). *The Psychology of Ordinary Explanations of Social Behaviour.* London: Academic Press.

Antaki, C. (1982). A brief introduction to attribution and attributional theories. In C. Antaki and C. Brewin (Eds.) *Attributions and Psychological Change.* London: Academic Press.

Antaki, C. and Brewin, C. (Eds.) (1982). *Attributions and Psychological Change.* London: Academic Press.

Antonovsky, A. (1979). *Health, Stress and Coping.* San Francisco: Josey-Bass.

Appel, J. and Rosen, S. R. (1950). Psychotic factors in psychosomatic illness. *Psychosomatic Medicine,* 12, 236–243.

Argyle, M., Furnham, A. and Graham, J. A. (1981). *Social Situations.* Cambridge: Cambridge University Press.

Aronson, E. (1968). Dissonance theory: progress and problems. In R. P. Abelson, E. Aronson, W. J. McGuire, T. M. Newcombe, M. J. Rosenberg and P. H. Tannenbaum (Eds.) *Theories of Cognitive Consistency: a Sourcebook.* Chicago: Rand McNally.

Aronson, E. and Mills, J. (1959). The effect of severity of initiation on liking for a group. *Journal of Abnormal and Social Psychology,* 59, 177–181.

Averill, J. R. (1979). The functions of grief. In C. E. Izard (Ed.) *Emotions in Personality and Psychopathology.* New York: Plenum.

Bahnson, C. B. (1969). Psychophysiological complementarity in malignancies: past work and future vistas. *Annals of the New York Academy of Sciences,* 164, 319–334.

Bahnson, M. B. and Bahnson, C. B. (1969). Ego-defenses in cancer patients. *Annals of the New York Academy of Sciences,* 164, 546–559.

Bandura, A. (1977). *Social Learning Theory.* Englewood Cliffs, N.J.: Prentice-Hall.

Bartrop, R. W., Lazarus, L., Luckhurst, E. and Kiloh, L. G. (1977). Depressed lymphocyte function after bereavement. *Lancet* 1, 834–836.

Bem, D. J. (1967). Self-perception: an altertive interpretation of cognitive dissonance phenomena. *Psychological Review,* 74, 183–200.

Berkman, L. F. and Syme, S. L. (1979). Social networks, lost resistance, and mortality: a nine-year follow-up study of Alameda County residents. *American Journal of Epidemiology,* 109, 186–204.

Bloor, D. (1983). *Wittgenstein: A Social Theory of Knowledge.* London: Macmillan.

Blumberg, E. M., West, P. M. and Ellis, F. W. (1954). A possible relationship between psychological factors and human cancer. *Psychosomatic Medicine,* 16, 277–286.

Boden, M. (1981). *Minds and Mechanisms.* Brighton: Harvester Press.

Bonami, M. and Rimé, B. (1972). Approche exploratoire de la personalité precoronarienne par analyse standardisée de données projectives thematiques. *Journal of Psychosomatic Research,* 16, 103–113.

Bonfils, S. S. and DeM'uzan, M. (1974). Irritable bowel syndrome vs. ulcerative colitis: psychofunctional disturbance vs. psychosomatic disease? *Journal of Psychosomatic Research,* 18, 291–296.

Booth, G. (1965). Irrational complications of the cancer problem. *American Journal of Psychoanalysis,* 25, 41–60.

Bowlby, J. (1969). *Attachment and Loss. Vol.1. Attachment.* New York: Basic Books.

Bowlby, J. (1979). *The Making and Breaking of Affectional Bonds.* London: Tavistock.

Brehm, J. W. and Cohen, A. R. (1962). *Explorations in Cognitive Dissonance.* New York: Wiley.

Brehm, S. (1976). *The Applications of Social Psychology to Clinical Practice.* New York: Hemisphere.

Brenner, M. (Ed.) (1980). *The Structure of Action.* Oxford: Blackwell.

Brenner, M. (1982). Actor's powers. In M. von Cranach and R. Harré (Eds.) *The Analysis of Action.* Cambridge: Cambridge University Press.

Brenner, M. H. (1979). Mortality and the national economy: a review, and the experience of England and Wales, 1936–1976. *Lancet,* 2, 568–573.

Brenner, M. H. and Mooney, A. (1982). Economic change and sex-specific cardiovascular mortality in Britain 1955–1976. *Social Science and Medicine,* 16, 431–442.

Breuer, G. (1982). *Sociobiology and the Human Dimension.* Cambridge: Cambridge University Press.

British Broadcasting Corporation. (1983, March). *A Gentler Way with Cancer* [Verbatim transcript from videotape]. BBC: London.

Brown, L. H. (1970). *Eagles.* London: A. Barker.

Brown, G. W. (1974). Meaning, measurement, and stress of life events. In B. S. Dohrenwend and B. P. Dohrenwend (Eds.) *Stressful Life Events: Their Nature and Effects.* New York: Wiley.

Brown, G. W. and Harris, T. (1978). *Social Origins of Depression.* London: Tavistock.

Brown, G. W. and Harris, T. (In Press). Establishing causal links: The Bedford college studies of depression. In H. Katschnig (Ed.) *Life Events and Psychiatric Disorders.* Cambridge: Cambridge University Press.

Bruhn, J. G., Paredes, A., Adsett, C. A. and Wolf, S. (1974). Psychological predictors of sudden death in myocardial infarction. *Journal of Psychosomatic Research,* 18, 187–191.

Bruner, J. S. (1982). The organization of action and the nature of adult–infant transaction. In M. von Cranach and R. Harré (Eds.) *The Analysis of Action.* Cambridge: Cambridge University Press.

Buchwald, A. M., Coyne, J. C. and Cole, C. S. (1978). A critical evaluation of the Learned Helplessness Model of Depression. *Journal of Abnormal Psychology,* 87, 180–193.

Buckley, W. (1968). *Modern Systems Research for the Behavioral Scientist,* Chicago: Aldine.

Burchfield, S. R., Holmes, T. H. and Harrington, R. L. (1981). Personality differences between sick and rarely sick individuals. *Social Science and Medicine,* 15E, 145–148.

Butler, R. N. (1964). The life review: An interpretation of reminiscence in the aged. In R. Kastenbaum (Ed.) *New Thoughts on Old Age.* New York: Springer.

Byrne, D. G. and Whyte, H. M. (1980). Life events and myocardial infarction revisited: the role of measures of individual impact. *Psychosomatic Medicine,* 42, 1–10.

Caffry, B. (1967). A review of empirical findings. In S. L. Syme and L. G. Reeder (Eds.) Social stress and cardiovascular disease. *Milbank Memorial Fund Quarterly,* 45.

Calhoun, J. B. (1973). Death squared: the explosive growth and demise of a mouse population. *Proceedings of the Royal Society of Medicine,* 66, 80–88.

Caplan, G. (1981). Mastery of stress: psychosocial aspects. *American Journal of Psychiatry,* 138, 413–420.

Cassel, J. C. (1964). Social science theory as a source of hypotheses in epidemiological research. *American Journal of Public Health,* 54, 1482–1488.

Cassel, J. C. (1974). Psychosocial processes and "stress": theoretical formulation. *International Journal of Health Statistics,* 4, 471–482.

Chambers, W. N. and Reiser, H. F. (1953). Conjestive heart failure. *Psychosomatic Medicine,* 15, 39–60.

Chapanis, N. P. and Chapanis, A. (1964). Cognitive dissonance. *Psychological Bulletin,* 61, 1–22.

Cobb, S. (1974). A model for life events and their consequences. In B. S. Dohrenwend and B. P. Dohrenwend (Eds.) *Stressful Life Events: Their Nature and Effects.* New York: Wiley.
Cobb, S. (1976). Social support as a moderator of life stress. *Psychosomatic Medicine,* 38, 300–314.
Cobb, S., Schull, W. J., Harburg, E. and Kasl, S. V. (1969). The intrafamilial transmission of rheumatoid arthritis: an unusual study. *Journal of Chronic Diseases,* 22, 193–194.
Colledge, M. (1982). Economic cycles and health. *Social Science and Medicine,* 16, 1919–1927.
Collett, P. (Ed.) (1977). *Social Rules and Social Behaviour.* Oxford: Blackwell.
Comstock, G. W. and Partridge, K. B. (1972). Church attendance and health. *Journal of Chronic Diseases,* 25, 665–672.
Cottington, E. M., Matthews, K. A., Talbott, E. and Kuller, L. H. (1980). Environmental events preceding sudden death in women. *Psychosomatic Medicine,* 42, 567–574.
Cotton, J. L. (1981). A review of research on Schachter's theory of emotion and the misattribution of arousal. *European Journal of Social Psychology,* 11, 365–395.
Coveney, P. (1967). *The Image of Childhood.* Harmondsworth: Penguin Books.
Cox, T. and Mackay, C. (1982). Psychosocial factors and psychophysiological mechanisms in the aetiology and development of cancers. *Social Science and Medicine,* 16, 381–396.
Culler, J. (1976). *Saussure.* London: Fontana
Cumming, E. and Henry, W. E. (1961). *Growing Old.* New York: Basic Books.
Davidson, D. (1980). *Essays on Actions and Events.* Oxford: Clarendon Press.
Dawkins, R. (1976). *The Selfish Gene.* Oxford: Oxford University Press.
Dembroski, T. M. and MacDougall, J. M. (1982). Coronary-prone behaviour, social psychophysiology, and coronary heart disease. In J. R. Eiser (Ed.) *Social Psychology and Behavioral Medicine.* Chichester, England: Wiley.
Dilman, V. M. (1981). *The Law of Deviation of Homeostasis and Diseases of Aging.* Boston: John Wright.
Dongier, M. (1974). Psychosomatic aspects in myocardial infarction in comparison with angina pectoris. *Psychotherapy and Psychosomatics* 23, 123–131.
Douglas, M. (1980). *Evans-Pritchard.* Glasgow: Fontana.
Doust, J. W. L. (1952). Psychiatric aspects of somatic immunity. *British Journal of Social Medicine,* 6, 49–67.
Draeger, J. H. (1983). The problem of truth in psychotherapy: a phenomenological approach. *Social Science and Medicine,* 17, 371–378.
Driscoll, R., Davis, K. E. and Lipitz, M. E. (1972). Parental interference and romantic love: the Romeo and Juliet effect. *Journal of Personality and Social Psychology,* 24, 1–10.
Durkheim, E. (1952). *Suicide.* (G. Simpson, Ed.; J. A. Spaulding and G. Simpson, Trans.) London: Routledge and Keagan Paul. (Original work published 1897)
Elms, A. C. and Janis, I. L. (1965). Counter-norm attitudes induced by consonant versus dissonant conditions of role-playing. *Journal of Experimental Research in Personality,* 1, 50–60.
Engel, G. L. (1955). Studies of ulcerative colitis III. The nature of the psychologic process. *American Journal of Medicine,* 19, 231–256.
Engel, G. L. (1971). Sudden and rapid death during psychological stress. *Annals of Internal Medicine,* 74, 771–782.
Engel, G. L. (1978). Psychological stress, vasodepressor (vasovagal) syncope, and sudden death. *Annals of Internal Medicine,* 89, 403–412.
Fabris, N. (1983). Thymus-neuroendocrine network during development and aging. In *Breakdown in Human Adaptation to Stress. Towards a Multidisciplinary Approach II. Proceed-*

ings of the E.E.C. Workshop on Psychoneuroimmunology, Utrecht. The Hague: Martinus Nijhoff.

Festinger, L. (1957). *A Theory of Cognitive Dissonance.* Evanston, Illinois: Row, Peterson.

Feyerabend, P. K. (1981). *Problems of empiricism.* Cambridge: Cambridge University Press.

Flarscheim, A. (1958). Ego mechanisms in three pulmonary tuberculosis patients. *Psychosomatic Medicine,* 20, 475–483.

Fredrick, J. R. (1976). Grief as a disease process. *Omega,* 7, 297–305.

Freud, S. (1960). *The Psychopathology of Everyday Life.* London: Hogarth Press.

Funch, D. P. and Marshall, J. (1983). The role of stress, social support and age in survival from breast cancer. *Journal of Psychosomatic Research,* 27, 77–83.

Gallagher, B. J. (1980). *The Sociology of Mental Illness.* Englewood Cliffs: Prentice-Hall.

Garber, J. and Seligman, M. E. P. (1980). *Human Helplessness: Theory and Applications.* New York: Academic Press.

Gerard, H. B. and Mathewson, G. C. (1966). The effects of severity of initiation on liking for a group: a replication. *Journal of Experimental Social Psychology,* 2, 278–287.

Gergen, K. J. (1978). Toward generative theory. *Journal of Personality and Social Psychology,* 36, 1344–1360.

Gergen, K. J. (1980). Towards intellectual audacity in social psychology. In R. Gilmour and S. Duck (Eds.) *The Development of Social Psychology.* London: Academic Press.

Gilmour, R. and Duck, S. (1980) (Eds.) *The Development of Social Psychology,* London: Academic Press.

Glass, D. C. (1977). *Behavior Patterns, Stress and Coronary Disease.* Hillsdale, NJ: Lawrence Erlbaum.

Goffman, E. (1969). *The Presentation of Self in Everyday Life.* London, Allen Lane.

Goodall, J. (1971). *In the Shadow of Man.* London: Collins.

Goodall, J. (1979). Life and death at Gombe. *National Geographic Magazine,* 155, 591–621.

Green, W. A. and Miller, G. (1958). Psychological factors and reticuloendothelial disease: IV. *Psychosomatic Medicine,* 20, 124–144.

Greer, S. and Morris, T. (1975). Psychological attributes of women who develop breast cancer: a controlled study. *Journal of Psychosomatic Research,* 19, 147–153.

Grossarth-Maticek, R., Siegrist, J. and Vetter, H. (1982). Interpersonal repression as a predictor of cancer. *Social Science and Medicine,* 16, 493–498.

Gumperz, J. J. (Ed.) (1982). *Language and Social Identity.* Cambridge: Cambridge University Press.

Hacking, I. (1981). *Scientific Revolutions.* New York: Oxford University Press.

Hagburg, B. and Malmquist, A. (1974). A prospective study of patients in chronic hemodialysis—IV. Pre-treatment psychiatric and psychological variables predicting outcome. *Journal of Psychosomatic Research,* 18, 315–319.

Hall, N. R., McGillis, J. E., Vahouny, G. H. and Goldstein, A. L. (1983). Immune regulation of the adrenal axis. In *Breakdown in Human Adaptation to Stress. Towards a Multidisciplinary Approach, II. Proceedings of the E.E.C. Workshop on Psychoneuroimmunology, Utrecht.* The Hague: Martinus Nijhoff.

Hamilton, V. and Warburton, D. M. (1979). *Human Stress and Cognition.* Chichester: Wiley.

Hammer, M. (1983). "Core" and "extended" social networks in relation to health and illness. *Social Science and Medicine,* 17, 405–411.

Hanna, N., and Fidler, I. J. (1980). Role of natural killer cells in the destruction of circulating tumor emboli. *Journal of the National Cancer Institute,* 65, 801–809.

Harré, R. (1979). *Social Being.* Oxford: Blackwell.

Harré, R. (1983). *Personal Being.* Oxford: Blackwell.

Harré, R. and Secord, P. S. (1972). *The Explanation of Social Behaviour.* Oxford: Blackwell.

Harvey, J. H., Ickes, W. and Kidds, R. F. (Eds.) (1978). *New Directions in Attribution Research,* Vol.2. Hillsdale, NJ: Lawrence Erlbaum.
Harvey, P. H. (1980) (Rapporteur). Mechanisms of kin-related behavior. In H. Markl (Ed.) *Evolution of Social Behavior: Hypotheses and Empirical Tests. Report of the Dahlem Workshop.* Berlin: Dahlem Konferenzen.
Heider, F. (1958). *The Psychology of Interpersonal Relations.* New York: Wiley.
Henderson, S. and Byrne, D. (1977). Towards a method for assessing social support systems. *Mental Health and Society,* 4, 164–170.
Henry, J. P. (1982). The relation of social to biological processes in disease. *Social Science and Medicine,* 16, 369–380.
Henry, J. P. and Cassel, J. C. (1969). Psychosocial factors in essential hypertension. Recent epidemiologic and animal experimental evidence. *American Journal of Epidemiology,* 90, 171–200.
Henry, J. P. and Stephens, P. M. (1977). *Stress, Health, and the Social Environment: A Sociobiologic Approach to Medicine.* New York: Springer-Verlag.
Hinkle, L. E. (1974). The effect of exposure to culture change, social change, and changes in interpersonal relationships on health. In B. S. Dohrenwend and B. P. Dohrenwend (Eds.) *Stressful Life Events: Their Nature and Effects.* New York: Wiley.
Holinger, P. C. and Klemen, E. H. (1982). Violent deaths in the United States 1900–1975. *Social Science and Medicine,* 16, 1929–1938.
Hollis, M. and Lukes, S. (1982). *Rationality and Relativism.* Oxford: Blackwell.
Holroyd, K. A. and Gorkin, L. (1983). Young adults at risk for hypertension: effects of family history and anger management in determining responses to interpersonal conflict. *Journal of Psychosomatic Research,* 27, 131–138.
Horwitz, A. V. (1982). *The Social Control of Mental Illness.* New York: Academic Press.
House, J. S. (1981). *Work, Stress and Social Support.* Reading, MA: Addison-Wesley.
Howard, J. H., Cunningham, D. A. and Rechnitzer, P. A. (1977). Work patterns associated with Type-A behavior: a managerial population. *Human Relations,* 30, 825–836.
Huesmann, L. R. (1978). Cognitive processes and models of depression. *Journal of Abnormal Psychology,* 87, 194–198.
Hughes, M. and Gove, W. R. (1981). Living alone, social integration and mental health. *American Journal of Sociology,* 87, 48–74.
Huxley, J., Mayr, E., Osmond, H. and Hoffer, A. (1964). Schizophrenia as a genetic morphism. *Nature,* 204, 220–221.
Jacobs, T. J. and Charles, E. (1980). Life events and the occurrence of cancer in children. *Psychosomatic Medicine,* 42, 11–24.
Jacobs, M. A., Silken, A. Z., Norman, M. M. and Anderson, L. S. (1970). Life stress and respiratory illness. *Psychosomatic Medicine,* 32, 233–243.
Janet, P. M. (1925). *Psychological Healing. A Historical and Clinical Study.* (E. and C. Paul, Trans.) London: Macmillan.
Jenkins, C. D. (1976). Recent evidence supporting psychologic and social risk factors for coronary disease. *New England Journal of Medicine,* 294, 987–994, 1033–1038.
Jones, E. E. and Gerard, H. B. (1967). *Foundations of Social Psychology.* New York: Wiley.
Joynson, R. B. (1974). *Psychology and Common Sense.* London: Routledge and Kegan Paul.
Jupp, T. C., Roberts, C., and Cook-Gumperz, J. (1982). Language and disadvantage: the hidden process. In J. J. Gumperz (Ed.) *Language and Social Identity.* Cambridge: Cambridge University Press.
Kahle, L. R. and Berman, J. J. (1979). Attitudes cause behaviours: a cross-lagged panel analysis. *Journal of Personality and Social Psychology,* 37, 315–321.

Katz, J., Gallagher, T., Hellman, L., Sachar, E. and Weiner, H. (1969). Psychoendocrine considerations in cancer of the breast. *Annals of the New York Academy of Sciences,* 164, 509–516.

Kelley, H. H. (1967). Attribution theory in social psychology. In D. Levine (Ed.) *Nebraska Symposium on Motivation.* Lincoln: University of Nebraska Press.

Kelman, H. C. (1974). Attitudes are alive and well and gainfully employed in the sphere of action. *American Psychologist,* 29, 310–324.

Kiesler, C. A., Collins, B. E. and Miller, N. (1969). *Attitude Change.* New York: Wiley.

Kissen, D. M. (1966). The significance of personality in lung cancer in men. *Annals of the New York Academy of Sciences,* 125, 820–826.

Kleiner, R. J. and Parker, S. (1969). Social mobility, anomie, and mental disorder. In S. Plog and R. B. Edgerton (Eds.) *Changing Perspectives in Mental Illness.* New York: Holt, Rinehart and Winston.

Kohn, M. L. (1969). *Class and Conformity: A Study in Values.* Homewood, IL: Dorsey Press.

Kohn, M. L. (1976). Occupational structure and alienation. *American Journal of Sociology,* 82, 111–130.

Kohn, M. L. and Schooler, C. (1978). The reciprocal effects of the substantive complexity of work and intellectual flexibility: a longitudinal assessment. *American Journal of Sociology,* 84, 24–52.

Kook, A. I. and Trainin, N. (1974). Hormone-like activity of a thymus humoral factor on the induction of immune competence in lymphoid cells. *Journal of Experimental Medicine,* 139, 193–205.

Kovel, J. (1981). *A Complete Guide to Therapy.* New York: Pantheon.

Kuhn, A. (1976). *The Logic of Social Systems.* San Francisco: Josey-Bass.

Kuhn, T. S. (1978). *The Essential Tension.* Chicago: University of Chicago Press.

Kuo, W. (1976). Theories of migration and mental health: an empirical testing on Chinese Americans. *Social Science and Medicine,* 10, 297–306.

LaRocco, J. M., House, J. S. and French, J. R. P. (1980). Social support, occupational stress, and health. *Journal of Health and Social Behavior,* 21, 202–218.

Laudan, L. (1981). A problem-solving approach to scientific progress. In I. Hacking (Ed.) *Scientific Revolutions.* Oxford: Oxford University Press.

Layden, M. A. (1982). Attributional style therapy. In C. Antaki and C. Brewin (Eds.) *Attributions and Psychological Change.* London: Academic Press.

Lazarus, R. S. (1966). *Psychological Stress and the Coping Process.* New York: McGraw-Hill.

Leaf, A. (1973). Getting old. *Scientific American,* 229, 44–52.

Leavy, R. (1983). Social support and psychological disorder: a review. *Journal of Community Psychology,* 11, 3–21.

Lehr, I., Messinger, H. B. and Rosenman, R. H. (1973). A sociobiological approach to the study of coronary heart disease. *Journal of Chronic Diseases,* 26, 13–30.

Lemon, B. W., Bengtson, V. L. and Peterson, J. A. (1972). An exploration of the activity theory of aging: activity and life satisfaction among inmovers to a retirement community. *Journal of Gerontology,* 27, 511–523.

Le Shan, L. (1966). And emotional life history pattern associated with neoplastic disease. *Annals of the New York Academy of Sciences,* 125, 780–793.

Liesse, M. van Imschoot, K., Mertens, C. and Lauwers, P. (1974). Charactéristiques psychologiques et réactions physiologiques au stress de sujets normaux et coronariens. *Journal of Psychosomatic Research,* 18, 101–113.

Lin, N., Ensel, W. M., Simeone, R. S. and Kuo, W. (1979). Social support, stressful life events and illness: a model and an empirical test. *Journal of Health and Social Behavior,* 20, 108–119.

Linder, D. E., Cooper, J. and Jones, E. E. (1967). Decision freedom as a determinant of the role of incentive magnitude in attitude change. *Journal of Personality and Social Psychology,* 6, 245–254.

Lindzey, G. and Aronson, E. (1968). *A Handbook of Social Psychology.* Vol. I. Reading, MA: Addison Wesley.

Lipinski, M., Virelizier, J-L, Tursz, T. and Griscelli, C. (1980). Natural killer and killer cell activities in patients with immunodeficiencies or defects in immune interferon production. *European Journal of Immunology,* 10, 246–249.

Locke, D. and Pennington, D. (1982). Reasons and other causes: their role in attribution processes. *Journal of Personality and Social Psychology,* 42, 212–223.

Luborsky, L., Docherty, J. P. and Penick, S. (1973). Onset conditions for psychosomatic symptoms: a comparative review of immediate observation with retrospective research. *Psychosomatic Medicine,* 35, 187–204.

Maddison, D. C. and Viola, A. (1968). The health of widows in the year following bereavement. *Journal of Psychosomatic Research,* 12, 297–306.

Maddison, D. C. and Walker, W. L. (1967). Factors affecting the outcome of conjugal bereavement. *British Journal of Psychiatry,* 113, 1057–1067.

Mahler, H. Y. (1977, August 4). Quoted by R. Bates, Medicine: a worrying diagnosis. *The Listener.*

Mandler, G. (1979). Thought processes, consciousness and stress. In V. Hamilton and D. M. Warburton (Eds.) *Human Stress and Cognition.* Chichester: Wiley.

Marks, R. (1967). A review of empirical findings. In S. L. Syme and L. G. Reeder (Eds.) *Social Stress and Cardiovascular Disease. Milbank Memorial Fund Quarterly,* 45.

Markl, H. (1976). *Aggression and Altruismus: Coevolution der Gegensätze im Verhalten der Tiere.* Konstanz: Universitätsverlag.

Marmot, M. G. (1983). Stress, social and cultural variations in heart disease. *Journal of Psychosomatic Research,* 27, 377–384.

Marsh, P., Rosser, E. and Harré, R. (1978). *The Rules of Disorder.* London: Routledge and Kegan-Paul.

McClary, A. R., Meyer, E. and Weitzman, E. L. (1955). Observations on the mechanism of depression in some patients with disseminated lupus erythematosus. *Psychomatic Medicine,* 17, 311–321.

McGuigan, F. J., Sime, W. E. and Wallace, M. (Eds.) (1980). *Stress and Tension Control.* New York: Plenum.

McGuire, W. J. (1973). The yin and yang of progress in social psychology: seven koan. *Journal of Personality and Social Psychology,* 26, 446–456.

McGuire, W. J. (1976). The concept of attitudes and their relation to behaviours. In H. N. Sinaiko, and L. A. Broedling (Eds.) *Perspectives on Attitude Assessment: Surveys and their Alternatives.* Champaign, IL: Pendleton.

McGuire, W. J. (1980). The development of theory in social psychology. In R. Gilmour and S. Duck (Eds.) *The Development of Social Psychology.* London: Academic Press.

McQueen, D. V. and Celentano, D. D. (1982). Social factors in the etiology of multiple outcomes; the case of blood pressure and alcohol consumption patterns. *Social Science and Medicine,* 16, 397–418.

McQueen, D. V. and Siegrist, J. (1982). Social factors in the etiology of chronic disease: an overview. *Social Science and Medicine,* 16, 353–367.

Medalie, J. H., Kahn, H. A., Neufeld, H. N., Riss, E., Goldbourt, U., Perlstein, T. and Oron, D. (1973). Myocardial infarction over a five year period. I. Prevalence, incidence and mortality experience. *Journal of Chronic Diseases,* 26, 63–84.

Mertens, C. and Segers, M. J. (1971). L'influence des facteurs psychologiques dans la genèse des affections coronariennes. I Données bibliographiques. *Bulletin de l'Académie Royale de Medécine de Belgique,* 11, 155–199.

Merton, R. K. (1957). *Social Theory and Social Structure.* Glencoe, IL: Free Press.

Mestrovic, S. and Glassner, B. (1983). A Durkheimian hypotheses on stress. *Social Science and Medicine,* 17, 1315–1327.

Midgley, M. (1981). *How Humans Adapt: A Biocultural Odyssey.* Washington, DC: Smithsonian Institution.

Miller, S. M. (1980). Why having control reduces stress: If I can stop the roller coaster, I don't want to get off. In J. Garber and M. E. P. Seligmen (Eds.) *Human Helplessness: Theory and Applications.* New York: Academic Press.

Millet, J. A. P., Lief, H. and Mittelmann, B. (1953). Raynaud's disease. Psychogenic factors and psychotherapy. *Psychosomatic Medicine,* 15, 61–65.

Minc, S. (1965). Psychological factors in coronary heart disease. *Geriatrics,* 20, 747–755.

Monjan, A. A. (1983). Stress and the immune response in animals: fact and artifact. In *Breakdown in Human Adaptation to Stress. Towards a Multidisciplinary Approach, II. Proceedings of the E.E.C. Workshop on Psychoneuroimmunology, Utrecht.* The Hague: Martinus Nijhoff.

Moos, R. H. (1964). Personality factors associated with rheumatoid arthritis: a review. *Journal of Chronic Diseases,* 17, 41–55.

Morgan, M. (1982). Theoretical interpretations of over-justification effects. *Current Psychological Reviews,* 2, 213–230.

Morris, T., Greer, S., Pettingale, K. W., Watson, M. (1981). Patterns of expression of anger and their psychological correlates in women with breast cancer. *Journal of Psychosomatic Research,* 25, 111–117.

Moscovici, S. (1976). *Social influence and social change.* (European Monographs in Social Psychology, 10). London: Academic Press.

Moss, S. (1973). *Illness, Immunity and Social Interaction.* New York: Wiley.

Newcombe, R. D. and Rutter, D. R. (1982). Ten reasons why ANOVA theory and research fail to explain attributional processes: 2. Methodological problems. *Current Psychological Reviews,* 2, 153–170.

Nisbett, R. E. and Bellows, N. (1977). Verbal reports about causal influences on social judgments: private access versus public theories. *Journal of Personality and Social Psychology,* 35, 613–624.

Nisbett, R. and Valins, S. (1971). Perceiving the causes of one's own behavior. In E. E. Jones, D. E. Kanouse, H. H. Kelley, R. E. Nisbett, S. Valins and B. Weiner (Eds.) *Attribution: Perceiving the Causes of Behavior.* Morristown, NJ: General Learning Press.

Nisbett, R. E. and Wilson, T. D. (1977). Telling more than we can know: verbal reports on mental processes. *Psychological Review,* 84, 231–259.

Orne, M. T. (1962). On the social psychology of the psychological experiment: with particular reference to demand characteristics and their implications. *American Psychologist,* 17, 776–783.

Owen, H. P. (1969). *The Christian Knowledge of God.* London: The Athlone Press.

Packer, C. (1977). Reciprocal altruism in Papio anibus. *Nature,* 265, 441–443.

Parens, M. D., McConville, B. J. and Kaplan, S. M. (1966). The prediction of frequency of illness from the response to separation. *Psychosomatic Medicine,* 28, 162–171.

Parkes, C. M., Benjamin, B. and Fitzgerald, R. G. (1969). Broken heart: a statistical study of increased mortality among widowers. *British Medical Journal,* 1, 740–743.

Parkes, C. M. and Brown, R. (1972). Health after bereavement: a controlled study of young Boston widows and widowers. *Psychosomatic Medicine,* 34, 449–461.

Pavlidis, N. and Chirigos, M. (1980). Stress induced impairment of macrophage tumoricidal function. *Psychosomatic Medicine,* 42, 47–54.

Peters, R. S. (1958). *The Concept of Motivation.* London: Routledge and Kegan-Paul.

Peterson, C. (1982). Learned helplessness and attributional interventions in depression. In C. Antaki and C. Brewin (Eds.) *Attributions and Psychological Change.* London: Academic Press.

Philippopolous, G. S., Wittkower, E. D. and Cousineau, A. (1958). The etiologic significance of emotional factors in onset and exacerbation of multiple sclerosis. *Psychosomatic Medicine,* 20, 458–474.

Pilisuk, M. and Froland, C. (1978). Kinship networks, social support, and health. *Social Science and Medicine,* 12B, 273–280.

Potter, J. (1981). The development of social psychology: consensus, theory and methodology in the British Journal of Clinical Psychology. *British Journal of Clinical Psychology,* 20, 249–258.

Rahe, R. H. (1972). Subjects' recent life changes and their near future illness reports. *Annals of Clinical Research,* 4, 250–265.

Raven, B. H. and Rubin, J. Z. (1976). *Social Psychology: People in Groups.* New York: Wiley.

Regan, D. T. (1978). Attributional aspects of interpersonal attraction. In J. H. Harvey, W. Ickes and R. F. Kidd (Eds.) *New Directions in Attribution Research,* Vol.2. Hillsdale, NJ: Lawrence Erlbaum.

Reiff, P. (1966). *The Triumph of the Therapeutic.* New York: Harper.

Riley, L. (1981). Psychoneuroendocrine influences on immunocompetence and neoplasia. *Science,* 212, 1100–1109.

Rimé, B. and Bonami, M. (1973). Specificité psychosomatique et affections cardiaques coronariennes: essai de verification de la theorie de Dunbar au moyen du MMPI. *Journal of Psychosomatic Research,* 17, 345–352.

Romaine, S. (Ed.) (1982). *Sociolinguistic Variation in Speech Communities.* London: Edward Arnold.

Rommetveit, R. (1980). On "meanings" of acts and what is meant and made known by what is said in a pluralistic social world. In M. Brenner (Ed.) *The Structure of Action.* Oxford: Blackwell.

Romo, M., Siltanen, P., Theorell, T., and Rahe, R. H. (1974). Work behavior, time urgency and life dissatisfactions in subjects with myocardial infarction: a cross cultural study. *Journal of Psychomatic Research,* 18, 1–8.

Rorty, R. (1980). *Philosophy and the Mirror of Nature.* Oxford: Blackwell.

Rosenberg, M. J. (1965). When dissonance fails: on eliminating evaluation apprehension from attitude measurement. *Journal of Personality and Social Psychology,* 1, 28–42.

Rosenman, R. H. and Friedman, M. (1974). Neurogenic factors in pathogenesis of coronary heart disease. *Medical Clinics of North America,* 58, 269–279.

Rotter, J. B. (1966). Generalized expectancies for internal versus external control of reinforcement. *Psychological Monographs, 80* (Whole No. 609).

Rowland, K. F. (1977). Environmental events predicting death for the elderly. *Psychological Bulletin,* 84, 349–372.

Russek, H. I. (1958). Emotional stress and the etiology of coronary artery disease. *American Journal of Cardiology,* 2, 129–134.

Sabani, J. and Silver, M. (1982). *Moralities of Everyday Life.* New York: Oxford University Press.

Sade, D. S. (1980). Can 'fitness' be measured in primate populations? In H. Markl (Ed.) *Evolution of Social Behavior: Hypotheses and Empirical Tests.* Berlin: Dahlem Konferenzen.

Saussure, F. de. (1916). *Cours de Linguistique Générale.* Paris: Payot. (see also W. Baskin (trans.), *Course,* 1974. London: Fontana).

Schachter, S. and Singer, J. E. (1962). Cognitive, social and physiological determinants of emotional state. *Psychological Review,* 69, 379–399.

Scheff, T. J. (1966). *Being Mentally Ill: A Sociological Theory.* Chicago: Aldine.

Scheff, T. J. (1974). The labelling theory of mental illness. *American Sociological Review,* 39, 444–452.

Schmale, A. H. and Iker, H. P. (1966). The psychological setting of uterine cervical cancer. *Annals of the New York Academy of Sciences,* 125, 807–813.

Schmale, A. H., Meyerowitz, S. and Tinling, D. C. (1970). Current concepts of psychosomatic medicine. In O. W. Hill (Ed.) *Modern Trends in Psychosomatic Medicine,* 2. London: Butterworth.

Schrodinger, E. (1968). Quote from *What is life.* In W. Buckley (Ed.) *Modern Systems Research for the Behavioural Scientist.* Chicago: Aldine.

Schulz, R. (1978). *The Psychology of Death, Dying and Bereavement.* Reading, MA: Addison-Wesley.

Schulz, R. and Brenner, G. (1977). Relocation of the aged: a review and theoretical analysis. *Journal of Gerontology,* 32, 323–333.

Schumacher, E. F. (1973). *Small Is Beautiful: A Study of Economics as if People Mattered.* London: Bland and Briggs.

Schwenck, T. L. and Hughes, C. C. (1983). The family as patient in family medicine: rhetoric or reality. *Social Science and Medicine,* 17, 1–6.

Scotch, N. A. and Geiger, H. J. (1963). The epidemiology of essential hypertension: a review with special attention to psychologic and sociocultural factors: II. *Journal of Chronic Diseases,* 17, 167–177.

Searle, J. R. (1969). *Speech Acts.* Westford, MA: Murray.

Seligman, M. E. P. (1975). *Helplessness: on Depression, Development and Death.* San Francisco: Freeman.

Selye, H. (1956). *The Stress of Life.* New York: McGraw-Hill.

Semin, G. R. and Manstead, A. S. R. (1983). *The Accountability of Conduct.* London: Academic Press.

Shannon, C. and Weaver, W. (1949). *The Mathematical Theory of Communication.* Urbana: University of Illinois Press.

Shapiro, A. K. (1959). The placebo effect in the history of medical treatment: implications for psychiatry. *American Journal of Psychiatry,* 116, 298–304.

Shaver, K. G. (1977). *Principles of Social Psychology.* Cambridge, MA: Winthrop.

Shaw, M. E. and Costanzo, P. R. (1982). *Theories of Social Psychology.* New York: McGraw-Hill.

Shekelle, R. B., Raynor, W. J., Ostfeld, A. M., Garron, D. C., Bieliauskas, L. A., Liu, S. C., Maliza, C. and Paul, O. (1981). Psychological depression and 17-year risk of death from cancer. *Psychosomatic Medicine,* 43, 117–125.

Shirley, J. (1983, April 3). The longest year. *Sunday Times Magazine.*

Shotter, J. (1980). Action, joint action and intentionality. In M. Brenner (Ed.) *The Structure of Action.* Oxford: Blackwell.

Shotter, J. (1981). Telling and reporting: prospective and retrospective uses of self-ascriptions. In C. Antaki (Ed.) *The Psychology of Ordinary Explanations of Social Behaviour.* London: Academic Press.

Siegrist, J., Dittmann, K., Rittner, K. and Weber, I. (1982). The social context of active distress in patients with early myocardial infarction. *Social Science and Medicine,* 16, 443–462.

Siltanen, P., Lauroma, M., Nirrko, O., Punsar, S., Pyrola, K., Tuominen, H. and Vanhala, K.

(1975). Psychological characteristics related to coronary heart disease. *Journal of Psychosomatic Research,* 19, 183–195.

Silver, R. L. and Wortman, C. B. (1980). Coping with undesirable life events. In J. Garber and M. E. P. Seligman (Eds.) *Human Helplessness: Theory and Applications.* New York: Academic Press.

Sklar, L. S. and Anisman, H. (1981). Stress and cancer. *Psychological Bulletin,* 89, 369–406.

Smith, P. (1980). An attributional analysis of personal learning. In C. P. Alderfer and C. L. Cooper (Eds.) *Advances in Experiential Social Processes,* Vol.2. New York: Wiley.

Solomon, G. F. (1981). Emotional and personality factors in the onset and course of autoimmune disease, particularly rheumatoid arthritis. In R. Ader, (Ed.) *Psychoneuroimmunology.* New York: Academic Press.

Solomon, G. F. (1982). Emotions, immunity and disease: an historical and philosophical perspective. *Proceedings of the E.E.C. Workshop on Psychoneuroimmunology, Utrecht.* The Hague: Martinus Nijhoff.

Solomon, G. F. and Amkraut, A. A. (1979). Neuroendocrine aspects of the immune response and their implications for stress effects on tumour immunity. *Cancer Dectection and Prevention,* 2, 197–224.

Solomon, G. F. and Amkraut, A, A. (1981). Psychoneuroendocrinological effects on the immune response. *Annual Review of Microbiology,* 35, 155–184.

Sonne, J. L. and Janoff, D. S. (1982). Attributions and the maintenance of behaviour change. In C. Antaki and C. Brewin (Eds.) *Attributions and Psychological Change.* London: Academic Press.

Stahl, S. M., Grim, C. E., Donald, E. and Neikirk, H. J. (1975). A model for the social sciences and medicine: the case for hypertension. *Social Science and Medicine,* 9, 31–38.

Sterling, P. and Eyer, J. (1981). Biological basis of stress-related mortality. *Social Science and Medicine,* 15E, 3–42.

Storms, M. D. and Nisbett, R. E. (1970). Insomnia and the attribution process. *Journal of Personality and Social Psychology,* 16, 319–328.

Straker, N. and Tamerin, J. (1974). Aggression and childhood asthma: a study in a natural setting. *Journal of Psychosomatic Research,* 18, 131–135.

Stroebe, W., Stroebe, M. S., Gergen, K. J. and Gergen, M. (1982). The effects of bereavement on mortality: a social psychological analysis. In J. R. Eiser (Ed.) *Social Psychology and Behavioral Medicine.* Chichester, England: Wiley.

Syme, S. L. (1967). Implications and future prospects [Editorial]. In S. L. Syme and L. G. Reeder (Eds.) *Social Stress and Cardiovascular Disease. Milbank Memorial Fund Quarterly,* 45.

Tabachnick N.(1973). *Accident or Suicide? Destruction by Automobile.* Springfield, IL: Charles C. Thomas.

Tajfel, H. and Fraser, C. (1981). *Introducing Social Psychology.* Harmondsworth: Penguin Books.

Tajfel, H. (1981). *Human Groups and Social Cognitions.* Cambridge: Cambridge University Press.

Theil, H. G., Parker, D. and Bruce, T. A. (1973). Stress factors and the risk of myocardial infarction. *Journal of Psychosomatic Research,* 17, 43–57.

Theorell, T. and Rahe, R. H. (1972). Behavior and life satisfaction of Swedish subjects with myocardial infarction. *Journal of Chronic Diseases,* 25, 139–147.

Thomas, C. B. and Duszynski, K. R. (1974). Closeness to parents and the family constellation in a prospective study of five disease states: suicide, mental illness, malignant tumor, hypertension and coronary heart disease. *Johns Hopkins Medical Journal,* 134, 251–270.

Thomas, C. B. and Greenstreet, R. L. (1973). Psychobiological characteristics in youth as predictors of five disease states: suicide, mental illness, hypertension, coronary heart disease and tumor. *Johns Hopkins Medical Journal,* 132, 16–43.

Totman, R. G. (1979a). What makes "life events" stressful? A retrospective study of patients who have suffered a first myocardial infarction. *Journal of Psychosomatic Research,* 23, 193–201.

Totman, R. G. (1979b). *Social Causes of Illness.* London: Souvenir Press.

Totman, R. G. (1982). Psychosomatic theories. In J. R. Eiser (Ed.) *Social Psychology and Behavioral Medicine.* Chichester: Wiley.

Totman, R. G., Kiff, J., Reed, S. E. and Craig, W. (1980). Predicting experimental colds in volunteers from different measures of recent life stress. *Journal of Psychosomatic Research,* 24, 155–163.

Trivers, R. L. (1971). The evolution of reciprocal altruism. *Quarterly Review of Biology,* 46, 35–57.

Valins, S. and Ray, A. (1967). Effects of cognitive desensitisation on avoidance behavior. *Journal of Personality and Social Psychology,* 7, 345–350.

van der Pligt, J. (1981). Actors' and observers' explanations: divergent perspectives or divergent evaluations? In C. Antaki (Ed.) *The Psychology of Ordinary Explanations of Social Behaviour.* London: Academic Press.

van Dijl, H. (1975). Myocardial infarction patients and work attitudes—an empirical study. *Journal of Psychosomatic Research,* 19, 197–202.

Vilensky, J. A., van Hoesen, G. W. and Damasio, A. R. (1981). *The limbic system in human evolution.* Paper presented at the Proceedings of the 50th Annual Meeting of the American Association of Physical Anthropologists, Detroit, MI.

von Cranach, M. and Harré, R. (1982). *The Analysis of Action.* Cambridge: Cambridge University Press.

von Schilcher, F. and Tennant, N. (1984). *Philosophy, Evolution and Human Nature.* London: Routledge and Kegan-Paul.

Waldron, I., Nowotarski, M., Freimer, M., Henry, J. P., Post, N. and Witten, C. (1982). Cross-cultural variation in blood pressure: a quantitative analysis of the relationships of blood pressure to cultural characteristics, salt consumption and body weight. *Social Science and Medicine,* 16, 419–430.

Walker, K. N., MacBride, A. and Vachon, M. L. S. (1977). Social support networks and the crisis of bereavement. *Social Science and Medicine,* 11, 35–41.

Watson, G. (1966). *Social Psychology: Issues and Insights.* Philadelphia: Lippincott.

Weblin, J. E. (1963). Psychogenesis in asthma; an appraisal with a view to family research. *British Journal of Medical Psychology,* 36, 211–225.

Weiner, B. and Litman-Adizes, T. (1981). An attributional expectancy-value analysis of learned-helplessness and depression. In J. Garber and M. Seligman (Eds.) *Human Helplessness: Theory and Applications.* London: Academic Press.

Wilkinson, S. (1981). Personal constructs and private explanations. In C. Antaki (Ed.) *The Psychology of Ordinary Explanations of Social Behaviour.* London: Academic Press.

Williams, W, G. (1980). Civil education in a stressful society: a program of value clarity and tension reduction. In F. J. McGuigan, W. E. Sime and J. M. Wallace (Eds.) *Stress and Tension Control.* New York: Plenum.

Wilson, E. O. (1975). *Sociobiology: The New Synthesis.* Cambride, MA: The Belknap Press of Harvard University.

Winch, P. (1958). *The Idea of a Social Science and its Relations to Philosophy.* London: Routledge and Kegan-Paul.

Winnubst, J. A. M., Marcelissen, F. H. G. and Kleber, R. J. (1982). Effects of social support in the stressor-strain relationship: a Dutch sample. *Social Science and Medicine,* 16, 475–482.

Wirsching, M., Steirlin, H., Hoffman, F., Weber, G. and Wirsching, B. (1982). Psychological identification of breast cancer patients before biopsy. *Journal of Psychosomatic Research,* 26, 1–10.

Wittgenstein, L. (1953). *Philosophical Investigations.* Oxford: Blackwell.

Wittgenstein, L. (1958). *The Blue and Brown Books. Preliminary Studies for the "Philosophical Investigations."* Oxford: Blackwell.

Wolcott, D. L., Wellisch, D. K., Robertson, C. R. and Arthur, R. J. (1981). Serum gastrin and the family environment in duodenal ulcer. *Psychosomatic Medicine,* 43, 501–506.

Worchel, S. and Cooper, J. (1976). *Understanding Social Psychology.* Homewood, IL: Dorsey Press.

Wortman, C. B. and Dintzer, L. (1978). Is an attributional analysis of the Learned Helplessness phenomenon viable?: A critique of the Abramson-Seligman-Teasdale reformulation. *Journal of Abnormal Psychology,* 87, 75–90.

Young, A. (1980). The discourse on stress and the reproduction of conventional knowledge. *Social Science and Medicine,* 14B, 133–146.

van der Zanden, J. W., (1977). *Social Psychology.* New York: Random House.

Zanna, M. P. and Cooper, J. (1976). Dissonance and the attribution process. In J. Harvey, W. J. Ickes and R. F. Kidd (Eds.) *New Directions in Attribution Research,* Vol.1. Hillsdale, NJ: Lawrence Erlbaum.

Zajonc, R. (1968). Cognitive theories in social psychology. In G. Lindzey and E. Aronson (Eds.) *The Handbook of Social Psychology,* Vol I. Reading, MA: Addison-Wesley.

Zimbardo, P. G. (1969). *The Cognitive Control of Motivation.* Glenview, IL: Scott Foresman.

Index

V

W